The Collected Letters of Charles Olson and J. H. Prynne

Recencies Series: Research and Recovery in Twentieth-Century American Poetics
Matthew Hofer, Series Editor

This series stands at the intersection of critical investigation, historical documentation, and the preservation of cultural heritage. The series exists to illuminate the innovative poetics achievements of the recent past that remain relevant to the present. In addition to publishing monographs and edited volumes, it is also a venue for previously unpublished manuscripts, expanded reprints, and collections of major essays, letters, and interviews.

ALSO AVAILABLE IN THE RECENCIES SERIES:
RESEARCH AND RECOVERY IN TWENTIETH-CENTURY AMERICAN POETICS:

The Charles Olson Codex: Projective Verse and the Problem of Mayan Glyphs edited by Dennis Tedlock
The Birth of the Imagination: William Carlos Williams on Form by Bruce Holsapple
The Maltese Falcon to Body of Lies: Spies, Noirs, and Trust by Robert von Hallberg
The Oppens Remembered: Poetry, Politics, and Friendship edited by Rachel Blau DuPlessis
How Long Is the Present: Selected Talk Poems of David Antin edited by Stephen Fredman
Loose Cannons: Selected Prose by Christopher Middleton
Amiri Baraka and Edward Dorn: The Collected Letters edited by Claudia Moreno Pisano
The Shoshoneans: The People of the Basin-Plateau, Expanded Edition by Edward Dorn and Leroy Lucas

The Collected Letters of CHARLES OLSON and J. H. PRYNNE

EDITED BY **Ryan Dobran**

University of New Mexico Press • Albuquerque

Printed in the United States of America

Library of Congress Cataloging-in-Publication Data
Names: Dobran, Ryan, editor.
Title: The collected letters of Charles Olson and J. H. Prynne / edited by Ryan Dobran.
Description: Albuquerque : University of New Mexico Press, 2017. |
Series: Recencies Series: Research and Recovery in Twentieth-Century American Poetics |
Includes bibliographical references and index.
Identifiers: LCCN 2016039545 (print) | LCCN 2016042420 (ebook) |
ISBN 9780826358325 (cloth : alk. paper) | ISBN 9780826358332 (electronic)
Subjects: LCSH: Olson, Charles, 1910–1970—Correspondence. |
Prynne, J. H., 1936- —Correspondence. | Poets, American—20th century—Correspondence. |
Poetics—History—20th century.
Classification: LCC PS3529.L655 Z48 2017 (print) | LCC PS3529.L655 (ebook) |
DDC 811/.54 [B] —dc23
LC record available at https://lccn.loc.gov/2016039545

Designed by Felicia Cedillos
Composed in Minion Pro 10.5/14.25

Contents

Introduction

This volume contains nearly all of the letters written from 1961 to 1970 between American poet Charles Olson (1910–1970) and English poet J. H. Prynne (b. 1936).[1] Prynne initiated the correspondence by writing to Olson on November 7, 1961 in search of work for *Prospect*, a small literary magazine published in Cambridge, England. Prynne also closed out the correspondence with a dedicatory epigraph to *Fire Lizard*, a short poem sequence written on New Year's Day, 1970, that would reach Olson just days before his death. I have collected the letters from two sources: the Charles Olson Research Collection in the Thomas J. Dodd Research Center at the University of Connecticut, and Prynne's private archive in Cambridge.

The Charles Olson Research Collection is well-trodden territory, containing an expansive and well-lit archive of the poet's notes, letters, and manuscripts as well as books from his personal library. Olson's archival materials have been a wellspring for frequent posthumous publications, including the reconstructed third volume of his *Maximus Poems*. The many volumes of correspondence, essays, and poems testify to the enthusiasm and diligence of scholars such as George F. Butterick and Ralph Maud, among others.

Prynne's private collection of correspondence and manuscripts is scarcely known at all, and does not yet exist as an archive available to a scholarly public, although several letters to others besides Olson have been published in small magazines such as *The English Intelligencer*, *Grosseteste Review*, *Parataxis*, and *Quid*.[2] That said, Prynne took care to organize these correspondence materials

1. I have excluded Olson's letter to Prynne dated September 9, 1965, because it seems quite obviously to have been addressed to him by mistake. I have also left out Prynne's brief, confused reply of November 21, 1965.
2. A comprehensive bibliography may be found in the relevant section of Tencer, *The Bibliography of J. H. Prynne*.

chronologically, which made reconstructing a timeline of their exchange relatively straightforward. Prynne also photocopied his letters prior to sending them, and even transcribed some of Olson's early letters to ease his consultation of the older poet's notoriously turbid script. Prynne's letters to Olson have long been available at the University of Connecticut, but, with one exception, this is the first time Olson's letters to Prynne have been published.[3]

For those familiar with the cavalier, mischievous, and omnivorous attention paid to various discourses by both writers, the fact that these letters are dappled with citations from and allusions to various source materials—from Anglo-Saxon chronicles to quantum field theory—should come as no surprise. Indeed, one of the most distinguishing characteristics of this correspondence is the quantity of texts and bibliographical information that Prynne sent to Olson.[4] Because it is not possible to reprint such materials in full, I have supplemented any missing bibliographical details in the notes for each accompanying letter; when such materials were sent under separate cover without an attached note, I have given the bibliographical details in italics within the body of the text. In many instances, Prynne's own citation made additional reference superfluous. My own citations correspond to items listed in the bibliography.

If Olson and Prynne share a passion for knowledge, they share much less in terms of style. The difference in the two poets' sentence structure, punctuation, and handwriting is remarkable. Prynne typed the majority of his letters onto Gonville and Caius College letterhead, though there are some postcards and several letters from elsewhere: nearby Grantchester, Kent, and even Buffalo, New York, where he taught during the summer of 1965. Olson wrote the majority of his letters by hand on whatever seemed readily available, including advertisements for his own poetry readings and construction paper. In my transcriptions, I have attempted to produce a readable book while retaining idiosyncrasies that seem to express authorial intent. I have not converted Olson's abundant use of plus signs (+) to ampersands (&), and I have maintained his peculiar use of prose line breaks only when it seems to have been rhetorical, rather than a consequence of page margins. I have also silently corrected what seem to be obvious spelling or typing errors by both writers, and preserved underlining rather than converting it to italicization.

The letters are arranged chronologically according to the date of composition or postmark, although this retrospective order sometimes disturbs the interpersonal timeline of sending and receiving letters across the Atlantic. The

3. Olson's letter to Prynne dated May 14, 1966, appears in Olson, *Selected Letters*, 361–62.
4. See Maud, *Olson's Reading*, 153–56 for a partial list.

transmission delays, however minor, often resulted in one writer's initiating a new line of inquiry before the other had the chance to respond. Notably, there is a general decline in their letter writing from 1967 to 1970, which, I would suggest, is a direct consequence of the poets meeting in England in the autumn of 1966. For all of their mutual admiration and intimacy, as demonstrated in these letters, they did not seem to get along in person. Despite several trips to Europe during the 1960s, including extended visits to London and Dorchester, it seems that Olson never made it to Cambridge.

Various scholars on both sides of the Atlantic have recognized and written about the Prynne-Olson connection. Robert von Hallberg's monograph on Olson mentions the elder poet's influence on Edward Dorn and Amiri Baraka, as well as Prynne.[5] Butterick's "Editor's Afterword" to his edition of the collected *Maximus Poems* acknowledges Prynne's assistance with the typescript preparation of the second volume.[6] The revised second edition of *Muthologos* reveals Prynne as a guide for Olson's thought in both "Reading at Berkeley—The Day After" and "The *Paris Review* Interview."[7] In his biography of Olson, Tom Clark refers to Prynne as Olson's "loyal, assiduous poetic research assistant."[8] Maud's polemical follow-up biography, *Charles Olson at the Harbor*, which takes aim at the evidence in Clark's, mentions Prynne once in passing.[9] Despite these mentions, the transatlantic relation between Prynne and Olson remains somewhat obscure, though this is changing.[10]

Often loosely assembled via Eric Mottram's term the "British Poetry Revival," Prynne and his contemporaries were eager to renovate the stagnant ironies of the Movement poets prominently on display in postwar England. One instrument of breaking the hegemony of official verse culture was reading, discussing, teaching, publishing, and distributing postwar American poetry and prose. Very early on in these letters, Prynne mentions the condescension with which the English university and "Betjeman's England (the logical successor to Auden's) sees modern US writing" (November 26, 1961). For Prynne, as for so many of his generation, it is that loosely affiliated but dynamic organon of queer, anticapitalist, mythopoetic, new age, and anachronistic attitudes and forms nominated by Donald Allen in his anthology *New American Poetry* that catalyzed new forms of expression after 1960.[11]

5. See von Hallberg, *Charles Olson*, 208–10.
6. See Olson, *Maximus*, 637–45.
7. See Olson, *Muthologos*, 193–203 and 355–414, respectively.
8. Clark, *Charles Olson*, 299.
9. Maud, *Charles Olson at the Harbor*, 200.
10. See especially the work of Brinton, Mellors, Owens, Rodríguez, Sheppard, and Sutherland.
11. See Hickman for a discussion of the influence of this anthology.

But even before the occasion of that anthology, Olson had already touched down in Cambridge. The English poet and novelist Elaine Feinstein founded and edited the Cambridge literary magazine *Prospect*, and she had reached out to Olson in 1959 to ask for a statement of poetics, which was later published in *New American Poetry* alongside the highly influential essay "Projective Verse." Olson's poetics, focused on the poet's body as a verse-making instrument, as well as on the equivalence of history and experience, continued to crystallize throughout the 1960s in *Prospect* and the subscriber-only worksheet *The English Intelligencer*.[12] Olson had also been in communication with the Cambridge-educated Scottish poet Gael Turnbull as early as June 1957 concerning his plan to view the seventeenth-century English merchant records pertaining to Gloucester, Massachusetts, where Olson spent summers as a child and later settled. Olson would not arrive in England until nearly ten years later, at that point having already received Prynne's detailed notes and microfilm of the relevant Port Books from the Public Records Office in London.[13]

Prynne's first exposure to Olson may have been through having seen the latter's work in earlier issues of *Prospect*, though his yearlong fellowship at Harvard provided an invaluable introduction to the American scene by way of Gordon Cairnie's Grolier Poetry Book Shop. Prior to writing to Olson, Prynne had corresponded with the poet and editor of *Origin*, Cid Corman, himself an extensive correspondent with Olson during the 1950s and 1960s. At this point, *Prospect* had passed to Prynne, and in 1961, he was actively writing to American poets for new work, among them Robert Creeley, Robert Duncan, and Edward Dorn.

Prynne had already achieved some recognition as a poet—enough, at least, to land him a spot on Peter Orr's BBC radio program, *The Poet Speaks*. Shortly after this correspondence began, Routledge & Kegan Paul published Prynne's *Force of Circumstance and Other Poems* (1962), but it is clear that this was not the type of poetry that Prynne wanted to write. In a letter to Olson dated September 28 of that year, he refers to his book as "96% of no interest to me. Zip-fastener type of thing—dead as no door-nail would be, given any decent chance." Prynne's second stage of "early work," written between 1965 and 1968 and split between *Kitchen Poems* (1968) and *The White Stones* (1969), is informed by Olson's dedication to the use of source materials, but delivered in a languid, philosophical style, furnished out of the moral ecology of English and German romanticism. From the current vantage, with over a half century of retrospective distance, this era in Prynne's work appears to

12. See the thorough study by Alex Latter.

13. Olson, "Reading at Berkeley—The Day After," *Muthologos*, 194n2.

be epiphenomenal to the vast body of rhapsodic, often militantly paratactic experimentation that comprises the bulk of his poetic career from 1969 to the present.

When considered at all, the transatlantic transmission of attitudes, forms, and ideas about this poetry has been viewed largely as an eastern linear movement from Olson to Prynne, from American to British poetics. The overwhelming prestige of modern American poetry has perhaps obscured the entanglement. In this regard, these letters suggest various ways that Prynne influenced the course of Olson's thinking in the last decade of his life: by making large swathes of information readily available for consultation, by providing an initial typescript for his *Maximus Poems IV, V, VI* (1968), and by articulating Olson's own poetics to the older poet. One of the first published mentions of their relationship is embedded within Olson's wild interview with Gerard Malanga that appeared in the *Paris Review* in 1969. Now that the full recording has been transcribed and published, it's curious to read just how much time Olson spent gushing about Prynne, who had just mailed his review of *Maximus Poems IV, V, VI* to Gloucester.

Prynne is "knowing like mad," Olson remarks to Malanga.[14] In his review, Prynne seems to have articulated something about *Maximus* that Olson did not or could not see. When asked about the relation between Gloucester and the concept of knowledge, Olson defers to Prynne, "who today in a review has answered it immaculately."[15] When asked about his "care with such matters as line units and indentation," Olson brings in Prynne again:

> Wow, if I only knew I did it, it would be marvelous! . . . I read that piece of Prynne's, and, I mean, he says everything right, accurately, and I'm sitting here and I'm thinking, 'Isn't it terrible? You know, until somebody says it to you, I don't know nothing, I didn't know I did any—I didn't know what he says I did. Then I know I did what he said I did.' It's that wonderful business. Are you following me?[16]

Throughout the letters, Prynne's eloquence and resourcefulness as an interlocutor seem to invert Olson's typically authoritative position, while Olson's Promethean ambitions about the powers of poetic writing seem to drive Prynne's own consideration of language not as the material out of which verse gets made, but as the condition of being that emerges with writing. One of the most interesting

14. Olson, "The *Paris Review* Interview," in *Muthologos*, 357.
15. Olson, *Muthologos*, 359.
16. *Muthologos*, 377.

passages in Prynne's review casts light on Olson's practice, as well as the power Prynne sees in Olson's *Maximus Poems*, which is "not secondary assemblage, but primary writing; with this difference, that man's current position of knowing what he does brings in the great unifying sentimentalities of dream as surely as it offsets merely naive forward narrative. The result is a lingual and temporal syncretism, poised to make a new order."[17] Prynne's use of the concept of syncretism allows for a generous reading of a text infatuated with details that will not be put into order, a text whose creator oscillates between a desire for positivist facts and the flux of lyric invention. But then again, from very early on, Prynne's experience of reading Olson was uncanny: as he writes in the opening paragraph of the inaugural letter, "reading your various things was like reading for the first time the back of my own hand." And as he would remark later in his "Draft Bibliography on England," dated September 25, 1964, Olson's writing is "where the rich, pure language took on its new (and maybe only) life into this century."

Prynne wrote the review between January and February of 1969, well after the beginnings of his misgivings about the anarchic foundationalist research that galvanized Olson's *Maximus*. In a letter to Olson written on December 29, 1964, Prynne describes this paradigm shift in his thinking as a kind of degradation of confidence in the prospect that origins (cultural, linguistic, cognitive) could be *grasped* for poetic practice; he has "less sense now that I know the ground on which the thing might proceed." Part of his reluctance to participate in the wild reconstruction of culture active in Olson's imagination is that he does not know Greek, nor any of the ancient languages (Assyrian cuneiform, Sanskrit) that would be necessary for such a philologically sound reconstruction to take place. How can one know despite not knowing? "That is, to get at the coming to know, by weighing the language against its ethical and physical substance, you do need to be very close. Or I would need it."

Prynne's uncertainty seems to issue from a fundamental priority about the relation between language and knowing. Language must be a condition of being prior to the "coming to know," so that the condition whereby knowledge is possible means foremost knowing the language the way an artisan knows materials. It also requires the capacity to test the linguistic materials against the various uses to which they can be put: that is, not merely writing, but speaking. It is speech that does the work of ethical comportment within the poem because it is the breathing body that inspires the text. The poet must leverage the linguistic order not to conceptualize a subject position, but to negotiate the dimensions of knowing via the embeddedness of larger social and natural movements, which

17. Prynne, "Review of *Maximus*," 66.

cannot be furnished by a translated corpus. Prynne is interested in something "perhaps more local and less historistic."

Olson would reply emphatically: "Lord, Jeremy, I don't know Greek myself" on January 6, 1965. While he concedes that "one has no basis of experience of poems or anything of that sort in a language unless that language is your own," he nevertheless views etymology as a kind of linguistic archaeology necessary to uncover the roots.

Both poets are dedicated to the power of etymological derivation to augment poetic writing. By summoning an entire string of language development, the poet can mobilize the speculative reconstructions of root-word senses. Instigated by Olson's mention of derivation in his letter to Elaine Feinstein, Prynne brings up Indo-European philology in his very first letter, an interest that continues throughout the decade, amid other discursive fields: runic inscription, transformational grammar, the origins of merchants' proper names, geography, archaeology. In this view, the language corpus is not only a kind of world, but also a partial index of a world that is no longer. That's why Julius Pokorny's *Indogermanisches etymologisches Wörterbuch* sits on Prynne's "shelf like a bomb, ready to explode at a touch with the most intricately powerful forces caged up inside, a storehouse of vectors."

Maximus is not a futural project, but an ancestral one. Its atavistic tendencies are of a peculiar kind, however, because its principal aim is not a restitution of culture, but its construction. In any such project, there is a necessary tension between the desire for an intelligible ground of understanding that yields facts and the daunting if ineluctable problem of historical transmission via material culture; and between a transhistorical model of ideation that supervenes upon a latent collective spirit, and a philological materialism sensitive to the vicissitudes of text interpretation.

In his own poetry of this period, Prynne shies away from the grandiose and iconoclastic structure of *Maximus*. He largely rejects the hyperfocus on specific historical facts for adumbrations of the experience of knowledge as song:

> I am moved
> by the condition of knowledge, as the
> dispersion of form.[18]

One dimension of these adumbrations is the fluency between thinking and landscape. Enclosing "Moon Poem" in his letter of March 3, 1966, Prynne writes that

18. "Quality in that Case as Pressure" in *Poems*, 78–79.

it was written from a "quiet of spirit & desire." It is a nocturne inscribed to elaborate "a community of wish" against the narrow ossifications of "the mercantile notion of choice." This quiet poem registers the pleasure of wishing as love, and the recognition of such love as knowledge. Prynne's desire for "knowledge of the unseen" has no object.

> We disperse into the ether
> as waves, we slant down into a precluded notion
> of choice which becomes the unlearned habit of
> wish: where we live, as we more often are than
> we know.[19]

Emotional acts such as hoping, wishing, and desiring metamorphose into diffuse spaces of becoming. Prynne's focus on "wish" is consistent with his transformation of apparently abstract nouns into toponyms. Olson would register this when he wrote back to Prynne on March 11 to praise the enclosure: "What delights me here in your new poem (which you well yourself know, for the gravity as well of your recognition, in yr letter to me the next day, of the <u>place</u> the vocabulary has, in your hands, turned <u>its</u>elf to the possession of. . . ." It may have been "Moon Poem" to which Olson referred when he proclaimed in an interview conducted on that same day, "A poem was sent to me [last week], and I went for it hook, line, and sinker. And I couldn't really tell you what the fucking thing all amounted to, but, good god, was I hooked!"[20]

Elsewhere in *The White Stones*, Prynne would adopt some of the Olsonian methods of using scholarly resources in his poetry, particularly in "The Glacial Question, Unsolved" and "Aristeas, in Seven Years," both of which include a list of references. Temporally distant cultures are brought into sharp relief; the historical divorce is consoled not by Olson's "primary writing," with its map of names, but by the realization of nonhuman timescales and the intrication of mortality and place. Throughout *The White Stones*, assertions such as "the history of person / as an entire condition of landscape" and "the Pleistocene is our current sense, and / what in sentiment we are" testify to the refusal of the distance presumed by historicism, but equally to history as a mode of experience.[21]

One of the most obscure historical nooks within these letters involves the Weymouth Port Books, which give (and refuse) details about the various ships that may have entered into Gloucester harbor, particularly those operated by

19. *Poems*, 53.
20. See Olson, *Muthologos*, 214n12.
21. Prynne, *Poems*, 69, 66.

Matthew Craddock and Maurice Thomson, two English merchants involved in the Massachusetts Bay Company's colonization of the Cape Ann area. The letters reveal an asymmetrical interaction concerning the Port Books, not only because it is Olson who asks if Prynne knows any Cambridge scholars clued in to the provenance of the ones not yet accounted for in the pioneering scholarship of Frances Rose-Troup, but also because of Olson's lack of response to Prynne's research. When Olson wrote to Prynne on September 24, 1962, to inquire about these matters, he did not know what he was in for.

In "The Reading at Berkeley—The Day After," a talk with Richard Moore of National Educational Television and Edward Dorn recorded after the Berkeley Poetry Conference in July 1965—during which Prynne was teaching at Olson's own institution in Buffalo as a visiting lecturer—Olson recounts the excitement and dread that accompanied his receipt of Prynne's Port Books research: "And the frustration and just some night of just feeling bad led me to sit down and write to Prynne, and, you know, it was the worst mistake you make. This guy is the greatest researcher, and I haven't ever heard of anything like it."[22] The sheer quantity of information seems to have been too much for Olson to handle. It was the type of comprehensiveness that silenced the ludic, para-epistemic modes of thinking necessary for Olson's writing practice. Because Prynne "found all the goddamn records of all the boats that crossed the Atlantic Ocean after Columbus that might have bearing on entering Gloucester harbor," Olson wrote the poem "And now let all the ships come in." It was a direct response to abundance: the "ships" were iconic of the transmission of the Port Book materials mailed by sea from Cambridge to Gloucester.[23]

Throughout 1965, Dorn and Prynne pleaded with Olson to visit them for research and friendship. But it was not until late 1966 that Olson finally did so. He arrived in London and visited Essex, where Dorn taught. It is likely that Prynne met Olson in Essex at Dorn's house, and probably also in London. Not long after his arrival, Olson made his way to West Berlin, where he wrote to Prynne quite regularly. He was back in London at the beginning of 1967, travelling to Dorchester for research in May of that year and then back to Gloucester a month later, only to return to London for the much-publicized poetry reading with Allen Ginsberg and others at the Albert Hall in July.[24]

Olson's first volume of *Maximus* and his most influential prose works had already been published by the time he received Prynne's first letter. In a sense, the decade of the 1960s reveals Olson's institution as a significant influence

22. *Mutthologos*, 194.
23. See Olson, *Maximus* II, 290.
24. For details of Olson's travels in England, see Clark, *Charles Olson*, 332–36, and Selerie.

on many of the younger New American Poets, and also his decline in health and lyric powers. In his lectures, letters, and essays, he gives the impression of rancorous and boisterous exhortation strung together with wild frames of reference. He did things fast and with large strokes. Olson's rapid scrawl, which pulled in ready-to-hand surfaces, contrasts starkly with Prynne's meticulous penmanship and lapidary style. For Prynne, these letters reveal a committed experimentation with Olson's theories about poetry writing, as well as a thinking through of European modernity. I hope that the presentation of these texts allows for greater attention to postwar poetry written in English, particularly regarding Olson's reception by an entire generation of poets on the other side of the Atlantic, including Roy Fisher, Tom Raworth, R. F. Langley, Peter Riley, John James, Lee Harwood, John Hall, John Temple, and Andrew Crozier, among numerous others.

From the inception of this project, I have felt a lingering temptation, undoubtedly exacerbated by these two poets' omnivorous desire for information, to fill all of the possible referential gaps found within the letters, so that even the most obscure referents appear transparent. Yet, the converse of this apparent generosity is that letters principally about poems and poetics become easily overburdened by narrow biographical inference and speculations about unknowable intentions. What makes the present collection interesting is not what these letters offer in terms of personal details, but rather the way they bind knowledge and writing, information and composition, feeling and articulation, history and poetry. Furthermore, there is something to be said for a presentation whose editorial heuristic avoids preloading a reference before the reader has had a chance to think about what is written. Throughout, I have erred on the side of letting a term or name stand alone, rather than supplying a reference easily gleaned by any curious reader with an Internet connection.

I would like to extend my gratitude to Jeremy Prynne for his support of this project. When we began discussing it in 2012, he provided candid advice concerning the scope of the letters and its requirements. He made the consultation of archival materials at Gonville and Caius College entirely comfortable. I would also like to thank Melissa Watterworth Batt for her assistance during my visit to the Thomas J. Dodd Research Center at the University of Connecticut in Storrs; my consultation of the archive was funded by a Strochlitz Travel Grant. Matt Hofer and Elise McHugh gave this project a home at the University of New Mexico Press, for which I am grateful. Katherine Harper's editorial suggestions were invaluable. A special note of thanks to Jackqueline Frost for her loving encouragement during the final stages of this book.

CHAPTER 1
1961

Gonville and Caius College
Cambridge
November 4, 1961

Dear Charles Olson,

You won't know who I am, but I have just taken over as editor of PROSPECT, which published two of the Maximus letters when Elaine Feinstein was running the show.[1] Being immoderately reticent, I have for a long time been looking for a pretext on which to write, and now I have one: I hope you will send us something if and when you feel disposed to waste time with the English, rotting in a provincial squeamishness that seems inescapably built into the present situation. I spent last year in Boston, and via the angelic ministrations of Gordon Cairnie, found the wrought world of the mind and voice unfurling as I followed.[2] It will surely sound foolishly ecstatic, but you cannot imagine the sense of fabled release, the expansiveness, the new air. Most of it was new; but reading your various things was like reading for the first time the back of my own hand. IN COLD HELL, IN THICKET speaks for me out of the fast centre, I know why the traceries and knots and topology of the imagination, the arching spaces, the instant that flows, the law of outward and object, the care and use of one's eyes, I know why they turn as they must, fill out their necessary & musical spaces: you cannot imagine what intense excitements I have been drawn to—RECOGNITION. Switch to Anna Karenina: Levin discovers himself saying "The answer has been given me by life itself, through my knowledge of what is right and what is wrong. And this knowledge I did not acquire in any way: it was given to me as it is to everybody—given, because I could not have got it from anywhere."[3] True,

1. *Prospect* (1959–1964), a Cambridge-based magazine founded by Elaine Feinstein and later edited by Tony Ward and eventually by Prynne, ran for six issues. Prynne refers to Olson's *Maximus Poems*, published in three volumes between 1960 and 1975, the last of which was constructed by Charles Boer and George F. Butterick after Olson's death.

2. Gordon Cairnie (1895–1973), owner and proprietor of the Grolier Bookshop in Cambridge, Massachusetts.

3. Tolstoy, *Anna Karenina*, 832.

but to learn the sounding of one's own depth, the reach of one's own limbs and eyes, the outward pressure of real concern—the revelation of others can support and further the whole endeavor, by setting its own fierce limits. Each must follow his own grammar, I suppose, the syntax of his personal station, but learning as he can & must from the push of another's desperate honesty. I don't know whether you consider that all the small detail of Projective Verse still stands; but "to be as clean as wood," it rings (or should) perennially through the air, choked here with such wan confusion.[4]

All of which bloated paean is simply by way of gratitude—and interest. I am permanently astonished by the malicious blindness of English Bloomsbury (still in the saddle here); Tomlinson (Charles) comes the closest to seeing his way out, but though his review of the Maximi was carefully intelligent, he has written me that he sees no coherence there, only "angry jabber."[5] So there are wrongs to right; I shrink to recall the Spectator's wagging a reproving finger at Distances, out of their blessed English sanity (including a lordly gesture towards "someone called Creeley").[6] Perhaps I shall be able to get a review of Rbt. Creeley's collection into the next PROSPECT; I sure as hell hope so.[7]

I am waiting to see MAXIMUS IN DOGTOWN with maximum concern; and if you can spare time to put down any new directions or shapings you are currently interested in, I should be pleased to hear from you. Incidentally, you talked about tracking words along their lines of force, back to their roots; this is an aspect of the whole speech complex which I had hoped to see more in action in the big Grove Press anthology. And I don't know if anyone answered your query about a new dictionary of roots, which has in fact been done; by Julius Pokorny, Indogermanisches Etymologisches Wörterbuch (Franke Verlag, Bern und München, 1947–1959).[8] The dictionary is now complete, the introduction, notes & technical preamble still awaited. Pokorny has drawn on all the Celtic tongues, Tokharin and Hittite, and a whole range of little-known Romance dialects: Phrygian, Thracian, Messapian, Venetian, Illyrian, Ligurian &c; it makes tremendously exciting reading. In the section given to KAR-, for example, with a root signification of 'hard' or 'rough,' he shows an astonishing range of derived cognates embracing European words for 'rock,' 'crab,' 'shell, peel, nut,' 'strong, bold, heavy, difficult, firm,' perhaps also 'cliff, crag, crevice,'

4. Olson, "Projective Verse," in *Collected Prose*, 247.
5. Tomlinson, "From Both Sides of the Atlantic," 352.
6. "Names and Things," *Spectator*, July 28, 1961, 149.
7. Prynne's review of Creeley's *For Love: Poems 1950–1960* (1962), entitled "Its Own Intrinsic Form" (written c. December 1962) remains unpublished. See Edward Dorn Papers, I.A., Box 19, Folder 328.
8. Probably a reference to Olson's comment in "The Letter to Elaine Feinstein" (1959) regarding the need for "some 'dictionary' of roots which wld include Hittite at least." See Olson, *Collected Prose*, 250.

'stone, scarp,' 'cairn, burial-mound, temple.' And it merely confirms my own feeling to find 'keel, hull, ship' also included here; part 6 of the first Max. letter reveals the rationale behind this. Pokorny's whole book sits on my shelf like a bomb, ready to explode at a touch with the most intricately powerful forces caged up inside, a storehouse of vectors. But perhaps you know about this already. For myself, having learned German & Anglo-Saxon and tried to do the same with Old Icelandic, I have always felt this deep drive at the heart of all north-European languages, this reservoir of latent energy never quite fully discharged even by the most direct of sentence-constructions (though I have absolutely no knowledge of the Slavonic group).

Finally, though the nature of this place makes it necessary to pretend that PROSPECT is respectable & harmless, I hope to print some genuine kinetics now and then, if not more often. Not that I can expect much of this order from hereabouts; but if you know of anyone new that might be interesting, I should be thankful if you would put him on to us.

Best,
J. H. Prynne

P.S. I should be interested to hear whether you see anyone on the English scene that there may still be hope for. Have you seen any of Tomlinson's things, and do you think them completely stifled by their own prissy carefulness . . .?

---

28 Fort Square
Gloucester, MA
November 9, 1961

My dear J. H. Prynne:

I'm terribly gratified to have your letter—and to learn of Pokorny's word-book, which you are the first to tell me of, and delighted that you did treat that question as non-rhetorical.

Right off the top like this there isn't any new poem which comes to my mind to send you, mostly because most of them recently sit inside the poems which followed Maximus from Dogtown I (which is the one you refer to, and I hope you can get—it was published by Auerhahn, in San Francisco, and is a 6 or 7 page one. The longer ones tend to seem so relentless, and I should imagine dull, and the rest come out so small—2 or 3 lines, almost—I hesitate to assume they will seem anything but slight. But maybe the moment I think about it, or look, I'll have something, and surely send it.—Actually that whole feeling of derivation seems to have overtaken me more than any projection; or better the projection has become literal (the more usual meaning, which I certainly didn't have any known awareness of, when I used the word, as you will know from projectile etc—that sense of outward push), and the sense of where anything comes from into one, seems to have taken me over in the last few years. . . . or with some deliberateness I let it, or had to, or tried to. And am not at all happy.

By the way Robt. Duncan has just sent me a remarkable good old fashion essay (mind you with all new powers via some crazy use of what one does mean by old fashion . . . classical English prose or something) called, IDEAS OF THE MEANING OF FORM—it's 10 pages mimeographed on legal size paper, and might therefore be too much, but if you wanted it and could get it from him I believe you'd have something like what would fit happily into Prospect, and give the scene a look-on. For he does a thing here—or starts a thing, he plans to do two more such pieces, this one is clearing the ground of reason and convention, and from 1492 and the 17th century there in England to Miss *[Marianne]* Moore Mr *[Robert]* Lowell and W C Williams here. It's superb. His address, in case it does interest you, is 3735 20th St San Francisco 10, California.

Also, do you know the current mimeographed house organ coming out of NY the past 6 months, Floating Bear? (O by the way if you wanted to reprint that thing of mine in FB called Grammar a Book it wld be more of what you catch so quickly of what that derivation matter does lead on towards).[9] In any case the editor Leroi Jones is hot as hell, and in hell too, and he was doing some translations of the African story from *[the Leo]* Frobenius Atlantis collection, as well as a long Notes on Dante's Inferno, one part of which brought the Post Office down on the magazine![10] His address, and of FB, which you ought to feel free to ask for the whole lot—some 20 maybe to date—is: 324 East 14th, NYC 3.

I wanted also to call your attention to the work of Edward Dorn, in case it may not yet have come your way. He's a triple or quadruple threat man, and if he has anything it wld be worth your time: address Barton Road, Pocatello, Idaho.—I also hear that John Wieners, the young poet who had two bad years, is now writing again, and his address is (Can't find it. try? Milton Ave,) Milton, Mass.

Also there is a short story writer who hasn't yet shown much but what he has printed you may have seen: it seems to me much of what you do mean by kinetic, and that's Michael Rumaker, whose address is 66 North Broadway, Nyack, New York.[11]

OK. Not to snow you, and it may be you'd rather I suggest to these they send to

9. "GRAMMAR—a 'book'" was originally published in *Floating Bear* 7 (1961) and collected in *Proprioception* (1965). See Olson, *Collected Prose*, 191–95.
10. An excerpt from Leroi Jones, *The System of Dante's Hell*, appeared in *Floating Bear* 9 (1961).
11. Michael Rumaker (b. 1932), American prose writer, graduated from Black Mountain College in 1955.

you, and will when and if I am in touch with any of them but they are scattered, and in any case I am now writing you and shoot the wad. Creeley of course. His address you probably have: 1835 Dartmouth NE, Albuquerque, N.M. And Mike McClure: his new address is: 229 East 4th St apt. 2, NYC 9.

As of England I'm very fond of Michael Shayer's work (do you know it? Worcester).[12] You've probably seen Tom Raworth's Outburst, from London?[13] I don't know Tomlinson's poems at all, alas, and was hoping he'd have his say about The Distances as well as he did abt The Maximus: it was a pleasure to have him speak up, and though I dig he does think the trouvaille is what it does amount to he cld I believe be persuaded that picking one's way (among debris, was it?) was, at least, a possibility—then. I don't much any more think it is allowable, art suddenly has to be as straight as such thought as Levin utters, there isn't any time or place except for the goods delivered into public place to sit and stare for ever right there in front of all our eyes; and each of us to heat our life at those most ordinary fires[14]. The back of our hand for sure.

I appreciate hearing from you, as you will judge. Hope I haven't gone on too much, and please write again. I'll be happy to do anything on this side which I can, or you may ask of me. Any of your own further thoughts on the etymological, or runs like you send of KAR-, wld stir me up as this does. Certainly word-wise it ought to jump the system for years ahead, and what you say of sentence-construction is really where the work hasn't even begun. (In that Grammar a Book piece I felt as though I was at least pushing into parts of speech—the thing, as I recall, comes on strong on demonstrative pronouns, and on the old lost middle voice (Of Greek); but none of us—or maybe the effects are already taking place?—seem to front to the sentence (?). (I note that Duncan makes a big pitch for linguistic science, in the IDEAS mentioned above. He says it beautifully, tying it to a Carlyle quote from the Hero as Poet: "Carlyle's thought going toward the inner structure of Nature had intuitions of the inner structure of language. The science of *[Edward]* Sapir and *[Benjamin Lee]* Whorf has its origins in the thought of The Hero as Poet."[15]

Because you brought the word up in front of me let me leave it then with the whole open question of derivation: what does that mean? where [one] does come from?

Best, and many thanks,
Charles Olson

12. Poet and coeditor of *Migrant* with Gael Turnbull.
13. Between 1961 and 1963, Raworth published three issues of *Outburst*.
14. Olson refers to Prynne's quote from Tolstoy's *Anna Karenina* in the previous letter.
15. Duncan, "Ideas of the Meaning of Form," in *A Selected Prose*, 26.

Also did a thing called Proprioception—what seems to be a part of derivation—in Kulchur (N.Y.) Spring 1960.

---

28 Fort Square
Gloucester, MA
November 24, 1961

My dear Prynne:

I like the enclosed very much—and hope you will.[16] At least it gives me something fresh to send you, and it wld seem to be so law-abiding on its face that none of the established wld do anything but think it harmless XXX? I shld think so.

Ok, am spreading word of yr editorship: heard back fr Creeley, and John Wieners by accident came here the day before yesterday, and I now have his correct address—165 Eliot St Milton, Mass.

Hope all goes well, and look forward to hearing fr you again.

Charles Olson

---

109 Grantchester Meadows
Cambridge
November 26, 1961

Dear Charles Olson,

Very many thanks for yours, which was strangely exciting to have down here in the depths of the museum. I have written off to Robert Duncan to ask for his IDEAS, which sounds full of interest; but I doubt I could hope to print it. You can have no idea how hostile the parochial mediocrity of an English university can be—hence I intend giving the wiseacres no foothold in prose theory. I would rather work to a private circulation & print what needs to come out (like ORIGIN), but don't have the choice as things are. So my main hopes are for high and various quality in the verse itself, where readers will have to earn their insights. I just can't begin to convey how Betjeman's England (the logical successor to Auden's) sees modern US writing: its prime aim is to convert it into a kind of freely available slapstick garrulity, or else to patronise it by feigning 'interest.' And so I look for the verse carapace, not the vital but soft underside of theory, think I must do this, the way things stand. Cid Corman put me on to the FLOATING BEAR; I have been getting it since # 3 (just

16. Olson included a typescript of "Going out of the Century," dated November 19, 1961, which Prynne published in *Prospect* 6 (1964), and which later became part of *Maximus IV, V, VI*. See Olson, *Maximus* II, 244.

in time to catch Ed Dorn's vastly moving The Landscapes Below), and indeed saw your GRAMMAR—a "book." My concerns are very close to yours here, but perhaps at a slight angle: thus I am launched into the derivation problem, and hope you will bear with it.[17]

I am struck with the need to readjust parts of THE CHINESE WRITTEN CHARACTER, as a chap-book, towards some sense of the hinges in European language or its northern groupings considered in general. "The transference of force from agent to object," writes Fenollosa, "which constitute natural phenomena, occupy time. Therefore, a reproduction of them in imagination requires the same temporal order." Here EP interposes the gloss, "Style, that is to say limpidity, as opposed to rhetoric."[18] Hence the simple declarative sentence with one transitive & active verb, furnishes the kinetic type. But where are the sources of this force, how is access to them won out of the ambient silences which surround the man on the brink of speech? From the things themselves has been the answer, and in the final reckoning always must be. Things are nouns, and particular substantives of this order are storehouses of potential energy, hoard up the world's available motions. But there are other energies: the compelling human necessities, the exhaling of breath, the sugar which feeds the muscles of the diaphragm & lung. It seems probable that this source was channeled into speech simultaneously with if not before, the substantive pictogram or derived lexigraph. To sing is to modulate and make audible the breathing, declare the body's functioning, its various rhythms, like shouting or the groan of agony. Phonetic and imagistic unit in this way may have evolved side by side, as Doblhofer suggests: "Until quite recently it was believed that all writing without exception originated from a pictorial representation of concepts subsequently evolving, as was the case in the East, 'from the image to the letter.' Today we are inclined to believe that the letter existed from the very outset and that the principal creators of 'Western' writings (Anatolian, Alpine and possibly Old Iberian) had already discovered the isolated sound by the time the Greeks adopted and adapted the Phoenician alphabet, bringing about a reciprocal fusion and fecundation of the image and the letter." (Zeichen und Wunder)[19]

Even Chinese is not as exclusively visual an idiom as one might have assumed from THE CHARACTER; phonetic compounds appear very early, and are

17. Cid Corman (1924–2004), poet, translator and editor of *Origin*, corresponded extensively with Olson, and also with Prynne.

18. Ernest Fenollosa and Ezra Pound, "The Chinese Written Character as a Medium for Poetry" (1919), in *Ezra Pound's Poetry and Prose: Contributions to Periodicals*, III, 491. The first phrase should read: "The transferences of force from agent to agent."

19. Ernst Doblhofer, *Zeichen und Wunder: die Entzifferung verschollener Schriften und Sprachen* (Berlin: Paul Neff, 1957). Prynne's translation.

very extensive. Thus the name of a tree might be borrowed to make up a new compound, shedding its tree determinative, just for its sound ([*pi*]for example). Complex abstract notions are, it seems, commonly formed in this way, on the basis of transferred or borrowed sound values. Similarly unvisual are the 'cenematic' elements in the Chinese vocabulary, less numerous but much more common than the 'plerematic' elements. These function not as representational signs but as grammatical, syntactical, modal structuring agents; number, gender, case, person, tense, mood are cenematic functions, as are conjunctions, correlatives, causal, temporal, conditional, interrogative and other such constructions. Only the plerematic words (though the categories overlap) function primarily as content-words, and it is these that THE CHARACTER most considers—the substantive furnishings of the universe, the nouns among which and the verbs along whose lines we live. But a language must accommodate both these aspects ('locative' & 'instrumental,' perhaps), and as *[W.A.C.H.]* Dobson points out, Chinese is no exception: "In a language in which the pitch and contour of words is part of their intrinsic phonetic shape, pitch and contour ('intonation') if used as an emphatic or modal device, cannot be imposed on the word itself, but is, as in the case, imposed upon a class of morpheme in its environment, existing specifically for that purpose." (Late Archaic Chinese; a Grammatical Study) Thus it makes a difference to write

WINDS : BENDING TREES

rather than

THE WINDS ==> BEND ==> THE TREES

but we are still in Fenollosa's world with either version. But the human agent, once on the scene, immediately introduces his own impalpable forces. I BREAK THE TREE depends for its kinematics on our belief in the 'I' as a source of the necessary energies, in the pitch and contour of his actions. The agent must be grounded in some credible forcefulness, so fixed down and planted that his exertions can have direction outward and away from himself. In a more fluid medium, for example drifting through sea-water, the human agent may take his choice between I BUMPED A PIECE OF DRIFTWOOD or I WAS BUMPED BY A PIECE OF DRIFTWOOD or simply CONTACT OCCURRED BETWEEN ME AND A PIECE OF DRIFTWOOD.

What makes the difference then, so articulates the sentence that it may move with purpose & effect along its own line, outward from the agent, the object, the lungs? Its continued momentum, it seems to me, past and round and athwart changes in course and direction, and the credible certainty of its starting point. The two depend inseparably one upon the other. The movement founds the origin and the origin impels the movement: equal and opposite reaction perhaps.

And if it needs no question how the rocks on the shore may allow us to push on them to start out to sea, how is the human agent so endowed, with the right to function as the noun (pro-noun) subject of the sentence (his own life)? Commonly of course humanity is not so endowed, lives on the most fragile of credit, on a purely virtual instrument devised and maintained by the tacit agreement of others never to ask to see the map for themselves. Access to the fundament is earned by the mind's geologers, the passions which will forge out availably valid starting points and lend them to those few others prepared to profit. Writers have always done this, and poets have always gone deeper & more tenaciously than any into these soundless risks. What is brought to the encounter is patience and restraint and a developed sense of personal dimension, the casualness of a respect rooted in desperation. What is finally earned is place—the object—the first noun with its own weight. It is *[Martin]* Heidegger who sees this most clearly, being the one philosopher to recognise his dependency on the poet (in this case *[Friedrich]* Hölderlin), and the insights buried in etymology. "Alles, was sich an Auffassung und Aussage über das Ding zwischen das Ding und uns stellen möchte, muss zuvor beseitigt werden. Erst dann überlassen wir uns dem unverstellten Anwesen des Dinges. Aber diesen unvermittelte Begegnenlassen der Dinge brauchen wir weder erst zu fordern noch gar einzurichten. Es geschiet längst" (Der Ursprung des Kunstwerkes, in Holzwege).[20] And by an inverse law his shapes will make their own way, for sure, out from this achieved centre.

Once the noun is won and the right to the pro-noun earned, the simple declarative sentence becomes kinetically feasible. Not simply the locative gesture, SEE OVER THERE A TREE, but all the implicit passion of I SEE A TREE or even I DO SEE THIS TREE, NOW, FROM WHERE I AM STANDING; the poet has won his first melody, is singing. The tree has entered his voice, because he knows, with terrible certainty, where he stands. He has founded a race of pronouns, and these bring in the potential accuracies of adverb and adjective in regulation of this commerce, the passage of vital airs over his teeth & tongue & lips. Here are his certainties, and thus far little difficulty and perhaps little argument. But whence his confidence, whence his consciousness of such certainty—how can he not merely use his nouns in speaking, but know they are there when he is silent? One of the most far-ranging answers seems to lie (at least for European, or for English) in correlation, the syntax of articulated dependency. I SEE THE

20. "Everything that, by way of conception and statement, might interpose itself between us and thing must, first of all, be set aside. Only then do we allow ourselves the undistorted presence of the thing. But this allowing ourselves an immediate encounter with the thing is something we do not need either to demand or to arrange. It happens slowly." Martin Heidegger, "The Origin of the Work of Art," in *Off the Beaten Track*, 7.

TREE WHICH YOU TOLD ME OF: a new dimension has appeared by virtue of the right-angled bend about WHICH. Where does it take its pivotal certainty from, its fixity as a landmark by which to alter course? From the fundament of I and TREE. In the earlier Germanic tongues the leaning dependency of such syntax was much more stressed: I SEE THAT TREE, WHICH YOU TOLD ME OF, so that the turn was buttressed from both sides. Thus in the Anglo-Saxon Chronicle (entry for 755 A.D.) we find "Đā on morgenne gehīerdun þæt þæs cyninges þegnas þe him beæftan wærun, þæt se cyning ofslægen wæs; þā ridon hīe þider . . ." (When in the morning they heard that thing, those thanes of the king who were [i.e., had been left] behind him, that the king had been killed; then they rose thither . . .). Such constructions, even as densely interknit as this, were very frequent, as if every change in direction or introduced dependency had to be firmly rooted in an unambiguously demonstrative antecedent: place must exist before departure. In German the correlative construction for THE TIME . . . WHEN is still DIE ZEIT . . . WO (The time where). From here follows a whole range of clausal possibilities: for this reason . . . that; with this proviso . . . that; despite this fact . . . that; in order . . . that; so . . . that; and so on. (Consider the way a new nominative subject is introduced in the following: "Đā cōmon for forðȳ onweg ðe ðāra ōþerra scipu āsǣton."—"They got for this reason away, that there the others' ships went aground.")[21] Thus a reliable fundament (noun & pro-noun): roughly physical world and human body establishes innumerable pivots, and it is by the act of leverage upon these pivots that we feel their security and our motion. The sentence swings around its BECAUSE and ALTHOUGH and THAT (our native cenematics), and the inertial force which such a change of direction generates will confirm and corroborate the fundament while still depending upon it. Clauses joined in apposition across commas accumulate similar pressures: passion speaks out in the turns and joins, which regulate and so define the concern by the rhythms thus generated. (The bending of aluminum, say, as Against Wisdom &c.)[22] As *[George]* Williamson has suggested, "Periodic rhythm is a kind of punctuation which controls and directs the force of the sentence; it can be explained, Aristotle suggests, by analogy with antistrophic rhythm, for it includes a beginning movement and a returning or concluding movement, and it commonly involves a definite sense of a turn" (The Senecan Amble [47]).[23]

The sense of turn it is (I find) which generates its characteristically intense

21. Entry for AD 896.

22. See Olson, "Against Wisdom as Such" (1954), in *Collected Prose*, 263.

23. George Williamson, *The Senecan Amble: A Study in Prose Form from Bacon to Collier* (Chicago: University of Chicago Press, 1951), p. 47.

node of excitement, makes the construction of any sentence an absorbing venture. (It will have become evident by now that I cannot accept Sapir's hypothesis which you cite in your IVth section "ordering."[24] He would have a much harder job with conjunctions.) And throughout, the gravity of these induced concerns, this felt linkage, depends always upon the centre, which will be the substance of the originative nouns, the firm personal presence of the pro-nouns. The whole outward thrust into abstract utterance and totally non-referential syntax reaches back into the personal quadrant of now intersecting with here & giving definition to both FROM and TO (the prepositions which shape our lives). Sentences like HE WOULD PREFER NOT TO HAVE COME UNTIL AFTER YESTERDAY live on the efforts of other sentences; but it also may live through the breath across the teeth, and here again the fundament lies in the diaphragm, the speaking body, his last meal & his enduring concerns. In short, it has the occasion, and may live from this. Already in Shakespeare's time this was consciously known, and is the foundation of Ben Jonson's English Grammar: "All the parts of Syntaxe have already been declared. There resteth one general Affection of the whole, dispersed thorow every member thereof, as the bloud is thorow the body; and consisteth in the breathing, when we pronounce any Sentence; For, whereas our breath is by nature so short, that we cannot continue without a stay to speake long together; it was thought necessarie, as well as for the speakers ease, as for the plainer deliverance of the things spoken, to invent this meanes, whereby men pausing a pretty while, the whole speech might never the worse be understood" (Of the Distinction of Sentences).[25] Thus access to the pressure of solid bedrock & a fixed personal quadrant lies below and behind and at the root of every outward gesture: to comprehend HERE without shouting about it is to sing over the farthest horizon.

Thus anyway a sketch of how I have felt for some time about these problems, the energies that derivation may found and release. Your cosmogonic proem to MAXIMUS, FROM DOGTOWN—I tells me how you stand here, and demonstrates the matching concerns to those which started off the PROJECTIVE VERSE PIECE. "the man awake lights up from the sleeping"—kindles indeed into various passions, outward from the earth of which his body is made.[26] I need hardly say how excited and moved I am by this piece. I hope you will find something for PROSPECT, and perhaps find time to give me some of your reactions to it all, tell me if I run on too long. And I'll send a copy of PROSPECT #5

24. See Olson, "GRAMMAR—a 'Book,'" section IV, entitled "Syntax ('ordering')," which offers three quotations from Edward Sapir, *Language: An Introduction to the Study of Speech* (New York: Harcourt Brace Jovanovich, 1949), 113–14.

25. Ben Jonson, *The English Grammar* [c. 1619] (London, 1640), chapter IX, 83.

26. *Maximus* II, 2.

which has a piece of mine (dressed in impeccable academic prose, to keep the vultures out) about some closely related issues.[27] Meanwhile, I have followed up your leads, & am grateful for them.

Best wishes,
J. H. Prynne

P.S. re LIKE (from AS gelīc), it would perhaps be more accurate to say that 'ge-' here has the force of 'together, taken with.'[28] Hence gelīc has the force of 'having a body that could be taken together (or in common) with' and hence 'having a similar form.' But not 'having the same body or shape,' which implies identity rather than isomorphism. (A very small point, to be sure.) The German suffix '-lich' is similarly cognate with 'Leiche,' body or corpse; it is interesting to reflect that the original comparisons must have been largely external ones, as in all Germanic tongues this particular word for body rapidly narrows into the sense of dead or inanimate body. "He is like his brother"—in size and appearance, perhaps, rather than in temperament or other vital qualities. Pokorny takes it back to a root 'lĕig- or līg-,' which he glosses as 'of the form of someone, similar or resembling.' He cites the Old High German līh (body-form, appearance, body, corpse) and Gothic galeiks (= Modern German gleich, like, resembling), and also proposes a similar origin for the verb like (this a rather exciting possibility). Thus to like a person meant perhaps 'to feel oneself like a person,' hence 'to feel in sympathy with,' hence 'to find a person agreeable.' He cites AS līcian (= to like) and several other cognates with the force of 'suitable, fitting, appropriate.' (Compare Icelandic líka (+ dative), to be pleasing to, to satisfy: 'she is pleasing to me' = (of course) 'I like her.' Also archaic English, 'It belikes me' = I find it fitting to my present mood.) Thus the Lettish līgt (= agree, fall in with) is cognate & relevant here, and a whole range of Icelandic derivatives from lík (the living body; the dead body, or corpse): líkja (= to make like, to imitate, to resemble); líker (= like, resembling, likely, probable, promising, fit). &c . . .

---

28 Fort Square
Gloucester, MA
Monday Dec 4, 1961

My dear Jeremy Prynne:

Yr magazine in today and I have so far read yr last para. on resistance two or three times, which I find excellent. (Yr long letter via derivation also in the past

27. Prynne refers to his brief essay "Resistance and Difficulty."
28. See Olson's "GRAMMAR" in *Collected Prose*, 191, which refers to *gelīc*.

week and keeping it until my own mind is ready to have it, I hope you won't mind, it's like having mail ready when one craves it . . . not like the organist an American organist told me abt, at Oxford I think or it may have been Cambridge who placed each new coming mail carefully unopened on the top of the previous in a vertical case made to fit so that at least he had his own archaeology of mail received and a certain order of deposit if no knowledge of what had ever been written him or by whom!

Will write again soon—and please keep it coming

yrs
Charles Olson

---

28 Fort Square
Gloucester, MA
December 5, 1961

My dear Prynne:

I am very moved (as you'd expect me to be) by your 'piece' I want to call it—your letter—on derivation: or what is to give it its more interesting word an extension of etymology to found life and expression (yes?).

I've just read it and want to write a note to you simply off the top of it (I think you have 'thought' more than I, on the matter, and my report back would be only a sort of war-report, how it goes . . . e.g. yr word fundament knocks me right out of my seat, like . . . and that whole sense of how the rock is what one does launch oneself from when one does dive into the sea!

I hear you instantly on gelic as isomorphic, and my 'same' there was rather that than identical; or indeed just such import to the verb 'like' as you draw out of Pokorny: kin. In this whole area the engendering which comes about what I called in my letter to Elaine Feinstein types . . . in the meaning below imprint (the 'given' of your most valuable para. on resistance, to lay over that damned purposive thing which has so much kept swiftness out of the very best—and often the most limpid—language use.[29] (The prose of *[Ford Madox]* Ford's Good Soldier, e.g., gets as much of its freshness and present delight—after all the gains since 1914—because of that curious & marvellous way of returning to the same person over and over from another look at the familiar, with that saddest premise—I'm not even sure it felt to him, in his dog-like way of temperament hung-up on any governing human being as he was—of like: he the character of the 1st person liked Edward whateverhisname was.[30]

29. See *Collected Prose*, 250–52.
30. Edward Ashburnham is the central figure in Ford's *The Good Soldier: A Tale of Passion* (1915).

So much has all this area come in to play light on what was previously it wd seem a gender division—which tended to usurp human feeling so much that much of the mystery derivation can restore double and mobility to—that I think 'like' (simile—she sounds like a goddess, Simile) these are isomorphisms ((typos-es) which bring up huge structures of a different topology than was constructible by the long 'humanism' which existed after Indo-European root registers (((Scandinavian Britain, like))).

Just for my own thought or 'rocks,' don't mind if I somewhat doggedly pursue your letter via the other two terms of that idea, of tropos and—the easiest—topos. Isn't how one is bent much of that that you write about, of the I finding its identity and thus coming to control its own pronoun and thus any part of speech? That style isn't so much the man—or is, actually, but that that it is doesn't come so readily via that ratio—and that the limpid is equally more a social power, which comes after a previous achievement . . . I flow again into your 'resistance' place, the rock a person finds out they are jumping off of.

All right. I dare say this seems reluctant to the run of your own thought there—for it is delightful how encompassing and successfully analytical you are.

just for today, yrs
Charles Olson

---

109 Grantchester Meadows
Cambridge
December 10, 1961

Dear Charles Olson,

Thanks for notes, & yes of course I wd rather wait until pressure builds up for further speaking in these realms—feeling one's way through the soles of the feet perhaps. I much like Going Right out of the Century, and shd have it in print by Feb–March I hope. I have taken The Picture as gloss here, for the geodetic context, but do not know what 'shallops' are.[31] (One of the words I failed to search out in Webster while I had this to hand. Incidentally, the luck of fylfot as a running head in Webster must be lost on my countrymen.)

As one more 'random' observation, I have a sharp feeling on reading the 1st Letter on Georges that 'sway' has the most powerful centrifugal implications (in-foldings) arising from the root sense of 'bend, swing, turn.'[32] To hoist then perhaps contains the force of: sling upwards & into the wind current, to catch

31. Olson, *Maximus* II, 74.
32. See Olson, "1st Letter on Georges," in *Maximus* I, 140.

and belly out, bending before the onset. I haven't looked into this (pure conjecture), but Old Norse sveigja holds this notion of yielding partly but not wholly to pressure. The power swirling behind suchlike is quite intoxicating.

Best,
J. H. Prynne

---

28 Fort Square
Gloucester, MA
December 12, 1961

My dear Prynne

Would you give mime / (mimos) a run in your Pokorny—& im, my Greek lexicon says ("imititare" skk "___?)—+ see if he offers any connection of Mimir, in Norse mythology, to sd same root?

It wld interest me very much at the moment my—+ my thanks.

Yrs,
Charles Olson

CHAPTER 2
1962

109 Grantchester Meadows
Cambridge
January 8, 1962

Dear Charles Olson,

Very sorry for my delay in answering your last letter & query—I have been away for Christmas, and only yesterday got back to striking distance of a library. Your problem is a complicated one, and it's too bad I'm not even half qualified to give a proper answer. However, I'll cite as much material as seems relevant, and you can judge for yourself. If there is a connection between mimir and μῖμος, it seems it must be a remote & devious one; it does not seem to have been suggested before.

On the subject of Mimir the mythological figure, H. R. Ellis Davidson writes (Folklore, 69 [1958], p. 154): "Mimir, who is a smith in the medieval German poems, and in the 'Thiðriks Saga' appears as Weland's first teacher. . . . In Old Norse poetic tradition he is a giant associated with the Other World and with the spring beneath the World Tree. He is presumably to be identified with the 'satyr of the woods,' Mimingus, in Saxo's 'Danish History' (III, 70–1), from whom the hero Hotherus obtained a sword and a ring. To reach his dwelling it was necessary to make a long and difficult journey through a region of darkness and intense cold, fraught with obstacles and 'hard for mortal man to travel.' This suggests that his dwelling was in the Land of the Dead." The Well of Mimir figures in the Vǫluspǫ́ (stanza 21), and also in the Sigrdrífumál, where Mimir's severed head speaks wise words and true sayings (stanza 14). In her edition of this last text (printed in her The Hávámal, with Selections from Other Poems of the Edda [Cambridge, 1923], p. 120), D. E. Martin Clarke discusses some of the other appearances of Mimir, and notes that "In the Gylfaginning we are told that at the ragnar røk [end of the world] Óðinn will ride to Mimir's well to take counsel of Mimir for himself and his host." Thus the figure of Mimir is well established at the centre of early Teutonic mythology, with an important role to play. And as is the case with so many similar figures, the etymology of his name is by no means clear.

The most recent consideration of the problem is by Jan de Vries, *Altnordisches Etymologisches Wörterbuch* (Leiden, 1961), whose remarks I translate from the German as follows: *MIMIR*, m. 'mythical personage.' The *r* is not part of the word's root, as we also find the forms *Mími* and Mīmr. [In the *Sigrdrífumál* and the *Vǫluspǭ*, the same phrase, 'Míms höfuð' (= the head of Mimir), exhibits another form without the *r*.] *mīmeren*, Modern Dutch *mijmeren* (= to consider, meditate). *[Joseph]* Bosworth-*[T. Northcote]* Toller (*An Anglo-Saxon Dictionary* [Oxford, 1898]), gloss *mamorian*, *mamrian*, as 'to be deep in thought about anything (?)' and suggest a comparison with the later *mammering*. The *New English Dictionary*, however, observes that 'It is doubtful whether this [mammer] has any connection with the OE *mamrian*.' For the verbal noun *mammering* they give the meanings 'stammering; state of doubt, hesitation.' De Vries continues his comments on *Mimir* by citing these further cognates: Avestan *mimara*- (= mindful of, remembering), formed perhaps by reduplication **moi-mer*, **mi-mer*; cf. the root **mer* in Gothic *maurnan*. These words, he continues, can be traced further back to Latin *memor* (= remembering), Greek *μερμαίρω*, (= care, thought, worry, hesitation); Old Indian *smarati* (= to recollect, deliberate); Old Irish *airmert* (= prohibition, hinderance).

This is all de Vries has to say; but it seems to me fairly probably that also related to this *Wortfeld* are Old Icelandic *minna* (= to remind of, to remember, bear in mind), *minni* (= recollection; memorial), &c. Pokorny would seem to take this back to 3. *men*-, with the general meaning of 'think, be mentally active': under this heading he discusses Latin *meminī* and *mementō*, and Old Icelandic *mine* (= 'memory').

Turning to *mime*, we seem to be tantalizingly out of reach of the foregoing. The NED takes this back of course to *μῖμος*, Latin *mīm-us*, giving its root classical sense as '(A performer in) a kind of simple farcical drama among the Greeks and Romans, characterized by mimicry and the ludicrous representation of familiar types of character; a dialogue written for recital in a performance of this kind.' *[Henry]* Liddell & *[Robert]* Scott remark that it was typically 'without any distinct plot, which seems to have originated among the Dorians of Sicily.' Perhaps relevant here are Aristotle's cursory remarks in Chap III of the *Poetics*. The earliest English form of the word, Old English *mima* (900 a.d.) must almost certainly come direct from the Greek; otherwise *mimick*, *mimmick* are the earliest forms, from the Latic *mimic-us*, Greek *μιμίκός*. The word occurs in Shakespeare (1590), *[John]* Marston (1598), Ben Jonson (1599), with its central significance as 'exercising the profession of a mime or buffoon; having the characteristics of, or resembling, a mime.' *mimic* as a transitive verb does not appear until somewhat later. Under his heading *Mime* in *Origins* (London,

1958), Eric Partridge considers mime, mimesis, mimetic, mimetite; mimic, mimicry; mimosa; mimeograph; maya (magical power). He writes: "1. *Maya*, Sanskrit *māyā*, is perhaps akin to Bulgarian *izmama*, deception (? originally by imitation), and to Greek *mim*eisthai, to imitate, probably from *mimos*, a play of real life imitated grotesquely: Indo-European root **mei*-, variants **mai*-, **mi*-, to deceive—cf. Old High German *mein*, false, deceptive." J. B. Hofmann, in his *Etymologisches Wörterbuch des Griesischen* (München, 1949), similarly takes it back to Old Indian *māyā* (= change, transformation; illusory appearance; deception), and thence to the same conjectural roots as Partridge. Émile Boisacq, in his *Dictionnaire Étymologique de la Langue Greque* (Paris-Heidelberg, 1938), remarks that the etymology of *μῖμος* is obscure, and derives it from Sanskrit *máyatē*, citing Lettish *míju mít* (= 'troquer, échanger'); thus he is substantially of the same opinion as the others.

The relevant root in Pokorny is thus 2. *mei*-, with the basic signification of 'to change, deceive; hence, mutual, exchange gift, rendering.' He cites Old Indian *máyatē* (= exchange), Latin *mūnis* (= willing to serve) from archaic *moenus* (= service, function, tribute, gift, service of love [cf. the Old High German ethos of *Minne*, equivalent to the troubadour courtly love tradition &c.]), Lithuanian *maĩnas*, Lettish *mains* (= exchange), Old Bulgarian *měna* (= change, alteration), also various words for 'common, mutual,' and for 'revenge.' He refers finally to the associated roots *mei-gu-*, *mei-k-*, *mei-ti*-, from which derive such words as migrate, mix, mutate, &c. Unfortunately, as the index has still to be issued, I have not been able to locate the root under which he discusses *μῖμος*; but I have been carefully through all the roots with the initial letter *m*, and cannot see it there.

Last of all, *imitate*, which is unrelated to all the previous material; Boisacq makes a special point of noting that the Latin *imitō*, -*tor* has no connection with *μῖμος*. It derives from Latin *aemŭlus*, *aemŭlor* (= rivalling; to imitate, compete with).

Thus what I fear must seem an unfruitful enquiry; cross-relationships if any only of a most tenuous kind. I will keep my eyes open for further material, however, and let you know if anything crops up; if I knew Greek it would help, but my schooling so-called let me down unforgivably here, so I am stranded amongst the wreckage of assorted European dialects. I hope you'll write when you have time, with news of what goes and maybe something more for *Prospect*: & if you print anything & have a copy to spare, I should be most glad of it and surely interested.

Yours,
J. H. Prynne

---

109 Grantchester Meadows
Cambridge
January 16, 1962

Dear Charles Olson,

A brief nonletter, with this strong & agile account of tansy, written by a man who didn't know his prose was about to die under him:[1]

"Tanacetum vulgare & crispum. Tansie
Ovr Garden Tansie hath many hard greene leaues, or rather wings of leaues; for they are many small ones, set one against another all along a middle ribbe or stalke, and snipt about the edges: in some the leaues stand closer and thicker, and somewhat crumpled, which hath caused it to be called double or curld Tansie, in others thinner and more sparsedly: It riseth vp with many hard stalks, whereon growe at the tops vpon the seuerall small branches gold yellow floweres like buttons, which being gathered in their prime, will hold the colour fresh a long time: the seede is small, and as it were chaffie: the roote creepeth vnder ground, and shooteth vp againe in diuers places: the whole herbe, both leaues and flowers, are of a sharpe, strong, bitter smell and taste, but yet pleasant, and well to be endured."
PARADISI IN SOLE Paradisus Terrestris. or, A Garden of all sorts of pleasant flowers which our English ayre will permit to be noursed vp. . . . Collected by John Parkinson, Apothecary of London, 1629.

"But yet pleasant"—the acrid flavour is our pivot once more, round which we (may) turn to assess our own proper advantage. If only it were not so fine a task to separate this from rancour, the sharp from the merely sour, which sets up the astringent gesture as pure indulgence. Sometimes I cd wish there were not so much rancour in Maximus himself, about ownership & the ad-men; but at least thus he is feasibly human, & therefore of further pivotal value as a point of reference, ash-plant well to be endured. I am convinced that place has need of such nodes, axes to deploy their own symmetries; WCW *[William Carlos Williams]* is too often all circumference & periphery, because all demandingly relevant. How indeed deny that on which so much depends: but masts must be raised, or we shall never see where it was we departed from. I wish I had read something of *[Rainer Maria]* Gerhardt, but he is unobtainable; and I do not follow how

1. Prynne may be writing in response to the line, "o tansy city, root city" in Olson, "Letter 3," in *Maximus* I, 11.

you live "in a space we do not need to contrive."[2] Contrive, from con + turbare, to distract, perplex, implicate with the harassment of perspective: turbare has a strong vortical drive, which thus defines its axis in the sense I suggest above. Do you not feel the need to knit up your space into orbits, loops of arrival & departing, regrets mast-like against the horizon? Perhaps I run wild; but we here require urgently to un-knit our space, already congested with departures too distant to do more than entangle, as when Beowulf "himself led the way to the shore."[3]

But I must stop, as this is a non-letter.

Best,
J. H. Prynne

---

109 Grantchester Meadows
Cambridge
February 14, 1962

Dear Charles Olson,

We are delayed with PROSPECT 6, but should be out with your poem by April. Meanwhile I am sending the enclosed emblem of apprenticeship, for no very clear reason except that the attempt means nothing to anyone in this context over here.[4] It's a wordy gesture, I know, but some of the words concerned here have very deep roots—in any case the craft is to be learned, allegiances to be declared and fused with the changing weather. A landmark, if no more than this.

I hope to hear sometime, when & if it takes
you:

Best,
Jeremy Prynne

P.S. I passed Call Me Ishmael on to a friend here, Tony Ward, who is writing his second (totally ignored) novel & starving for want of the real community of concern he needs: he was stricken with excitement, & I think is going to write about this.[5] Hope you don't mind.

---

2. See Olson, "To Gerhardt, There, among Europe's Things of Which He Has Written Us in His 'Brief an Creeley und Olson,'" *Collected Poems*, 219.

3. See *Beowulf*, 11. 208–9: "sundwudu sohte secg wisade / lagucræftig mon landgemyrcu."

4. Prynne includes the typescript of his unpublished poem "After So Much Pride."

5. Olson's *Call Me Ishmael* (1947) is a study of Herman Melville and *Moby Dick*. Tony Ward was a contributor to *The English Intelligencer* and editor of *Prospect*.

109 Grantchester Meadows
Cambridge
March 6, 1962

Dear Charles Olson,

I thought you might be interested to see the enclosed broadsheet—insinuated under the guise of scholarship right into the heart of the academic machine.[6] Seriously, I hope you don't think this the wrong kind of tactic; the audience only got the list of authors & sources ten days after the first five pages, and the intention was purely to open up the field. Clear the sullen resonances of an irrelevant English tradition, the nervous ambiguities and "meddlesome elegance": listen closely to the unobstructed clarity of pure space: then the single human voice, right out of the physical centre, the shapes of its earned humanity. All dissembling as a chronological survey, but in pin-point earnest; someone might just see & hear why all this matters.

Best,
Jeremy Prynne

---

28 Fort Square
Gloucester, MA
Apr 26, 1962

Dear Prynne: A fine kettle of fish, you shld wait so long for any answer including your excellent poem, and letters (including that one, answering my query so completely.

Altogether thanks and if I don't sit right down now and write abt yr poem I'll at least enclose this quote from a 17 yr old who wrote me this week and sd he was writing verse "testing the limits of mind's comprehension of imagery." Which sounded fair enough, and I wrote back to him abt yr poem (his name is John Thorpe, and we may hear of him—if he gets out of a NeuroPsychiatric Institute he's in for what he says are existence problems: Wow, 17

6. The broadsheet is ten poems and an accompanying bibliography in six pages entitled "The Immediate World: Aspects of some Recent American Verse," sent to members of the Jesus College Literary Society in Cambridge. The poems are the following: Walt Whitman, "Song of the Open Road," section 13 (1856); Ezra Pound, "The Lake Isle," from *Lustra* (1916); Wallace Stevens, "An Ordinary Evening in New Haven," section III (early version, 1949); William Carlos Williams, "A Sort of a Song," *The Wedge* (1944), and "Flowers by the Sea," *An Early Martyr* (1935); Robert Creeley, "Air: Cat Bird Singing," *A Form of Women* (1959); Charles Olson, "tuesday may 23 L" [short poem written in letter to Vincent Ferrini dated May 23, 1950, and published in *Origin* I (1951)] and "In Cold Hell, in Thicket" (1950), section 2; Edward Dorn, excerpt from "The Landscapes Below," *The Floating Bear* 3 (1961) (also published as "The Land Below" in *Prospect* 6 and his 1964 collection *Hands Up*) and "The Common Lot," *The Newly Fallen* (1961).

I've either been in a drag or off somewhere reading (public readings of verse, by which one does finally make small earnings more than published work does! 50 dollars here—and once, on St. Valentine's Day, 200!

Please put us back on, and forever don't mind if I seem to go off out of orbit or something: it may be only now and then and at all it doesn't interfere with my sense that you are there and that makes much go on which may not get expressed

I was delighted by yr means of quotes unidentified for the Jesus Literary Society—and wish I were near enough to attend. Best, and quickly, to pick the whole thing up

Charles Olson

---

109 Grantchester Meadows
Cambridge
April 30, 1962

Dear Charles Olson,

It's a coincidence you should right at this moment reach me through the mail, since only last night I happened to see the nasus + torquere root of that particular pungency and thus to follow the linking there, across to the other singular accuracies. And I have been re-reading The Twist, with a closer sense of its movement.[7] On first reading I was worried over the blackberry blossom: the pressure of circumstance carried me with total conviction to this veracity, but the blossom seemed to carry itself as instance rather than fact, one out of a possible range of alternatives, any of which would have served. That is to say, the particular fact (by so devastating a sleight of hand) becomes an emblem of its own unique status, its place in the geographic; not itself real but a pointer to its own necessary reality. And I was wrong, I see, because it is the twist that the intersections of tidal motion define which furnishes the credible ground out of which this bramble can grow. The pungency of turning, the precision at the temporal zenith—here are the map references for this bramble's roots, a quadrant which because precisely local can belong to any interested person. Exactly there, the whole of it, personal history on the fulcrum of this day's sun.

Here is the matter put in rather more devious but equally geometric terms by a professional philosopher. He talks of the demonstrative identification of particulars, by which he means the use of terms like "this thing here" in contexts where this is not liable to misunderstanding, and then says: "By demonstrative

7. Olson, "The Twist," *Maximus* I, 86–90.

identification we can determine a common reference point and common axes of spatial direction; and with these at our disposal we have also the theoretical possibility of a description of every other particular in space and time as uniquely related to our reference point. . . . It cannot be denied that each of us is, at any moment, in possession of such a framework—a unified framework of knowledge of particulars, in which we ourselves and, usually, our immediate surroundings have their place, and of which each element is uniquely related to every other and hence to ourselves and our surroundings. . . . When we become sophisticated, we systematise the framework with calendars, maps, co-ordinate systems; but the use of such systems turns, fundamentally, on our knowing our own place in them." (P. F. STRAWSON, Individuals; An Essay in Descriptive Metaphysics [London, 1959], pp. 22, 24, 25.)

Such assurance about the average human's confident orientation within his landscape may be valid on this logical level; but inasmuch as this is a more complex matter of values and the knowledge of what it is to be a person, I am sure that the great majority have only surrogates for such a "framework," the sense of significant relation. He goes on to observe that "The identification and distinction of places turn on the identification and distinction of things; and the identification and distinction of things turn, in part, on the identification and distinction of places. There is no mystery about this mutual dependence" (p. 37). And later, "Clearly we do not, in ordinary conversation, make explicit the referential framework we employ. We do indeed often use demonstratives in reference to things in our immediate surroundings. But when our talk transcends them, we do not elaborately relate the things we speak of to the things we see. The place of the explicit relational framework is taken in part by that linguistic device which has so often and so justly absorbed the attention of logicians—the proper name. Demonstratives or quasi-demonstratives apart, it is proper names which tend to be the resting-places of references to particulars, the points on which the descriptive phrases pivot. Now, among particulars, the bearers par excellence of proper names are persons and places. It is a conceptual truth, as we have seen, that places are defined by the relations of material bodies; and it is also a conceptual truth, of which we shall see the significance more fully hereafter, that persons have material bodies" (p. 58). As regards the earlier mutual dependence, there seems in human terms to be every mystery, "something unknown but more importantly, cognizant, a crest, by which our common histories are made human again, and thrilling, for no other motive than they are ours" (Dorn on Maximus, p. 9).[8] And what is so fine about The Twist, I recognize (re-cognize), is the dense

8. See Dorn, *What I See in the Maximus Poems*, 9.

array of substantives which by virtue of their human disposition are all proper nouns, absolute resting-places. Ed Dorn notes the calmness of these nouns, "the shearings and simplicity of immediate knowledge," and he has this in the best of his poems too: not nouns simply, but names. The figure of Maximus himself I take to be the finally inclusive proper name, with the poems his body & sense of it, if you like, the force behind this day's sun.[9]

Best wishes, & I was most pleased to hear
Jeremy Prynne

---

28 Fort Square
Gloucester, MA
Sept 24, 1962

My dear Jeremy Prynne: This may be completely idle ((and above all please forgive the awful paper—only large piece in the house))— and if it is simply don't bother it, and think of it (as I also do) as the chance to write to you again, after so long:

I seem now—after 5 yrs!—to be some where near having some command of these miserable matters I stuck myself with. But there is one part—which was hanging there then, 5 years ago, and I had passport to come to go to Weymouth to examine Portbook 873 (which is it, in the poem???

That is my question: do you because you are yrself, and in addition are there Cambridge happen is there any present new English scholarship—as there strikingly is, Cambridge here (Harvard has now historians of the 17th century etc, excellent young men now seeing that sd time etc—the Great Migration it is called here. . . .

well: if you shld know any such chaps, it wld etc. For I do have problems: like, is there anything known, or knowable now there England of the London merchant MATHEW *[sic]* CRADDOCK, for example; or one I am even more interested in who was reported to have set up here Gl Harbor 1639 a fishery—MAURICE THOMPSON

Now I do know what the DNB etc has on such: what my question is, and solely to you, because it is a thought tonight, and I hate organized scholarship, believing (at least where my problem sits—like the bad tap in the sink!—that tonight once organization gets it (plumbers!), hopeless: the real stuff doesn't come through etc[10]

OK. I dare say it all is going on here in Massachusetts, and Kenneth McRobbie

9. Prynne includes the typescript of his poem "Quite Certain," *Force of Circumstance*, 49.
10. DNB stands for *The Dictionary of National Biography*, likely the 1921–1922 edition by Leslie Stephens and Sidney Lee, as pointed out by George Butterick, *A Guide to the Maximus Poems*, 757.

anyway (who was in Canada and wrote poems, and is in England permanently now I think) and was going to Weymouth to see if that Portbook—for 1623 and on—cld be better read than Frances Rose-Troup maiden lady did so wondrously for 50 years before 30 years ago![11]

just on a shot, that yr acquaintance might include some fellow who was dug in to the Admiralty/Privy Council—and Port Papers whateverso there is now—etc. there, I do believe, and even know such a "Keeper" the British Museum etc

la: hello Hope all goes well, especially the poems (my own seem all now gone or waiting on these issues of getting rid of that earliest go damn *[sic]* Gloucester

yessir, that's it: what was happening here in the years—or was it all turned back to wilderness after John White

Or (which is the suspicion rode up on me again tonight) that if Craddock had a wigwam Ipswich 1631, as well as a house which caught fire Marblehead 1631, then by the law he may have also been following earlier English uses of Gl. Harbor (???

and invoices ladings there anywhere England Westcountry—or by now all drawn into the Govt files, Lon-don?

That is, the Dorchester center for Cape Ann had been the 1623–1626 or 7 spot, Weymouth in particular

Gloucester again comes into the record 13 years later, with a Bridport man showing up here, along with Mr Maurice Thompson, London merchant, plans for a fishery backed by the Mass. Court

Now Craddock was the one known London merchant between these dates—during those 13 to 14 years—who was, for some of those years at least, still trying to do what English fishing interests had done previous to the failure of the Dorchester Company (Eng.) attempt to hold a winter station here 1623–26 or 7

The reason why (if you shld know some one who was already into such matters) that there seems reason to suspect is this:

a minister (of Gloucester here) in 1775 sd in a sermon that there were fishermen here, and a minister, as early as 1633

now no one has been able to support this, and a later situation may be what he is reflecting: that, 1639 at least, there were fishermen here, and an early meeting house, with a young Harvard student minister Thomas Rashleigh apparently comforting these few

11. Kenneth McRobbie, born in England in 1929, is a poet and historian who taught at the University of Manitoba until 1990. Olson visited him in Toronto in 1960 and mentioned Portbook 873 in a subsequent letter to McRobbie. See Olson, *Selected Letters*, 277–80. Frances Rose-Troup, a pioneering historian of sixteenth- and seventeenth-century New England, authored numerous studies, including *John White* (1930) and *The Massachusetts Bay Company and Its Predecessors* (1930), both of which were primary texts for Olson's *Maximus* research.

My own desire of course is totally to fill in all that might be caught up out of the possible story of what was GL in those years:

and (2) on what I do know of who were these person*[s]* as *[of]* 1639—one man named Osmund Dutch of Bridport, and one a Mr Thomas Millward, I'd guess if there were fishermen here anytime between 1627 and 1639 they wld have had to be ENGLISHMEN, and any fish caught WOULD HAVE BEEN LADED to ENGLISH PORTS (Bristol, possibly the old bunch at the mouth of the WEY—or such a London merchant as CRADDOCK, or this new fellow, 1639, THOMPSON

OK. Even to sit here and say it all out to you isn't wasting my time, even if it may be of no interest to you whatsoever—for which I believe you will forgive me, having that sense that this at least is one way someone might be going about etc

(by the way still the little poem I sent you for Prospect, abt that salt fr the Zouch Phoenix of London on 10 Lb island—what is the present state of publication. . . . interested party

Jonathan Wms plans now to issue Vols III and IV via Stuttgart again, and arrives in England abt the time of this letter:[12] I hope he plans to come see you, if not why don't you, if interested, dig him out, at:

Bertram Rota Lt Books, Bodley House, Vigo St London W 1

(he sailed Sept 21st on the Nieuw Amsterdam)

(also—as of previous subject—look for ballad called "Gulf of Maine" all the same jive of those materials in POETRY, Golden something or other issue just ahead: wld enjoy hearing yr response to sd jive[13]

Allright and happy as hell to have you to write to tonight: and worry no more abt this—unless it shld be a coincidentia oppositorum for the life—and happiness of you

Hope all is good, and better, and
my fondest to you,
Charles Olson

Have missed very much hearing fr you—don't mind I am buried in same such matters as now disclose / will END SOON.[14]

---

12. Jonathan Williams (1929–2008), student of Olson's at Black Mountain College, and founder of Jargon Press, who published *The Maximus Poems 1–10* (1953) and *The Maximus Poems 11–22* (1956) in Stuttgart, West Germany.

13. Olson, "Gulf of Maine," *Poetry* (Oct–Nov. 1962), 85–88. See *Maximus* II, 108–10.

14. Olson wrote this letter on the rear side of an advertisement for his reading at The Hammond Museum in Gloucester on September 3, 1962.

Gonville and Caius College
Cambridge
September 28, 1962

Dear Charles Olson,

Your letter arrived this morning. If I use the typewriter at this hour of the night I shall waken any number of kids below. In addition, I am in the process of moving [to the above address, my finding tag for the future]. I am more or less camping among packing cases and trunks of clothes, papers and so on. Consequently I am personally in some disorder, as I take such shifts as a kind of affront: either move, often and with little, or stay put. These will sound like invented pieties, to fix one's self-esteem: but a painter friend of mine has 150 yds of road which deploy all the spaces he needs & that matter to him, and I feel a similar claim on patterns of incidence which converge on this spot. Perhaps any spot; like (to use your idiom) this locality doesn't matter more than what makes it central to one's concourse, anywhere can be here. The throwing towards can use any rock—but such casualness is all plausible lies, like *[Edmund]* Husserl's theory of consciousness (the world is "world-for-me," and world-for-me is mine before it is world, ergo I "constitute" the world by allowing it to have meaning). Is this more than that there are things which happen suddenly or a long time ago, shake out into more immediate needs? I was looking at a patch of good cabbages a while ago, and was gripped by this. Not epiphanic insight, not one of those damned 'moments,' but <u>in the reverse direction</u>. Far from removing out of the time and place, it opened out that lie of the land: I knew they would be cropped and eaten—sudden acts. Not for one instant did this kind of pointing happen over there when I was nearer your world. Like a camper, I rummaged in the bag to see what carelessly might have been brought. [Query: why don't you over there know the shape of your own contours—footpaths not to the Concord log cabin & overwrit diary, but as a matter of <u>course</u>.]

Hence as you'll see your letter fires right off for me, instantly. How should it not, as you might guess? This is no answer to you, because I must cast about for advantage, and shall need some time for this. And you know my task will be not to care too much for these things, and the workings of Craddock and Thompson. I will grab at what I can find, and not learn to consult archives with proper care & attention, by which your needful line could be broken up. To now though I know NOTHING, and shall take care whom to ask, &c. Over here antiquaries ask the right questions, not historians (mostly), for whom information tends to be illustrative or irrelevant. I may be wrong about this, as you could have asked re. gourds with greater immediate profit. All these are thoughts as I go, with your letter in front of me and most pleased to hear, having not written but thought often enough and can make little of the Poetry review of The Distances: why do they do that kind of arcadian fan-dance any more, as I think, back to that Creeley insert to the Stuttgart printing (such a fine job, though too expensive now to have).[15]

Transcripts is what you will need, of the exact utterance, so I take it, from whoever put it to record. I should know more about the nature & method of such things: mistakes & ignorance of a person nearer to it than photostat with footnotes—up to some point. Time and enquiry will tell. Later I will pull this together and write a letter, instead of taking how pleased I am to think of such-like into an envelope without delay. I am trying to get Ed Dorn into book shape over here, & there are possibilities here. I wd. like to see Jonathan Williams (and be sure of Vols III & IV), and will try to get moved and out into London for this. Why don't you come over here? I passed through Gloucester while in Massachusetts, but didn't stop because Englishmen alas don't do that kind of thing and besides, I must confess to a cordial dislike of the visible surface right there. To pass through, there was nothing to catch at: I am wary of shores at the best of times, as they have to be taken very suddenly . . .

It's getting later and later and I must stop turning it over and over. But also pleased to write from the waste lot and such matters are still strange ones. I will ask. There will be enquiries. [N.B. When an Englishman says pleased he means happy: this is a mean circumstance but here built-in, which is why my own vol. of poems (out November) is 96% of no interest to me.[16] Zip-fastener type of thing—dead as no door-nail would be, given any decent chance. Cid is unsparing with the rod of correction, but (a) he is too thin now, life is more explicit or to be thought about than that; and (b) roots are where they are, and the past must be at least treated with. But it's true of course, nothing there nor even a pointer (except privately, two or three)—maybe.]

With all affection,
Jeremy Prynne

Gonville and Caius College
Cambridge
October 2, 1962

Dear Charles Olson,

This to you and in haste, to report progress at the very start of your problem. Some notes on purely printed sources herewith, & I expect none of this is

15. See George Oppen, Review of *The Distances*: "Three Poets," *Poetry* 100 (August 1962), 329–33.
16. Prynne refers to his first (and later suppressed) collection, *Force of Circumstance and Other Poems* (London: Routledge and Kegan Paul, 1962).

strange. But I put myself more clearly in context, and you may possibly notice something here in passing, as a lead. And no time spent reading that truly excellent book of *[Bernard]* Bailyn's could be thought wasted: it brings me closer to it than anything else I've yet seen. Fact, and with much generous insight—or so it seems to me?

The enclosed are set out in polite jargon, so that I can use the carbon I've kept to pursue enquiries. I have spoken to economic historians here, and they agree that this particular area is very badly served. Port books and archives relating to ladings, invoices, customs &c, where they survive, will apparently be in the local depositories concerned, NOT centralised in London. (I'll be pleased to go & look if we can trace a useful reference.) The State papers can be seen at the Public Records Office, London; but I'm told that the summarised account of contents given in the Calendars is usually very complete where proper names are concerned. Of course, there is no reason why early trading voyages across the Atlantic should invoke dealings with the Privy Council.

Let me hear how this first stage strikes you, if you have time, and maybe fill out the information you already have re Craddock and Thompson [I haven't pursued your obvious local sources]. And as soon as a chance presents itself, I'll take the whole matter a stage further. Have you the names of any vessels involved?

Without much time,
Jeremy Prynne

P.S. Weymouth is too far I think, until the Spring at least—but it would be a great thing if you could come yourself—great for me.

Your inquiry about traceable trading activities of MATTHEW CRADDOCK and MAURICE THOMPSON, both sixteenth century merchants based on London, have so far yielded few positive results. Most of the material I refer to at this stage will already be familiar to you; I include it just to sketch in the background and to cover any possible gaps.

The information from your end about these two merchants centres on these two pieces of evidence, both unconfirmed:

> that Matthew Craddock tried after the failure of the Dorchester Company to establish a settlement on the Cape Ann, New England coast (c. 1623–27);
> that Maurice Thompson, with the backing of the Massachusetts Court, tried to set up a permanent fishing station at Gloucester Harbour, in about 1639.

Both propositions are quite feasible, and would fit in with existing general notions of the situation: "During the 1620's, groups from both London and the west country helped to finance expeditions resulting in the first organized settlements in the area. The inhabitants of these plantations were the Pilgrims, the Old Planters of Salem, the first Maine and New Hampshire colonists, and that wayward band of half-legendary characters, the original settlers of Massachusetts Bay. . . . The theory was simple and convincing: costs could be reduced and profits greatly increased by sending settlers to New England, where, as self-sufficient residents, they could catch fish, collect furs, and process other products for shipment to the entrepreneurs in England" (Bernard Bailyn, The New England Merchants of the Seventeenth Century [Cambridge, Mass., 1955], p. 10; cf. also pp. 78–82).

As Craddock's career is quite well documented (with, for example, a longish entry in the DNB and citations from his letters in Bailyn [op. cit., above]), background material is more readily available from printed sources. The earliest mention of him in the Calendar of State Papers (Colonial) refers to his Petition to the Privy Council of 1630. In company with Samuel Aldersey, Nath. Wright, Jo. Humphrey [see Bailyn, p. 17 & note thereto] and others, he petitioned "on behalf of the Governor and company of the Massachusetts Bay in New England . . . " for permission to tranship to settlers a quantity of provisions supplementary to their original supplies, to ease hardship. (See W. N. Sainsbury [ed], Calendar of State Papers, Colonial Series, 1574–1660, Preserved in the State Paper Department of Her Majesty's Public Record Office [London, 1860], p. 120.) It would from this appear likely that the settlers had been transported in the spring or summer of 1629, and were experiencing the usual immediate difficulties of making ends meet. Craddock's Petition was presented on 29th September 1630, when the need for stores to endure the coming winter would have become serious. In a subsequent entry concerning Minutes of the Council for New England (dated June 1632), Sainsbury reports that "Mr. Humphreys and Matthew Cradock [sic, with one d throughout] reproved for falsely accusing Sir Ferd. Georges *[sic]* at the last meeting, of not suffering any ship or passenger to pass to New England without licence" (op. cit., p. 153). There are no entries before these dates that concern Craddock, so that it would seem on the face of it that earlier activity, if such there was, went unrecorded in this context (see also Bailyn's note on Cradock *[sic]*, op. cit., p. 17).

Maurice Thompson is a much more enigmatic figure. There are frequent mentions of his activities in connection with foreign trade in the State Papers, but none in connection with trade in this particular area. According to Sainsbury, Thompson was eventually a "Commissioner for the Somers Islands [i.e., the Bermudas]." Such officials were appointed to govern local affairs, and also "to establish the advancement of the colony, and make proposals to encourage adventurers to plant there" (op. cit., intro, p. xvii). This would indicate some considerable degree of success. It seems likely that he eventually purchased an Estate in England, as his son John Thompson (c. 1648–1710) was created 1st Baron Haversham. Maurice Thompson married Dorothy [but according to Collins, Ellen], daughter of John Vaux of Pembrokeshire; she died c. 1678. Maurice Thompson was buried at Haversham, in Buckinghamshire, in 1671 (George Lipscomb, The History and Antiquities of the County of Buckingham [4 vols, London, 1847], IV, 187–188 [the full pedigree is given; the family papers are unlikely to survive, as the line eventually became extinct]).

Charles Judah cites the entry in *[Governor John]* Winthrop's Journal (I, 310), where the start of Cape Ann's fishing trade is attributed to "Mr. Maurice Thomson [sic, without the p], a merchant from London" (C. B. Judah, "The North American Fisheries and British Policy to 1713," Illinois Studies in the Social Sciences, XVIII, Urbana, 1933, p. 66).

However, information about the trading careers of seventeenth-century merchants is very hard to come by, as the records are extremely patchy: "The annual customs accounts ceased to be enrolled in the Office of the King's Remembrancer at the accession of James I. The Inspectors-General of Imports and Exports did not begin to compile their ledgers until 1696. For the intervening years, the historian is driven back to sources that are both discontinuous and difficult to correlate. . . . There still remain a few of the original Port Books in which all imports or exports were required to be entered; but years of neglect have reduced a once complete series to a sample . . ." (F. J. Fisher, "London's Export Trade in the Early Seventeenth Century," Economic History Review, 2nd Ser., III [1950], 151). The situation regarding Shipping Registers is not a great deal better: of the outports in the British Isles, "only Liverpool has preserved its shipping register for the colonial period" (B. & L. Bailyn, Massachusetts Shipping, 1697–1714; a Statistical Study [Cambridge, Mass., 1959], p. 5 note; Excerpts from the American material in the Liverpool Register are printed in American Neptune, I [1941], 167, 297). In addition, the central register and related papers of the London customs house "seem to have disappeared for the whole period from its beginnings to 1835" (G. N. Clark, Guide to English Commercial Statistics, 1696–1782 [London, 1938], p. 50). One set of important documents for Bristol do survive, however; these will be mentioned later.

General surveys of the merchant entrepreneurs and their background are also very scarce, mostly concentrating not on the fisheries but on the cloth trade (e.g., B. E. Supple, Commercial Crisis and Change in England, 1600–1642; a Study in the Instability of a Mercantile Economy [Cambridge, 1959]). The main source for linked records of Thompson's career is thus the State Papers, from which it appears that he owned a number of ships, commissioned several more, and carried on trade with various colonial and other settlements. In 1632 it is recommended that "Tucker, Stone, and Maurice Thompson should contract for three or more years for all the tobacco of the growth of Virginia" (Sainsbury, p. 151). While this contract was still current, Thompson is mentioned in connection with trade about Canada and with the Caribee Islands. In September 1632 he is petitioned against for unlicensed "trading about Canada," and ordered to be fined 400 marks; he refused to pay this on two successive occasions (Sainsbury, p. 155 ff).

An important entry for "1634?" details "Petition of Maurice and Edward [not a son or relative recorded in Lipscomb] Thompson and Geo. Snelling to the Privy Council. Have Hired the Discovery and the Sampson for a voyage to the Caribee islands. Pray for licence to transport 500 dozen of shoes, 200 muskets, and 200 swords for the use and defence of these plantations" (Sainsbury, p. 195). Now a ship of 200 tons named the Sampson was built in Bristol, and a half share in it acquired by a couple of Bristol merchants, as details of this are preserved in the fairly complete and surviving Deposition Books of this port (Patrick McGrath, "Merchant Shipping in the Seventeenth Century; the Evidence of the Bristol Deposition Books, Part I," Mariner's Mirror, 40 [1954], 283). If both Sampsons are, as seems quite possible, one and the same vessel, then Bristol would seem to be a likely port of operations for at least part of Thompson's trading voyages. (See further John Latimer, History of the Society of Merchant Venturers of the City of Bristol [Bristol, 1903], ibid, The Annals of Bristol in the Seventeenth Century [Bristol, 1900], and Patrick V. McGrath, "The Merchant Venturers and Bristol Shipping in the Early Seventeenth Century," The Mariner's Mirror, 36 [1950], 69–80). Unfortunately, the Deposition Books only cover the period 1643–1687; detail are as follows:

Vol I	(1643–1647)	Ed. H. E. Nott, Bristol Record Society
Vol II	(1650–1654)	Ed. Nott & E. Ralph (Bristol Record Doc)
Vol III	(1654–1657)	Still in MS
Vol IV	(1657–1661)	Still in MS
Vol V	(1661–1667)	Still in MS
Vol VI	(1673–1687)	Still in MS

The depositions "were sworn statements made before the magistrates by people who wished to put on record evidence which might later be required in legal or other proceedings" (McGrath, "Merchant Shipping . . . ," p. 282). Information included details of ownership, bills of lading, master & crew, tonnage and overall value, costs of chartering ships and charges for carrying freight, insurance, conditions of cargoes, and so on.

Thompson probably also traded from the Port of London; In May 1638 "the Star of London and other ships, owned by Maurice Thompson and others, [was] to be restrained from trading with Guinea and Binney," without licence from the Guinea Company (Sainsbury, p. 273). The name would seem to indicate in this case a London-based vessel. In 1639–40 Thompson is engaged on further opportunistic supply voyages, on these occasions to Providence Island [i.e., the Bahamas]. "Thompson to have a commission for taking Spanish prizes in the West Indies" (Sainsbury, p. 309). In 1640 the voyages to Providence were regularised on the contractual basis of two ships per year. Thompson is again mentioned in 1649, in connection with plans for subduing the rebellious Virginia, and his name occurs for the last time in 1653.

All of the above may help to fill in some of the background concerning the two merchants in question; but as you will see, nothing has come to light as yet which would contribute towards confirming or refuting your two pieces of evidence concerning activities on the New England coast. Please excuse the sketchy—and probably inaccurate—compilation of these notes.

Gonville and Caius College
Cambridge
October 3, 1962

Dear Charles Olson,

Herewith a few more fruits of current rummaging, including some corrections to what I last wrote. Notably, that all the Port Books are there to be seen, in London & no distance from where I am. I suggest that you go through what you know and what you still need with a tooth comb, and then let me know as precisely as possible what to look for; I will then go to the PRO and transcribe the relevant sections. It's too bad there's no centralised index of names, or by ships, destinations &c—but that's too much to hope for alas. By now it is clear to me that McGrath (at the University of Bristol) is the expert on Bristol shipping and trade records, and that this Williams knows more about Port Books than any man living; we should be able to go on from here. You'll realise that I've so far found nothing of remotest interest, and simply familiarised myself with the field and sources already printed; I have looked through dozens of other volumes & records etc., but have arranged to quote only from all the important things that turned up, so that you have the reference in case of need.

Hope things are well for you, and
apologise for great haste,
Jeremy Prynne

P.S. Entries shown on the enclosed as "Overseas" of course include trade with the New England colonial settlements as well as European markets.

NOTES

The above particulars are excerpted from the comprehensive index cited above, which has a short but valuable introduction. Books containing details of coastal trade, or trade conducted by aliens, have not been included here; neither have books devoted to specialist forms of trade, e.g., wine or wool &c.

Port Books were taxation documents and not commercial records, so that the actual commercial picture to be built up from them is sometimes disappointing. However, Fisher's comments (in "London's Export Trade . . .") on the fragmentary state of the Port Book records are not fully justified; there are indeed many incomplete or missing volumes, but the system entailed so much double & triple registration of identical particulars that few periods are without some form of record. Destinations and the names of ships and masters are often given, but as Williams remarks, "much more important than the names of ships are those of merchants. London merchants are happily given the name of the city company of which they were freemen, and membership of the fellowship of merchants adventurers or staplers is also often specified" (N. J. Williams, "The London Port Books," Transactions of the London & Middlesex Archaeological Society 18 [1956], 13–26; an excellent review article). McGrath reports on the Bristol Port Books as follows: "there are a considerable number of books relating to overseas and coastal shipping up to 1639, although a number of books are missing, and others imperfect. There is nothing on foreign trade between 1639 and 1667, and there are certain gaps in the series during the rest of the century" (Patrick McGrath, Merchants and Merchandise in Seventeenth-Century Bristol [Bristol, 1955], p. xxxvii). All these Port Books, for each of the several outports and during the whole period for which they were kept, are now kept in the Public Records Office, Chancery Lane, London W.C.2, and the finding references here cited are part of the classification scheme adopted by the PRO. In addition to Port Books, Bristol also preserves other types of record relating to shipping and marine trading (see McGrath's general survey, op. cit. above). Most important are the

Brief Details of Port Books Relevant to the Inquiry
(Extracted from N. J. Williams [ed.], Descriptive List of Exchequer, Queen's Remembrancer, Port Books; Part I, 1565 to 1700 [London, 1960])

Head Port Of London

Dates covered	PRO Finding Reference	Nature of Entries
1622–1623	E.190.26/7	Exports by denizens
1623–1624	E.190.28/6	Exports by denizens
1624–1625	E.190.28/1	Overseas outwards
1625–1626	E.190.29/4	Overseas outwards
1625–1626	E.190.31/3	Imports by denizens
1626–1627	E.190.31/4	Overseas outwards
1626–1627	E.190.31/1	Overseas outwards
1626–1627	E.190.32/2	Overseas: exports by denizens
1628–1629	E.190.34/4	Overseas: exports by denizens
1629–1630	E.190.34/2	Overseas inwards
1629–1630	E.190.35/4	Overseas inwards
1630–1631	E.190.35/5	Exports by denizens
1631–1631	E.190.36/1	Overseas outwards
1631–1632	E.190.36/7	Overseas: exports by denizens
1632–1633	E.190.38/1	Overseas: imports by denizens
1633–1634	E.190.38/2	Overseas inwards
1633–1634	E.190.38/4	Overseas inwards
1633–1634	E.190.38/5	Overseas imports by denizens
1633–1634	E.190.38/7	Exports by denizens
1634–1635	E.190.39/1	Overseas: outwards
1635–1636	E.190.37/13	Overseas inwards
1635–1636	E.190.40/4	Overseas: exports by denizens
1636–1636	E.190.40/5	Overseas outwards
1637–1638	E.190.41/5	Overseas inwards
1638–1638	E.190.42/1	Overseas inwards
1638–1639	E.190.42/3	Overseas outwards
1638–1639	E.190.43/6	Overseas: exports by denizens
1639–1639	E.190.43/2	Overseas: exports by denizens
1639–1640	E.190.43/1	Overseas: exports by denizens
1639–1640	E.190.43/5	Overseas: imports by denizens
1639–1640	E.190.43/4	Overseas: exports by denizens
1639–1640	E.190.44/1	Overseas: exports by denizens

Port Of Poole, Comprising The Head Port Of Poole And The Creeks Of Weymouth And Lyme (Weymouth volumes only listed)

1619–1620	E.190.872/6	Overseas
1621–1622	E.190.873/4	Overseas
1623–1623	E.190.873/5	Overseas
1625–1626	E.190.873/9	Overseas
1627–1628	E.190.874/5	Overseas
1632–1633	E.190.875/6	Overseas
1633–1634	E.190.875/8	Overseas
1634–1635	E.190.766/2	Overseas
1634–1635	E.190.876/1	Overseas
1635–1636	E.190.876/6	Overseas
1636–1636	E.190.876/10	Overseas
1636–1637	E.190.876/11	Overseas
1638–1639	E.190.877/8	Overseas
1638–1639	E.190.1036/7	Overseas
1645–1646	E.190.878/6	Overseas

Head Port Of Bristol

Dates covered	PRO Finding Reference	Nature of Entries
1620–1621	E.190.1134/11	Overseas outwards
1620–1621	E.190.1134/10	Overseas
1622–1622	E.190.1135/2	Overseas
1622–1623	E.190.1135/3	Overseas
1624–1625	E.190.1135/5	Overseas outwards
1624–1625	E.190.1135/6	Overseas
1625–1626	E.190.1135/8	Overseas outwards
1626–1627	E.190.1135/10	Overseas
1628–1629	E.190.1136/1	Overseas outwards
1636–1636	E.190.1136/5	Overseas
1636–1637	E.190.1136/8	Overseas outwards
1637–1638	E.190.1136/10	Overseas inwards
1638–1639	E.190.1136/6	Overseas inwards

Wharfage Books, 20 volumes of which have survived. Unfortunately, though "the wharfage books give details of goods imported into Bristol, the names of the ships in which they came, and the names of the merchants who paid the duty" (McGrath, p. liii), none of these documents survive for the period before 1654 (see McGrath, p. 174 & note). Bristol also preserves The [Bristol] Society of Merchant Venturers, Book of Trade, 1598–1693 (now located at the Merchants' Hall, Bristol). But by no means all merchants operating via Bristol joined this society (neither Cradock *[sic]* nor Thompson were members), and these records relate only to trade carried on by actual members: "the evidence of the Burgess Rolls and the Port Books shows that, apart from the petty dealers, there were many merchants who did not join the Merchant Venturers" (McGrath, Records Relating to the Society of Merchant Venturers of the City of Bristol in the Seventeenth Century [Bristol, 1952], p. xxi). Cf also C. M. MacInnes, Bristol A Gateway of Empire, and the History & Annals of Bristol published by John Latimer at the start of this century.

On Port Books in general, cf. M. S. Giuseppi, A Guide to the Manuscripts Preserved in the Public Records Office (2 vols, London, 1923–24): "Port Books. 1565 to 1798. 1,551 Bundles. These were entry books kept by the Customs Officers at the various ports. Though varying somewhat as to the amount of information they contain, they show usually the names of ships entering and leaving, the nature and value of their merchandise, the places whence they sailed and their destination" (p. 109). These volumes are technically part of the Records of the Exchequer—the King's Remembrancer, and are freely available for inspection by the public; for details and conditions of access, see V. H. Galbraith, An Introduction to the Use of the Public Records Office (corrected reprint, Oxford, 1952). There are also facilities for photostatic reproduction.[17]

---

28 Fort Square
Gloucester, MA
Saturday[18]

My dear Jeremy Prynne

You mustn't mind. You sent me every thing I could have possibly wanted. I have tried to write you every day. This is simply to get some word to you.

Yours,
Charles

---

17. Prynne wrote to N. J. Williams at the Public Record Office on October 3 to request additional information about the Port Books and a copy of Williams's article. He received a reply on October 5.
18. Letter is undated, but probably either October 20 or 27.

Gonville and Caius College
Cambridge
November 7, 1962

Dear Charles Olson,

Nor do I mind, in the least, since I have no occasion to do so; do not disturb yourself over transmitting the specific response, as I can divine this over a great distance. Dammit, there's more to life than bread-and-butter letters; the flow of information has grown thinner only because I am preparing for the eventual attack on the Port Books themselves. I have my reader's ticket for the PRO now, and am waiting for my opportunity. What strikes me as relevant I will try to have microfilmed, since this is the only way you will be sure of having the full authentic record; all that I need from you is a more general indication of what specifically to watch out for, the matters of concern. But there is no haste over this, just when you can & feel inclined; meanwhile I am also negotiating on Ed Dorn's behalf for an English printing of his poems. He has sent me the MS of his new collection, HANDS UP! which is a marvellous thing & full of great rarity. I have induced Donald Davie to like it, and he is a figure of such authority in these matters that we should be able to find a publisher without too much difficulty.[19] I certainly hope so: it might trigger off some sort of breakthrough in this dismal land, recapture a lost element of primary attention and its governance. My students are being exposed straight away, as you will see from the enclosed exercise.[20] I have added a prim rubric, to conceal the quality of my interest (which would not be proper), and hope for some rudimentary liveliness of attention; some of the minds are after all still more or less fresh to this thing, that there are poems outside the museums.

All best wishes,
Jeremy Prynne

P.S. I went down to London to see Jonathan Williams, but he had left on a trip to the Lake District without address. I have meant to write to him to await return, but would still prefer the unconstructed encounter, why I don't really know.

19. Donald Davie (1922–1995), poet, critic, teacher and colleague of Prynne at Gonville and Caius College.
20. Prynne refers to a Practical Criticism exercise on Dorn's poem "On the Debt My Mother Owed to Sears Roebuck" that he used for teaching. See Dorn, *Collected Poems*, 74–75.

CHAPTER 3
1963

London
Public Records Office
January 8, 1963

Dear Charles Olson,

Just a note written from the search room of the Public Records Office, where I am awaiting production of the next batch of port books. I have been going through these fairly steadily, though the state of affairs is not a very encouraging one. The port books themselves are mostly in a very poor state of repair, being sewn bunches of vellum that have evidently been exposed to accumulated dirt & dust, damp, and what looks like rats. The script appears to be a form of court hand (?), including a wide range of contracted forms and abbreviations, sometimes neat and sometimes not. Unfortunately I haven't a great deal of time here, so that I can't follow each ledger through and produce a digest of relevant information on the spot. However, I am ordering microfilm of all the important items, and enclose a more detailed note of what I am having thus copied. The staff here tell me that they are very behind with their work in the photographic department, and that a delay of up to ten or twelve weeks is to be expected; I have asked them to press on, and to send me the results as soon as they are ready. I imagine that you will not find them easy to decipher, since the brown ink used is often not far in tone from the darkened vellum sheets, and has sometimes either faded, or partly rubbed away. The damp has caused extensive deterioration. But you will have advantages over me, in knowing the names of merchants and vessels which matter, as well as the crucial dates, so that you will be able to concentrate on the really significant entries. You will see from my enclosed list that I have asked for film of all the pages actually containing entries in the Weymouth port books 1621–28 relating to overseas trade, and also (because this seems an important year) the similar records for 1623 from London and Bristol. You must let me know as the work goes forward if there are other periods or ports that you need to know about, as the film isn't all that costly, and it's only the delay that is rather frustrating.

Nor much else currently, except that I am hearing a good deal from Ed Dorn who is a great burning bush without knowing it. His new collection, Hands Up! sent me sprawling with sheer delighted admiration, and has also a very deep thrust at the rock level. He's sent me the whole MS, and I'm hoping to find him a London publisher, since he certainly needs that. I have several contacts, and thus considerable hopes for this. He has told me about *[John]* Ledyard, and I am just reading the Memoirs of the Life and Travels put together by Jared Sparks (London, 1828). It is the modesty of all this that excites so, throws down the roots: certainty.

Always the best,
Jeremy Prynne

Excuse haste. And P.S: I've had to abandon the idea of film of the London & Bristol 1623 books, since the London book is "unfit for inspection" and the Bristol books eaten away thus—but will send anything you know to be needful. J.P.

E.190. 872/6
Weymouth overseas (1619–1620). In advanced state of decomposition and unfit for inspection or for filming; according to PRO staff it would require a very expert archivist to retrieve what information still survived in this document.

E.190. 873/4
Weymouth overseas (1621–1622). Very brief and in bad state of preservation, with leaves very torn and crumpled; compiled in a bold and rather untidy hand. Microfilm ordered.

E. 190. 873/5
Weymouth overseas (1623). Brief (7pp. of text) and in extremely poor state of presentation; torn and crumbling at all edges, badly creased, and several pages partly inseparable. Severely affected by damp, esp. at lower edges, which has made parts of text almost undecipherable. Written in a bold hand not easy to follow. Microfilm ordered.

E.190. 873/9
Weymouth overseas (1625). Full record of an evidently busy period; in a neat hand and a good state of repair. Microfilm ordered.

E. 190. 874/5
Weymouth overseas (1627–28). Severely damaged in places by damp, and eaten

through at the top by what seem to have been rats. The top quarter of all the early pages is thus more or less lost. In a neat but rather faded hand. Microfilm ordered.

Gonville and Caius College
Cambridge
January 16, 1963

Dear Charles Olson:

Herewith from the Reverend William Barnes, Dorset poet and man of forgotten learning: "Dislike seems a bad word-shape. Mislike is the old and true English one. Like is from lic, a shape, as lich, the body of a dead man. "It liketh (lica[eth]) me well" is "it shapes itself (looketh) to me well." "It misliketh me" is "it misshapes itself to me" (looks bad). To seem is from the thing-name—sam, seam, seem, body or mass—and "it seems to me" is "it bodies itself to me." "That ship seems to be a French one," or "that man seems to be ill," bodies itself or himself to be a French one or ill" (An Outline of English Speech-Craft [London, 1878], p. 41). I can't trace this line from seem back to "body or mass," but it has the feel of being not far out. Under Seemly *[Walter W.]* Skeat cites Icelandic sæmiligr, "seemly, becoming; a longer form of sæmr, becoming, fit, with suffix -ligr answering to A. S. -líc, like, and E[nglish] -ly.—Icel. sama, to beseem, befit, become; cognate with Goth. samjan, to please. The lit. sense is 'to be the same,' hence to be like, to fit, suit, be congruent with. . . . Thus seemly = same-like agreeing with, fit; and seem is to agree with, appear like, or simply, to appear; the A. S. séman, to conciliate [bring together], is the same, with the act. sense 'to make like,' make to agree" (An Etymological Dictionary of the English Language [Oxford, 1882], p. 538). Pokorny's root forms are sem- (unified, brought together, same) and som- (together, along with). Same is thus the primary individual, known as essentially one by comparison with another.

And for all Barnes' love of Anglo-Saxon and his Dorset dialect, the result isn't the Wm Morris archaising without roots, but a noble voice: "The goodness of a speech should be sought in its clearness to the hearing and mind, clearness of its breath-sounds, and clearness of meaning in its words; in its fulness of words for all the things and time-takings which come, with all their sundrinesses, in their common life; in sound-sweetness to the ear, and glibness to the tongue." (p. 86). Or this from the Fore-Say: "Speech was shapen of the breath-sounds of speakers, for the ears of hearers, and not from speech-tokens (letters) in books, for men's eyes, though it is a great happiness that the words of man can be long holden and given over to the sight; and therefore I have shapen my teaching as that of a speech of breath-sounded words, and not of lettered ones" (p. iii).

I see from the latest Kulchur that McClure has got on to the great pressure of derivation, though someone ought to tell his editor about Anglo-Saxon sex and also female characters;[1] the foot-note on p. 69 is grossly ignorant and rank obstruction: one would refer to the sickening & ambiguous desire of the female speaker in Wulf and Eadwacer; the woman's recall of her husband's affection in The Lover's Message; the pregnancy of Beadohild in The Song of Deor; Wealtheow the Queen of the Scyldings in Beowulf, who is mild & generous but quick to protect her children from the consequences of thoughtless largesse proposed by her husband; the long poem on Judith & Holoferne; and from the Gnomic Verses:

Dear is the welcome one
to his Frisian wife, when his ship is at anchor;
his boat has arrived and her man come home,
her own husband; and she calls him in,
washes his sea-stained raiment and gives him fresh clothes,
grants him on the land what his love requires.[2] [94–99]

Well, so much for what has just come into view. I'm hoping that Ed Dorn's new collection may be printed here quite soon: I'm pushing for it. & I hope all goes well with you, and all around.

Best,
Jeremy Prynne

Gonville and Caius College
Cambridge
February 3, 1963

Dear Charles Olson,

No news yet from the PRO; such matters are slow in coming. When the films do reach you, I suspect that you'll need the aid of a palaeographer, or at least of someone used to seventeenth century bureaucratic script plus customs-house Latin. Though maybe if one looks with the right eyes the whole thing falls out plain enough. This note is anyway just out of the present mood and to celebrate the geographic in between: expanse. More especially because I have just come to

1. See Michael McClure, "Phi Upsilon Kappa" [i.e., 'Ph.U.K.'], *Kulchur* 8 (Winter 1962): 65–74; later published in the second edition of *Meat Science Essays* (San Francisco: City Lights, 1966).
2. See Martin Lehnert, *Poetry and Prose of the Anglo-Saxons* (Halle: M. Niemeyer, 1956), 77.

own a copy of Mayan Letters, after much searching, from a bookshop in Spain.[3] I am hardly into it yet, having read it through only five or six times so far; but the major push is clear, and the great resonance of it not to be missed. That it should be (almost) all on stone or clay, and not on birch-bark or untreated animal skin, and thus set down as link into a geographic field, without as you say calling in that former Mediterranean affair. So that while only this far there are several questions/topics, which I put as something between query and a first gathering of the lines.

1. The sense of history as field: the convergence of necessities & the imagination, the shaping of a language to climate, coastline: process held down firmly enough to yield the substantive kernels of it, the megaliths, the primary nodes. The spaces are intimate, the reality formal (even for us cartographic), but what shape is there of the sequence, the ordering of primary happening & its basic contour? The instant is always paradise if swathed simply in its own light; but the sentence carries it (history and the whole poetic) and draws us into its passing. History as what was being precipitates the survival of what was: is the difference of use/value, now?
2. What of *[J. Eric S.]* Thompson's new work: Bonampak, Chiapas, Mexico (1955), The Rise and Fall of Maya Civilisation (1956), A Catalogue of Maya Hieroglyphs (1962). From what you say of him generally there may be nothing here, but what's to be done from Engelonde?
3. The sea was also of first imaginative importance to the Anglo-Saxons, and I suspect to most of the early groups with coastal experience and a history of transition from nomadic to settled culture. The rhythms of thought are bound by the steady recurrence of passage as the prime idiom; the contour of a land economy mimes out the earlier voyages to the fishing-grounds or the more hopeful shores beyond.
4. Hence to this thing, of arrestment, which I do take aslant from your view, since the northern barrow and incised megalith are the idiom of culmination, gathering up the pressures of the past and summing them, that they may be carried forward (writing in the matrix of process, as the runic inscriptions of Sweden &c.). From which part of my query abt E.P. *[Ezra Pound]*, who has set up a great cartographic at the expense of the discovery (?). Which is not to say more than elsewhere, BUT the field of force is from above yet another nomination: the shape of interplay,

3. See Charles Olson, *The Mayan Letters* (Palma de Mallorca: Divers Press, 1953).

space as prime metaphor. Further back is Wyndham Lewis's Time and Western Man, where he says of *[Henri]* Bergson's musicalised world: "As much as he enjoys the sight of things 'penetrating' and 'merging,' do we enjoy the opposite picture of them standing apart—the wind blowing between them, and the air circulating freely in and out of them" (p. 428). Or again, in polemic contra the chronologic conspiracy: "In your turn, 'you' become the series of your temporal repetitions; you are no longer a centralized self, but a spun-out, strung-along series, a pattern-of-a-self, depending like the musical composition upon time; an object, too, always in the making, who are your states. So you are a history: there must be no Present for you. You are an historical object, since your mental or time-life has been as it were objectified" (p. 176).

5. Now, all this there & operative in the Cantos, where the stone temple and the castilian light are the paradisiac nodes within the great flux of irritated fluency—vide the importance of "now" as a breath-counter in the moments of prime certainty (in, for example, the conclusion to Canto 90). The whole manner of thought operates against the sequential contour of the sentence & its origin in natural process and human life, in favour of the medallion—history as pivot. And the ambiguity here extends further, and more challengingly: "The objects which occur at every given moment of composition (of recognition, we can call it) are, can be, must be treated exactly as they do occur therein and not by any ideas or preconceptions from outside the poem, must be handled as a series of objects in field in such a way that a series of tensions (which they also are) are made to hold, and to hold exactly inside the content and the context of the poem which has forced itself, through the poet and them, into being."[4] So that time is a governing absolute within the process, the immersal in the poem and its coming to be; but the achieved kinetics of the thing on the page are tensions, which is the idiom of poem as construct or diagram rather than passage or transit. WCW is defeated by his history not because of any failure in his reductive machinery, but because his command of the sentence (syntax, Aristotle's notion of 'plot') wasn't firm enough to confer substance on the great flowing process beneath him.
6. You would know that for me the noun is the holding of all the world's needful substance, it functions as the irreducible fact which has only (as if this is not sufficient) to be disposed into relevant contours to release what it most certainly is. I hold to that, but qualify: the root image now

4. Olson, "Projective Verse," in *Collected Prose*, 243–44.

seems to me the gerund, since all nouns imply their own continuity, which is what makes them blessed. The entire ambiguity of history is within that: the gerundial scope, the named happening. This is for me the whole fact of Maximus, as it would seem that Mexico wasn't at that time for you, as you then saw it.

7. What is GATE & C;[5] who is Slater;[6] does Section 9 of the Letters belong in right sequence between Sections 5 and 6; or does none of this not now approach what is still of importance.
8. Back to glyph as name, even if there used to record and compute the rate of passing. If Lewis's wind does indeed play around these final ("random") objects of speech, how is reference back to them not simply exercising the ego: the beak as instrument of nostalgia. I have a profound suspicion of this golden severance of sequence, that the past is idealised by standing beyond the reach of knowledge (not the reach of science & museum teams, but the passage of the imagination). To travel to the geographic of it is in part enactive of retrogression; but how to "come in quite fresh from the other end" (p. 59), to the choking beauty of inaccessibly remote nouns (that they are so, and survive)?[7] The mass and weight of it, this is no less than truth; but (from outside & afar) does this exclude the gerund of it: the stone, and also not far off, the sea?
9. Poem in wake of this.[8]

Best, always, and (always) in final accord,
Jeremy Prynne

---

28 Fort Square
Gloucester, MA
February 8, 1963

SB is Slater Brown, an earlier friend of Creeley's (who by the way lives now in Rockport—which, if you remember yr day when you went away from here [too fast for me] is 5 miles farther than Gloucester; and though I know he's there (and is married to a wealthy woman Gordon Cairnie told me) I've never met

5. Olson, "The Gate and the Center" (1951), *Collected Prose*, 168–73.
6. William Slater Brown (1896–1997), American novelist and translator, corresponded with Robert Creeley during the time of Olson's writing of *The Mayan Letters*.
7. Olson, *The Mayan Letters*, 59.
8. Prynne encloses a draft of "Lie of the Other Land," later published in *Prospect* 6 (Spring 1964), which he would also do with his letter of April 24, 1963.

him—except that it was the page Creeley's wife sent me with SB's tracing of Quetzalcoatl as a sea—which started all that (there then)—and as well, that my sense was, one night looking at a map of stars the Creeleys had sent with a flash-light while drawing it & laying on my back try*[ing]* by screwing my face up to locate the Southern Cross (!) that I had remembered Slater

He has a whole other history you may know of. Or be interested in—& Cr. says his impression is *[E. E.]* Cummings really stole the thing from SB (in the sense C reversed their roles) but SB is the companion of The Enormous Room.[9]

OK. Only one question answered but to get a word back to you in acknowl-edgment of all you have sent as well as what I am now to look for

Yrs,
Charles

Any contact yet with Le Grand Seigneur Americaine, Sir Jonathan Williams? His address is 2 Well Walk, Hampstead London N W 3

Quickly & with all—yrs

Gonville and Caius College
Cambridge
April 24, 1963

Dear Charles Olson,

I finally got to seeing Jonathan Williams a few weeks ago; I wrote him a note which apparently reached him on the same day as yours mentioning my name. Very pleasant: I like him, except that finally he's too mild to fix it for himself. I know all the feeling about localities, the jokes slipping into an important silence, but it's still too mild. But he (and it) are surely pleasing to know and keep facing in the right direction. While I was in London (which urgently awaits your visit) I phoned the Public Records Office about the microfilm, to ask when it might come. I lied about the needfulness, since who now believes in mūthos. They promised that the beginning of May should see it through, and I'll go and hammer them if nothing comes by then. Incidentally, on the books themselves it might be worth consulting R. C. Jarvis, "The Archival History of the Customs Records," Journal of the Society of Archivists, I (1955–1959), 239–250. I wrote off to an address on the cover for an offprint of this, but my letter was returned address not traceable. I've still not found anyone who really knows about such

9. William Slater Brown appears as "B." in E. E. Cummings's novel *The Enormous Room* (1922).

matters or can advise on tracking down Craddock or Thompson; but I keep my eyes open, and something may quite unexpectedly turn up. Meanwhile, perhaps more information has come through at your end, or from other sources.

Judging the time to be ripe, I shewed your (projectile (percussive (prospective to Donald Davie, a colleague & close friend of mine here, and an established academic critic of considerable repute. I transcribe from his note to me, dated 31st January 1963: "Projective Verse is wonderful!! My notes on it take the form of copying out the bulk of it longhand, as I've not done with any comparable document since I first read Fenollosa. Olson has pulled together into coherent shape all my own best insights of a decade, & locked them in along with others—his poems must be good." So far, however, he can't make the poems, and I suspect they're out of reach (for the present, at least). But he has established enthusiastic access to Robt. Creeley, if on slightly unusual terms, and is supporting all my efforts to get Ed. Dorn's new book of poems into print over here. I also loaned him the Mayan Letters, and he was very keen about that. While he was in the States a month or so back (lecturing at Cincinnati), he picked up for me a copy of the Incidents of Travel in Central America, Chiapas, and Yucatán. I've not read it yet as a friend just back from Mexico asked to have it while his own view was still in mind; but I have put together a brief (unchecked) sketch of a bibliography, and enclose a copy in case &c.

Davie (as you may know) has written a good & mostly valid book taking in the Fenollosa: Articulate Energy; an Inquiry into the Syntax of English Poetry (London, 1955). But he also there fails to contest Fenollosa's curious notions about the successive patterns of Chinese thought. One has little right to an opinion, of course, but I'd chance it and say that within that continent the process is more of an implied contrast between substantives (possibly reaching as far as gerunds—named happenings) than a primary directional thrust necessitating a nominal source & termination. Thus Confucius was for cheng ming, the "rectification of names"—names, one notes, not verbs or happenings. An article by Chang Tung-Sun spells it out for us; he emphasises the absence of any subject-predicate analogy in Chinese "sentence"-structure: "Chinese thought puts no emphasis on exclusiveness, rather it emphasises the relational quality between above and below, good and evil, something and nothing. All these relatives are supposed to be interdependent. In a sentence like yu wu hsiang sheng, nan i hsiang ch'eng, ch'ang tuan hsiang chiao, ch'ien hou hsiang sui . . . ('Something and nothing are mutually generative; the difficult and the easy are mutually complementary; the long and short are mutually relative; the front and the rear are mutually accompanying'), we have a logic of a quite different nature" (original Chinese version, Sociological World, X [1938]; reprinted in ETC, IX [1952], p. 213). I know that the reprint's in a pretty suspect milieu; but the original work is listed in the bibliography to Joseph Needham's _Science and Civilisation in China_, II: History of Scientific Thought (Cambridge, 1956), so that it may be attended to. All this goes back of course to my reactions to the Mayan matter, and the issues there raised, which seem to me of some considerable importance. What is more, the Fenollosa thesis comes under further fire (most recently) from Achilles Fang ("Fenollosa and Pound," _Harvard Journal of Asiatic Studies_, 20 [1957], 213–238). Fang is not intemperate, even though he scrutinises the Pound translations with the usual irrelevant categories in view; and in any case, dissenting from the feasibility of the Fenollosa _ars poetica_ is quite different from working out what Pound made of it. But the very complete wrong-headedness of the thing has precipitated some confusion (i.e., the "pictographic" thesis), so that the paradisiac nodes of the _Cantos_ are nominal-gerundial without this being noticed.

But I would infer that you have moved on from here, and so will not prolong the matter. Instead to the prospect of setting up an anthology of modern American Poetry that I have been offered. To be specific, Routledge & Kegan Paul have asked me to gather material for a distinctly current collection of the live (open & projective) writing as of now or quite recently. I am thinking on the lines of something like a work-book: four or five authors only, with poems, prose, discussion, letters & sheer "writing" for the need & delight of it. To give some sense of the scope and spread drawn up into the one mind and the world as he sees (has) it. It might even come as something of an eye-opener for fuddy old London. The actual book is to be made up with some care, and _not_ persuaded to look like a set of police regulations. If I can find the right kind of illustrator, this might well be possible—preferably a form of free graphic work that could be integrated into the typography so as to trigger it for the eye & ear. I hope you will consent to appear in such an ambience, since I plan (tentatively) to make Black Mountain the unspoken centre of the thing. To include you, Creeley & Dorn, and perhaps a couple of others. To establish how poems do still get written in this television age—hence the idea of the work-book. I should welcome any comments or suggestions you might have, especially about what of your own work you would like to see brought in and which other person(s) might fit with that company. I am hoping it may even be possible for me to come over this summer, to track down the needful material; maybe we could meet up and talk about the details. But in any case I should like some comment before this, if you can make it. (For example: a thought: a whole chunk of that first _Origin_? As you will gather, to get the rounded _sense_ of it will be the problem, as well as the sad but inevitable exclusions.)

I hope things are going well with you, or as can be expected. There's no doubt that Dorn is one of the finest contacts I have. Meanwhile I'm quite at sea, to know what to do with it all, how to dispose it to the necessary right advantage. I suppose one can never know, finally; but the number of ways to be wrong (timid) is frightening.[10]

Best, ever,
Jeremy Prynne

P.S. If you've recently written or printed anything, or have plans, I'd be pleased to hear; otherwise all is silence among the dunes.

J. L. Stephens: An Outline Bibliography

T.21.56. J. L. Stephens, Incidents of Travel in Egypt, Arabia, Petraea, and the Holy Land (2 vols, London, 1837 [BM]; the CUL copy is of the 1838 edition)

0.20.46 (&BM). J. L. Stephens, Incidents of Travel in Greece, Turkey, Russian and Poland (2 vols, London, 1838)

T.21.43 [&BM]. J. L. Stephens, Incidents of Travel in the Russian and Turkish Empires (2 vols, London, 1839)

8660.c.131. J. L. Stephens, Incidents of Travel in Central America, Chipas *[sic]*, and Yucatan (2 vols, London, 1841); the New York edition appeared in the same year and was reprinted in 1845, 1848, 1850, 1852, 1853, 1855, 1856, 1858, 1860, 1867, 1871. The work was reviewed or discussed in Little's Museum of Foreign Literature [Philadelphia], XLIII [1841]; Monthly Review, CLVI [1841]; New York Review, IX [1841]; North American Review [by J. G. Palfrey], LIII [1841]; Quarterly Review, LXIX [1841]; Dublin Review, XII [1842]; Dublin University Magazine, XIX [1842]; New Englander [New Haven], I [1843]; Edinburgh Review, LXXV [1842]; New Quarterly Review, III [1853]; Chamber's Edinburgh Journal, XLVIII [1871]

671.1.c.85.1 [&BM]. J. L. Stephens, Incidents of Travel in Central America, Chipas *[sic]*, and Yucatan (revised from the latest American edition by F. Catherwood, London, 1854)

8660.c.143-[&BM]. J. L. Stephens, Incidents of Travel in Yucatán (2 vols, London, 1843; the work was first translated into Spanish in 1848 [Viaje a Yucatán (BM)], and was reviewed or discussed in the Dublin University Magazine, XXII [1843]; Methodist Quarterly, III [1843]; Monthly Review, CLX [1843]; New Englander [New Haven], I [1843]; North American Review [by J. Inman], LVII [1843]; Southern Literary Messenger [Richmond], IX [1843]; Eclectic Museum, II [1844]; New Quarterly Review, III [1854])

664.ol.c.22.40. J. L. Stephens, Incidents of Travel in Yucatán, ed. V. W. von Hagen (2 vols, Norman, Okla., 1962)

Frederick Catherwood, Views of Ancient Monuments in Central America, Chiapas, and Yucatán (London, 1844)

J. L. Stephens, "An Hour with Humboldt," Little's *[sic]* Living Age, XV (1847) [first printed in the Literary World]

10. Prynne encloses his poem "Lie of the Other Land," later published in *Prospect* 6 (Spring 1964): 36–37, as well as "J. L. Stephens: An Outline Bibliography." The numbers along the left margin refer to catalogue numbers in the Cambridge University Library.

Acton.d.44.141. Pedro Velasquez, Illustrated Memoir of an Eventful Expedition into Central America, trans. from the Spanish by J. L. Stephens (New York, 1850; London, 1853)

J. L. Hawkes, "The Late John L. Stephens," Putnam's Monthly Magazine (New York), I (1853), 64–68

Roger Wolcott (ed.), The Correspondence of William Hickling Prescott, 1833–1847 (Massachusetts Historical Society; Boston, 1925)

671.12.c.90.2. H. E. D. Pollock, "Sources and Methods in the Study of Maya Architecture," in The Maya and their Neighbors (New York, 1941)

S670.c.94.4. C. Lizardi Ramos (ed.), Los Mayas Antiguos; Monografías de Arqueología, Etnografía y Linguística Mayas, publicadas con motive del Centenario de la Exploración de Yucatán por John L. Stephens y Frederick Catherwood en los Anõs 1841–42 (México, 1941; contains an article by Alfred M. Tozzer on "Stephens and Prescott, Bancroft and Others," which quotes extensively from Prescott's correspondence, and a bibliography listing surviving MS material by A. E. Gropp)

664·01.c.22.11. V. W. von Hagen, Maya Explorer: J. L. Stephens and the Lost Cities of Central America and Yucatán (Norman, Okla., 1947)

701·01.b.1.21. David Levin, History as Romantic Art; Bancroft, Prescott, Motley, and Parkman (Stanford, 1959)

Gonville and Caius College
Cambridge
April 30, 1963

Dear Charles Olson,

I heard from Ed Dorn today about the Dartmouth project. It must be a very difficult & uncertain time. Ed doesn't find it easy either, yet he lives with such steady certitude. I admire that so much, it's of use. He sent a poem about the NY visit, which you may have seen; honest and honourable. This has triggered off a personal sign from me, which I enclose in the same spirit.[11] I am impressed by the interval it has worked across, shaken even—it's like living on a planet. In deepest affection and respect, then, because it is all now very much in mind,

thus out of the blue
Jeremy Prynne

Gonville and Caius College
Cambridge
May 2, 1963

Public Record Office, London, Microfilm order number 751 (26th April 1963):

11. "Salt Water, Fresh Water," which would appear in *Prospect* 6 (Spring 1964): 34.

Weymouth Port Books
(1621–1628):
E.190.873/4
E.190.873/5
E.190.873/9
E.190.874/5

I hope these contain at least part of what you want; if not, let me know & I'll make further enquiries.

---

28 Fort Square
Gloucester, MA
May 6, 1963 [postmarked]

My dear Jeremy, I took care of all my publishing the day your letter and poem came in. And now today the film is here

Please write as often as you can—and go right ahead (so far as I am concerned) on your project (announced in previous letter)

Yours, Charles Olson

Gonville and Caius College
Cambridge
May 9, 1963

Dear Charles,

Thanks for the card, which arrived today; I'm glad the film arrived safely, and hope it may be of use. This is only a snippet note, to enclose some things which might interest you. These have been sparked off by discussion between myself and Donald Davie about Pound and the kinetic thrust of his verse line. My aim was to convince Donald of how wrong Fenollosa was about the transitive dynamics of Chinese sentence-structure, and also even to suggest that Pound himself came (in practice) to realise this: that the monolinear sequence allows too little breadth of narrative, too little space in which to deploy the larger patterns of awareness. The locus, that is, as well as the vector (or, as I revert to it, the noun as well as the verb). The overall Poundian structure, even, as a form of parallelistic gerundial patternment. And thus back to my earlier thoughts on this matter and on the Mayan Letters . . . I'll say no more, but hope these passages are coherent & perhaps of some interest.

Things are still just worth it, I trust,
Jeremy

"The key-word in the Old Chinese thought-system was Order, but this was an order based on organic pattern, and indeed on a hierarchy of organisms. The symbolic correlations or correspondences all formed part of one colossal pattern. Things behaved in particular ways not necessarily because of prior actions or chance impulsions of other things, but because their position in the ever-moving cyclical universe was such that they were endowed with intrinsic natures which made that behaviour inevitable for them. If they did not behave in those particular ways they would lose their relational positions in the whole (which made them what they were), and turn into something other than themselves. They were thus organic parts in existential dependence upon the whole world-organism. And they reacted upon one another not so much by mechanical impulsion or causation as by a kind of mysterious resonance."

Ho Ping-Yü and Joseph Needham, "Theories of Categories in Early Mediaeval Chinese Alchemy," *Journal of the Warburg and Courtauld Institutes*, XXII (1959), p. 188.

"He [Hsün Tzu] was sufficiently influenced by the Taoists to use the word Tao sometimes to mean the Order of nature, including the right Way of human society, but he exalted *li*, the essence of rites, good customs, traditional observances, into a cosmic principle, as if men in human society were but imitating at their own level the numinous dance of the stars and the seasons. Thus: '*Li* is that whereby Heaven and Earth unite, whereby the sun and moon are brilliant, whereby the four seasons are ordered, whereby the stars move in their courses, whereby rivers flow, whereby all things prosper, whereby love and hatred are tempered, whereby joy and anger keep their proper place. It causes the lower orders to obey, and the upper classes to be illustrious; through a myriad changes it prevents going astray. If one departs from it, one will be destroyed. Is not *Li* the greatest of all principles?' [*Hsün Tzu*, chap. 19, p. 7b; H. H. Dubs (trans.), *The Works of Hsün Tzu* (London, 1928), p. 223]"

Joseph Needham, *Science and Civilisation in China*, Vol 2: History of Scientific Thought (Cambridge, 1956), p. 27. Compare also the *Book of Changes*, Appendix IV (R. Wilhelm and C. F. Baynes [trans.], *The I Ching* [New York, 1950], II, p. 15), and Achilles Fang, Introduction to Ezra Pound (trans.), *The Classic Anthology Defined by Confucius* (London, 1955), p. xvi.

"Misch [G. Misch, *The Dawn of Philosophy*, trans. & ed. R. F. C. Hull

(London, 1950)] rightly maintained that Chinese thinkers in all the descriptions which they gave of the regularity of natural processes had in mind, not government by law, but the mutual adaptations of community life [pp. 122, 170, 206, 240]. Harmony was regarded as the basic principle of a world-order 'spontaneous and organic' [p. 210]. With this in mind, we can see in a new light the poetical philosophy of Hsün Tzu (cf. p. 27 above), who went so far as to exalt li (good customs and traditional observances sanctioned by generally accepted morality) to the level of a universal cosmological principle. Not in human society only, but throughout the world of Nature, there was a give and take, a kind of mutual courtesy rather than strife among inanimate powers and processes, a finding of solutions by compromise, an avoidance of mechanical force, and an acceptance of the inevitability of birth and doom for every natural thing."

Joseph Needham, op. cit., pp. 283–284.

"It would seem truer to visualise that there were (at least) two ways of advance from primitive participative thought, one (the way taken by the Greeks) to refine the concepts of causation in such a manner as to lead to the Democritean account of natural phenomena; the other, to systematise the universe of things and events into a pattern of structure, by which all the mutual influences of its parts were conditioned. On one world-view, if a particle of matter occupied a particular point in space-time, it was because another particle had pushed it there; on the other, it was because it was taking up its place in a field of force alongside other particles similarly responsive. Causation was thus not 'particulate' but 'circumambient.'"

Joseph Needham, op. cit., pp. 284–285; in a note he adds that "The Aristotelian account [of natural phenomena] had more in common with Chinese ideas, but it was too biological and modern science had to discard it in order to be born."

"In such a system [i.e., a universe viewed as a reciprocally adjusting harmony of its constituent members] causality is reticular and hierarchically fluctuating, not particulate and singly catenarian. . . . 'The conviction that the universe and each of the wholes composing it have a cyclical nature, undergoing alterations, so dominated (Chinese) thought that the idea of succession was always subordinated to that of interdependence. Thus retrospective explanations were not felt to involve any difficulty. Such and such a lord, in his lifetime, was not able to obtain the hegemony, because, after his death, human victims were sacrificed to him' [M. Granet, La

Pensée Chinois (Paris, 1934), p. 330]. Both facts were simply part of one timeless pattern."

Joseph Needham, op. cit., p. 289; in a note he adds: "It would be right here to point out that this kind of retrospective causality has some similarity with the final cause of Aristotle. But it would be necessary to add that one of the greatest efforts of Renaissance science was directed (successfully) to ridding itself of final causes (e.g. in Francis Bacon). The final cause may be considered an anomaly in European thought, due to the individual genius of Aristotle" (p. 289).

"Happiness, rage, grief, delight. To be unmoved by these emotions is to stand in the axis, in the center; being moved by these passions each in due degree constitutes being in harmony. That axis in the center is the great root of the universe; that harmony is the universe's outspread process [of existence]. From this root and in this harmony, heaven and earth are established in their precise modalities, and the multitudes of all creatures persist, nourished on their meridians. . . . Considering which things, the man of breed, in whom speaks the voice of his forebears, harmonizes these energies without losing his own direction; he stands firm in the middle of what whirls without leaning on anything either to one side or another, his energy is admirably rectificative; if the country be well governed, he does not alter his way of life from what it had been during the establishment of the regime; when the country is ill governed he holds firm to the end, even to death, unchanging. His is an admirably rectificative energy."

Ezra Pound (trans.), The Unwobbling Pivot [Chung Yung] & The Great Digest [Ta S'eu] (Washington, n.d.); Pivot, 4, 4; X, 5 (pp. 5,8). Pound's Confucian translations were made at Pisa in 1945, and first published by New Directions (New York, 1947). Compare also Canto LII, which is based on S. Couvreur's Li Ki (Ho Kien Fou, 1899), the Confucian Book of Rites compiled by the Elder and Younger Tai (Achilles Fang, "Fenollosa and Pound," Harvard Journal of Asiatic Studies, 20 [1957], Appendix II, p. 237).

"The 'section d'or,' if that is what it meant, that gave the churches like St Hilaire, San Zeno, the Duomo di Modena, the clear lines and proportions. Not the pagan worship of strength, nor the Greek perception of visual non-animate plastic, or plastic in which the being animate was not the main and principle quality, but this 'harmony in the sentience' or harmony of the sentient, where the thought has its demarcation, the substance its *virtue*, where stupid men have not reduced all 'energy' to an unbounded undistinguished abstraction. For the modern scientist energy has no borders, it is a shapeless 'mass' of force; even his capacity to differentiate it to a degree never dreamed by the ancients has not led him to think of its shape or even its loci. The rose that his magnet makes in the iron filings, does not lead him to think of the force in botanic terms, or wish to visualize that force as floral and extant (*ex stare*)."

Ezra Pound, "Cavalcanti: Medievalism" (1934); T. S. Eliot (ed.), *Literary Essays of Ezra Pound* (London, 1954), p. 154.

"Thus the *li* [as defined in the *Li Ki* or *Book of Rites*] perform two functions: that of regulating (*chieh*) human emotions; and that of refining (*wen*) them, that is, giving them a refined expression. This is necessary because human feelings and desires must be kept within the proper mean. This mean is the point of exact propriety in the expression of feeling, going beyond which means conflict either with other persons or with other aspects of oneself. The *li* constitute the mould imposed from without which will maintain men in this correct mean."

Fung Yu-Lan, *A History of Chinese Philosophy* (original Chinese ed., Shanghai, 1931–1934; trans. Derk Bodde, Princeton, 1937–1953), I, p. 338; see also pp. 297–299 on *li* according to Hsün-Tzu and pp. 337–378 on the general principles of *li*. The affinities of some Confucian interpretations of *li* with aspects of Aristotelian thought may be extrapolated from H. H. Dubs, *Hsün-tze; The Moulder of Ancient Confucianism* (London, 1927). Their operational and contextual views of moral behaviour contrast strikingly with the ethical idealism of the Platonic and Augustinian traditions.

---

28 Fort Square
Gloucester, MA
May 13, 1963

Bewray the Old Man he mistook the Proper Noun he thought it was rhyme or in the instance quoted is just an old Name Dropper—damn ole Idiot American finding out Wot it was all about: intellectual center my arse Civilization issues from precept

OK, burn.—All you say your*self* in letter seems to me to *apply* to work 'after "Air"' when mass and energy are *not* not located, and the distinction anyway is bullshit energy was a will idea [not as en-ergon]

fortune-sign in Ypsilanti or in the area of Kinlichee Wash >

< When you say deploy and a space in which to and a locus is not anything but pun or Proper Noun and either way is scalar—alsoweider only the demonstrative allows itself into the fundamental an expression of a proposition (? "each doth contain

---

"his organs of hearing and utterance"
Hawkes [another Cambridgeite?]

ø] 1 2 3

Energy but nobody knew it except some certain few already was busted certain (as a bad idea) by precisely date month year 1865 record must existing almost to the hour Clausius said[12]

los Americanos are victims of par excellence of continuing 'Civil War' la guerre civile beauty of l'univers

libido at least worth more than poor English word energy

How are you and if these jottings don't yield sense only because ain't Name enough yet

how the hell can we write this language as though it was directly after the ability to pick up anything?

Pleasure to hear from you and we'll get the time-signals over when they gone and left themselves into Venus

Yrs
Ex-Venusesian

Gonville and Caius College
Cambridge
May 29, 1963

Dear Charles Olson,

Energy was a will idea all right, even if they then thought of it as amor or lux, setting the universe in an order of luminous tendential movement. "Quapropter maxime unita et ad se per aequalitatem concordissime proportionate: proportionum autem concordia pulchritude est.—Quapropter etiam sine

12. Probably Rudolf Clausius (1822–1888), the German scientist considered a founder of modern thermodynamics.

corporearum figurarum harmonica proportione ipsa lux pulchra est et visui jocondissima" (Robert Grosseteste, Exameron secundum Lincolniensis, British Museum MS Roy.6E.V.12, f.148^{r}).[13] Edgar de Bruyne comments: "La couleur et la splendeur aussi bien que la figure et la proportion y sont déduites d'un principe unique: la lumière. On pourrait meme dire que dans ce systeme [de Grosseteste] la beauté de toutes les formes, sonores aussi bien que visuelles, découle du movement diffusif de l'energie lumineuse, obéissant à des proportiones fondamentales: l'esthétique est donc à la fois mécanico-géometrique et musicale; toute beauté est l'expression d'une energie qui se manifeste suivant les lois les plus simples de l'harmonie mathématique" (Etudes d'Esthétiques Médiévales [3 vols, Bruges, 1946], III, p. 124 [author's italics]).[14]

I suspect that we may not even have lost this, having simply rendered it into a language of more paramount abstraction; what, after all, lies just further than the enclosed notes snatched out of the unknown? Vector as gerund, perhaps, and the universal field an interplay of intentions with the placement of proper nouns. Your last note was through to me, but only just; don't let the lines get snarled up, as we need what clarity we can gather up for use. This isn't a letter, but just to say that an English bookseller is advertising William Bradford's History of "Plimoth Plantation" (Boston, 1897). If you don't own a copy yourself and would like it, write at once (in case it goes), and I'll get it for you. A pleasure.[15]

All the best I have,
Jeremy Prynne

"Dynamics"
"For convenience, dynamics is commonly divided into two branches called kinematics and kinetics. In kinematics we are concerned only with the space-time relationship of a given motion of a body and not at all with the forces that cause the motion. If we see that a wheel rolls along a

13. "Therefore, it is most uniform and, because of its equality, stands in most harmonious proportion to itself; and the harmony of proportions is beauty. Therefore, regardless of the harmonious proportions of physical shapes, light itself is beautiful and most pleasant to behold." See Tatarkiewicz, *History of Aesthetics*, II, 230.

14. The color and splendor as well as the figure and proportion are reduced to a single principle: light. One could even say that in this system (of Grosseteste) the beauty of all forms, sonorous as well as visual, stems from the diffuse movement of luminous energy, obedient to fundamental proportions: aesthetics is therefore at once mechanical-geometrical and musical; all beauty is the expression of an energy that manifests itself following the simplest laws of mathematical harmony."

15. Olson wrote extensively in pencil on this letter. Much of the text would later become part of "13 Vessels," *Maximus* II, 366–68.

straight level track with uniform speed, the determination of the shape of the path [i.e., the locus] described by a point on its rim and of the position along this path that the chosen point will occupy at any given instant are problems of kinematics. In kinetics we are concerned with finding the kind of motion that a given body or system of bodies will have under the action of given forces or with what forces must be applied to produce a prescribed motion. If a constant horizontal force is to be applied to a given body that rests on a smooth horizontal plane, the prediction of the way in which the body will move is a problem for kinetics."

S. Timoshenko and D. H. Young, Engineering Mechanics (4th ed., New York, 1956), pp. 245–246.

"The direction of a force is the direction, along a straight line through its point or application, in which the force tends to move a body to which it is applied. This line is called the line of action of the force. . . . Any quantity, such as force, that possesses direction as well as magnitude is called a vector quantity and can be represented graphically by a segment of a straight line, called a vector."

S. Timoshenko and D. H. Young, op. cit., p. 5.

"A system of line vectors is a sort of polarization of 'space,' of the space which is the seat of their lines of action. It is a geometrical entity, describable by the system of line vectors specified, but capable of being described by other systems of line vectors, which are then defined as being 'equivalent' to the original system. Just as the free vector is the class of its representations, so there exists an entity which is the class of all systems of line vectors equivalent to a given system of line vectors. This entity is something more fundamental than any particular system which describes or represents it. Such entities are worthy of study for their own sakes, quite apart from particular applications. Just as a geometrical entity may be built up out of points, lines and planes, so the geometrical entities here in question are built up out of line vectors. The line vector is a geometrical unit or 'brick' of the structure, which is something essentially different from a point, a line or a plane: it is a combination of a line, a length and a sense [i.e., a direction]."

E. A. Milne, Vectorial Mechanics (London, 1948), pp. 103–104. Crudely, the "line vector" may be described as a moment (or force) having specific magnitude and direction but not anchored at any point within the given linear direction. It is thus sometimes called a "sliding vector." Milne explicitly states that the study of systems of line vectors is that branch of mechanics called "abstract statics" (op. cit., p. 2), and hence (because of its generalised nature) it would seem to concern the conditions for dynamic phenomena rather than any such phenomena themselves.

Gonville and Caius College
Cambridge
November 11, 1963

Dear Charles Olson,

I spent part of this summer in the British Museum, and looked further into the doings of Maurice Thompson. In particular, I found that I had overlooked a very important entry in the Colonial State Papers, giving what looks in effect like details of the voyage by which Thompson first reached New England. I attach photocopies of the relevant notes and correspondence, so that you will have the full text and finding references.[16] It is now clear that Thompson lived in London, in the Billingsgate Ward (famous for its connection with the fishing industry), and that he operated from the Port of London. It looks as if the name of the vessel he crossed in was "The Planter" (naturally enough, one might say), with Nicholas Trevyse of Wapping (one of the London Dock areas) as master. A Mr. Foot is also mentioned as a partner with Thompson in this voyage; perhaps you have encountered this name somewhere at your end of things.

I then went to see the Librarian at the Guildhall Library, which is part of the City of London. The City still preserves its independent status as an autonomous mercantile community, and has quite a well-developed system of records. Various helpful suggestions were made about how I might enquire further into these matters, most of which, alas, lead nowhere very significant. The whizz idea that I should find out whether he was ever made a free man of the city looked extremely promising, but as you can see, also produced a negative result. On the Guildhall Librarian's advice I eventually wrote to R. C. Jarvis, who is chief Librarian and Archivist at the Customs and Excise Records Department and an expert on early English trade. Again as you can see, he can suggest nothing new, and points to the Port Books as the only real source of new information. Did

16. Prynne enclosed copies of the following: Prynne's letter to the Clerk to the Chamberlain's Court (September 18, 1963); four pages of Prynne's working notes related to further research about Thompson; the Clerk to the Chamberlain's Court's reply to Prynne (September 23, 1963); Prynne's letter to R. C. Jarvis at H. M. Customs & Excise in London (September 18, 1963); Jarvis's reply (October 4, 1963); Prynne's letter to Jarvis (October 16, 1963) and the latter's reply (October 24, 1963).

these yield anything, by the way? I had no chance to work through them before sending them off to you, and would be interested to hear if you were able to get much from them.

Or perhaps you have moved on from all this; I feel myself very much out of touch now. I keep battling on with British publishers over Ed Dorn's poems and novel, Creeley's poems and (now a new idea) your own collected prose. Only the most tenuous response. The firm which was to have done my anthology has withdrawn from the project, so that I have to try elsewhere. But this is dull and not the real matter of it. Creeley tells me you have now finished the next full instalment of Maximus, that you read it over there, in fact, and that it's another achieved segment of the whole arch (or trajectory, not to use too rooted a metaphor). How long do I have to wait to see this, I wonder; is it coming from Stuttgart again? Oh and what else have you been writing or thinking up of it all: I need to be put in the picture, as you see. Ed Dorn tells me anyway that you now have a job at the University of Buffalo; which is perhaps interesting. They certainly publish something that I'm reasonably interested in, a journal called Philosophy and Phenomenological Research (chew on that one, if you like). In fact, that's a whole area which I have made use of with profit, but only also (I imagine) at some risk.

I did meet Jonathan Williams while he was in London, on a brief occasion, which was something of a curious disappointment. Curious, because I liked the man; but none of it necessary enough, a certain equable assemblage of temper which left the smallest rancid flavour only because of what it conspicuously was not. That is, the lack of firmness in the man, with no real tautness of intention, although pleasant to know & to talk to. Maybe I should have listened harder, that there really was more to hear than that. But what I'm more interested in right now is Michael Rumaker, whose Butterfly has just got through to me. I recognise the contour at once, and suspect that he must have been at Black Mountain. Right from the punctuation I would say this, and from the attentiveness to the modes in which living does go on which such pointing of the breath encloses. I've written to him in Nyack, but perhaps he's not there any more, or prefers to be undisturbed.[17]

So, you see, I am right out of touch, with what to read and who is writing, where it goes on and can be seen, the further flow of it all. The primary directions out from, or back to, or some illusive circling insistence—anything rather than the diligent canter round the outer track. There's quite a little node of subversive

17. Prynne's letter to Rumaker about *Butterfly: A Story in Nine Parts* (1962) included a three-page review of the book, which remains unpublished. Rumaker registered his friendly disagreement with aspects of Prynne's review in a reply dated January 30, 1964. See Dorn Papers, I.A., Box 19, Folder 328.

activity in Cambridge here now, but I have to supply nearly all of the texts and promptings myself. Maybe now you have more time; anyway, I'd much appreciate some news or whatever.

My very best,
Jeremy

P.S. I'll send the photocopies by sea mail, as they're rather heavy.

Wyoming, NY
December 11, 1963
direct address (+ home—in the country 50 miles east of Buffalo

My dear Jeremy,

Never at all please mind that I would seem not to write. And I was so delighted to hear from you last month, and glad that you did know I had left Gloucester in July, and come here thereafter

At the moment I am writing at the request of this fellow Cook (who was responsible for asking me here, originally for this three months, and has asked me for an additional three months from January 17th, as well as to become a member thereafter but I haven't as of now accepted that nor has it officially been propounded—actually it would be more interesting to me if something as difficult for an English department, as they still call them as you'd well know, to imagine, as Research Professor in Mythology (so that work could be done there, with those sorts of funds, and actual persons working for themselves with one) and (which has been my present position, and would be again, in the spring, Visiting Lecturer in Poetry then

it might meet the case, but otherwise I find this takes a great deal, and like very much some of the persons, especially the rise all over the United States of a new class of young Americans who are excellently taught and prepared in Greek in particular

But the idea was (and would be of course mine always that your own self was what could be a thing for just the same persons I have found interesting, and I was myself fascinated to hear what you would do, or say, about Cook's offer to you; but I would not have anticipated your answer, except that Cook yesterday did ask me to ask you whether you were interested, and if so, would you write him.[18] (Simply this—no immediate commitment called for (how he does have

18. Albert S. Cook (1925–1998), professor at University of Buffalo from 1963 to 1978, wrote to Prynne on November 20, 1963 to offer him a visiting teaching position at Buffalo for a year, semester, or summer. On December 20, Prynne wrote back to say that while he would not be able to teach during the

the job for you, as I understand it.) In any case write me out of my own interest anyway, would you? (I rushed myself, when you wrote me about Farber's magazine here,[19] which I had never heard of, and found the current copy but Farber alas seems to have flown the place last year when it became the State University of New York at Buffalo and the magazine with it, which now is edited from Pennsylvania

Merleau-Ponty much on the present (not here, but in my own mind) scene[20] (via a young fellow named Sassoon met in Vancouver)[21] and also, what should interest you, a new magazine here ((which I wish you were editing)) the Niagara Frontier Review a grand idea,[22] to exploit this funny back-country of the States, the old strength of the Erie Canal, and delightfully hanging-up like the old folk of pre War I America, including, of course, the tycoon (crazy, and the triangle including Toronto, and Rochester, like, almost.

Ok. And too soon at all to say if anything really swinging can go (they have set up a mad middle summer session, with this stack of fellows known to us to be teaching the same courses on the same lot for the same five weeks:

Robert Kelly
Robert Creeley
Leroi Jones
and Edward Dorn

Yrs, and also rec'v the packet
packet *[sic]* mail, fondly, Charles

There is much on Trevyse of Wapping, mariner, in the John Winthrop Papers (MHS); and more on the Planter, + Thompson in Sainsbury's Col. of State Papers etc.; but what fascinates me is, are there summaries of Sainsbury got all the leads

---

academic year, he would be available during the summer. His one caveat was that he would not lecture on postwar English writing.

19. Marvin Farber (1901–1980), American philosopher, founder of the journal *Philosophy and Phenomenological Research*, and chairman of the Department of Philosophy at SUNY Buffalo until 1961.

20. Maurice Merleau-Ponty (1908–1961), French philosopher and author of *Phénoménologie de la Perception* (1945), among other works. Prynne endorsed the work of Merleau-Ponty in "Resistance and Difficulty" (1961).

21. Richard Sassoon, a student at the University of British Columbia in Vancouver who met Olson during the summer of 1963 and sent him excerpts from Colin Smith's English translation of Merleau-Ponty's *The Phenomenology of Perception* (1962) in November of that year. Olson used these excerpts in his talk on November 16, 1963 at Bill and Harriet Gratwick's home in Pavilion, New York, "Under the Mushroom." See *Muthologos*, 108–10 and Olson's letter to Sassoon in *Selected Letters*, 315–16.

22. Edited by Olson, Harvey Brown, and Charles Boer, *Niagara Frontier Review* ran for three issues from 1964–1966.

small as one might [eventually; God save us you have done the Thompson man] continue to run on such a fellow in Gloucester's, or Massachusetts' Year 1638–39? Like is item there BM.2073.143 all searched out? [I recall great Admiralty Papers Bundle told all of the John White John Watts 10 lb Island Case, looked at as dried paper][23]

Anyway simply to send back the complete use of what you have done!

Bramble Wood
The Glen
Farnborough Park
Kent
December 28, 1963

Dear Charles,

All through the middle of December I have been marking examination scripts, to decide who was to be let into Cambridge University next year. Which in addition to my other obligations left me with no single spare moment, to answer those letters from your Chairman Cook (whom I seem to recall as an Anglo-Saxonist) and from you yourself. I hope you'll not mind, that I was tied down so; and that I only managed to write to Cook just before Christmas; because what you propose or have perhaps managed to fix is more than somewhat breathtaking. A very special change from what was to be foreseen, to imply maybe a main shift in the current of what gets done. As you will realise I find it difficult to grasp the probability involved, and whether it would work out. Not that I have anything special at all to offer to those kids: but if the whole venture did really carry itself forward. . . . It may seem from this that I am less than wild about the idea, but it's not so at all. More shaken by even the thought, and anxious as hell that it might come out, to be of use.

I have written to tell Cook that the whole year would not be possible, for reasons quite beyond my reach. I have just this October taken on a new job here, and am due in addition for another in October 1964. And so I cannot break into the academic year, being even more deeply imbroiled than I knew. But if there were any way at all for me to come for the summer I would fall over myself to do this, on virtually any conditions provided I could somehow raise the fare money. I will have some restrained correspondence with Cook (since I imagine that's his idiom), but if the cash just isn't there I may be able to root around for part of it

23. Ten Pound Island is a very small island on the eastern side of the inner harbor of Gloucester. See *Maximus* I, 115, and Butterick, *Guide*, 171–72.

over on this side. And if the kids were really bright (or willing), I could make a very unsteady attempt to start them into Developments in the Phenomenology of Attention and Some Recent American Writers—which is how I have thought for some time that several themes I know to be important might be brought together and made to yield some insight. Merleau-Ponty would be important here . . . but I'll not write about this, since I'm at the moment a good way from books and such, being at home with the family. Instead I'll ask if you have a copy of the Proprioception piece which you could spare, since I've not been able to see it and would very much like to. In fact I haven't seen much at all in recent months; anything you had to send would at least be read with pretty close attention. It is difficult to keep up here in England, since none of the Libraries have anything or take any of the journals that matter, and I can only write for what I know to exist, if it's not too costly. Incidentally, two unlikely exceptions: the British Museum has a copy of In Cold Hell, in Thicket, and the Cambridge University Library has both volumes of the Stuttgart Maximus. Some under-librarian slipped up, perhaps.

Little real news from here, as you will see, propped up on the dining table amongst the plates and cups. I have copied out a few notes about field theory, however, which might be of interest, mainly concerned with electromagnetic and biological forms of energy and with patterns of process rather than atemporal configurations (i.e. Gestalt psychology not of much relevance here).[24] There seems to me a great need to take certain operating metaphors very literally indeed, to know as much as possible about them and in some detail. How certain notions came to be organised as they are, and whether their structures have really been coarsened in the ways that casual observers have often suggested.

24. Prynne included a nine-page annotated bibliography entitled "Field Theory," with lengthy excerpts from the following sources: Tertullian, *Adversvs Hermogenem*, cap. 44, in *Qvinti Septimi Florentis Tertvlliani Opera, ex Recensione Aemilii Kroymann*, pars III (Corpvs Scriptorvm Ecclesiasticorvm, vol. 48; Vindobonae & Lipsiae, 1906), 173–74; William Gilbert, *De Magnetate, Magneticisqve Corporibvs, et de Magno Magnete Tellure; Physiologia Noua, Plurimis & Argumentis, & Experimentis Demonstrata* (London, 1600), lib. II, cap. VII (77); J. Daujat, *Origines et Formation de la Theorie des Phenomenes Electriques et Magnetiques*, I, (Paris, 1945), 135, 200, 211, 215; Nicolaus Cabeus, *Philosophia Magnetica* (Coloniae, 1629), lib. II, cap. VI, 124; Michael Faraday, "Experimental Researches in Electricity, Twenty-Ninth Series," *Philosophical Transactions of the Royal Society of London* (1852), 156; Faraday, "On the Lines of Magnetic Force," [January 23, 1852] *Notices of the Proceedings at the Meetings of the Members of the Royal Institution*, I (1851–1854), 105; Faraday, "Experimental Researches in Electricity, Twenty-Eighth Series," *Philosophical Transactions of the Royal Society of London* (1852), 26; J. C. Maxwell, "A Dynamical Theory of the Electromagnetic Field," *Philosophical Transactions of the Royal Society* 155 (1865), 464; Sir Edmund Whittaker, *A History of the Theories of Aether and Electricity: The Classical Theories* (London, 1951), 241n1, 249, 250, 255, 258–59; L. D. Landau and E. M. Lifshitz, *The Classical Theory of Fields*, rev. 2nd ed. trans. M. Hamermesh (Oxford: Pergamon Press, 1962, 47); Joseph Needham, *Biochemistry and Morphogenesis* (Cambridge, UK: Cambridge University Press, 1942), 127–28, 129.

(Again I am thinking of that dolt E. P. whose local ignorance is unsurpassed: wrong about Chinese syntax, and hopelessly stupid about the modern scientist's "shapeless 'mass' of force."[25] If he really thought that "even his capacity to differentiate it to a degree never dreamed by the ancients has not led him to think of its shape or even its loci," why in hell didn't he look for the facts? There is indeed a poignant mythos attached to our thinking about the operative pressures that move our lives, and the role that this has played in the development of our modern cosmology; but it would take more than a certain precision of reference to disentangle this, and without such modest care all speculation is reduced to the merest complaint: shrill tone of the man without valid personal grounds.)

What's new to read over there which I could get hold of, and how does it feel to live without a shoreline? I spoke to the Curator of the Library at the (English) National Maritime Museum a few weeks ago; but he has only naval materials and nothing on commercial or entrepreneurial ventures. Meanwhile, I am trying endlessly but without success so far to place Ed Dorn's novel over here; it's an extremely fine piece of writing, and I hope something happens soon.[26]

Yours, & that the summer may work,
Jeremy

25. See Ezra Pound, "Cavalcanti," *Literary Essays*, 154.
26. Edward Dorn's *The Rites of Passage* would eventually be published by the Buffalo-based Frontier Press in 1965.

CHAPTER 4
1964

Niagara Frontier Review
85 Custer Street
Buffalo, NY
January 4, 1964 [postmarked]

My dear Jeremy,

Delighted to hear from you. (I don't know what to advise, had heard from Cook New Year's Eve, that he had heard from you—pushed him actually to add you, if possible, to the middle summer session the coming summer, the one with Ed, and Creeley, and Robert Kelly, whom you may not know, but who wrote some fine poems the past spring and is an attractive—he does weigh 350 lbs—person—from Brooklyn, and LeRoi Jones, but those jobs have run out and Cook says he has invited you for the summer of 1965. Which might be just the time to test the place. Of course if I were sure I were going to continue on here I'd have quite a different attitude, and wish for sure you were. Told in fact my older men—about a dozen teaching fellows, some of whom, say 5 or 6 include the editors of (the above) and another one, perhaps the best, and several of these are that new brand of Americans I may have mentioned to you, Classicists! Literally. An amazing development on these shores: men capable of handling and writing direct from Greek and Latin (with Dante of course always thrown in)

and they have been the answer for me to have that sort of training in front of me and we have had a 3 month period which, because of them (plus Havelock's Preface to Plato, which I have at least done notes on (again for the above—its first issue due this spring)[1]

but my point was I had teasingly and not naming you announced that <u>next year</u> they should have a chance to study <u>vocabulary</u> (after we had spent so much time on syntax, and, which will interest you, an extraordinary outburst against metaphor, and a reasonably interesting poke at Gorgias, as much of a villain

1. Olson's review of Eric Havelock's *Preface to Plato* was published in the first issue of *Niagara Frontier Review* later that summer. See *Collected Prose*, 355–58.

as Plato in inventing that Universe of Discourse which—the dictum is—must go! (A fellow who got that going I haven't mentioned, from Canada and one of *[Marshall]* McLuhan's men, who did honestly give the thing the gun.)

So you see you were looked forward to!

Many thanks for enclosures—and, as I said to Bet, I would have been completely happy if you had gone on for pages, among the cups and saucers of all which was of your concern or on your mind. This anyway to get back to you briskly while you may still be 'home.'

Yrs, on this side of the great ocean,
Charles

Bramble Wood
The Glen
Farnborough Park
Kent
January 7, 1964

Dear Charles,

I've just had a note from Cook, who writes as follows: "Thank you for writing so fully, and thank you for your interest in coming for a summer. I'm sorry you can't come for next academic year and that I can't offer you a summer post this year, since we're filled up and have our own staff waiting in line." So there seems not much to be done about that. He does ask about 1965–66, or the summer thereafter, but this is of course more than a fair way off, and even if possible might well not coincide with an occasion of value. Thus I will own to feeling disappointed, since there did seem a considerable potential, growing within the outlines of this project. In fact—but what the hell, if there are residents already standing in line, the thing is over the present horizon as far as I'm concerned. Quindi niente da fare, though I regret to say it.[2]

Meanwhile, here's an interesting resurgence of some very ancient notions which I have recently been exploring. "Let it stand therefore for certain, that all the principles were created the first day, even one in its masse; and that all things were afterwards composed out of them. . . . So also [following the similitude of the Confectioner] God first prepared his matter: then tempered it with a living spirit; then brought light into it, which by its heat and motion might mix and temper both together and bring it to certain forms . . . we see in every stone, hearb, and living creature: first a certain quantity of matter; secondly, a certain

2. The Italian expression may be translated as "So nothing to do."

inward virtue, whereby it is generated, it groweth, it spreads abroad its savour, and its odour and its healing virtue; thirdly, a form of certain disposition of parts with divers changes, which come from the heat working within. For,

Matter)) meerly passive,
Light) is a prin-) meerly active,
) ciple)
Spirit)) indifferent, for in re-

spect of the matter it is active; in respect of the light, passive.

The definitions of the principles

Matter, is a corpulent substance, of it self rude and dark, constituting bodies.

Spirit, is a subtile substance, of it self living, invisible and insensible, dwelling and growing in bodies.

Light, is a substance of it self visible, and moveable, lucid, penetrating the matter, and preparing it to receive the spirits, and so forming out the bodies. . . .

From the light therefore is the disposition and adorning of the whole World. For the light is the onely foundation both of visibility, and of motion, and of heat. take light out of the World, and all things will return into a Chaos. For if all things lose their colours and their formes, in the night when the sun is absent; and living creatures and plants die in Winter, by reason of the Suns operation being not strong enough, and the earth and the water do nothing but freeze: what do you think would be, if the luminaries of heaven, were quite extinguished? Therefore all things in the visible World throughout, are, and are made, of the matter, in the spirit, but by the fire or light." (J. A. Comenius, Naturall Philosophie Reformed by Divine Light: or, A Synopsis of Physicks. . . . Being a View of the World in Generall, and of the Particular Creatures therein Conteined; Grounded upon Scripture Principles [London, 1651], pp. 25–26, 37. The original Latin text was first published in Amsterdam in 1643; see K. B. Collier, Cosmogenies of our Fathers; Some Theories of the Seventeenth and Eighteenth Centuries [New York, 1934], esp. pp. 338–350.) This reminds me as much of the Valentinian gnosis as of Genesis; and I am always surprised at the imaginative persistence of the great anagogic patterns like these. A man could find himself and his own small coherence in these terms, if he kept accurately to the mythic fact and didn't allow his vision to go flatteringly cloudy. Sketch map of the sidereal meadows, though of use only to one with a firm sense of his own person, down here in (the) fact.

Well, this is all to carry me away from that first paragraph and my feeling about that. Do let me know what there is to be read, if you should find time, as no one can live indefinitely on the air of an uncertain past.

With all the best,
Jeremy

P.S. I may have managed to fix Ed Dorn a job over here for a while, which I gather is something he'd like (though I'm really not clear why this should be).

Wyoming, NY
January 11, 1964

that the analogy is itself inherent, that meaning is itself analogy, that there wld be nothing if it were not itself an image

---

Gonville and Caius College
Cambridge
January 21, 1964

Dear Charles,

So that analogy is the means by which we finally do come to know; the cognate, parallel utterance; the resemblance which can be carried across (transferred) just because it is less than complete identity. Always assuming that the whole pattern is allowed its substantive integrity, and not merely employed as rhetorical ornament. That is, the mind must venture some real weight on the proposed image, commit a portion of trust to its stability. Thus, the prose rhythm may offer itself as an image of what will support its own fact, which is the density of its hold on a footed point of view; the writing itself will contain & display that to which it may more publicly appear to refer. The proffered reference, in fact, as a realised inherence: the analogy of a man speaking with his own voice. And so by way of example, which is to hand & has impressed me:

> "In the next place, for the lightsome Passion of Joy. It was not that, which now often usurpes this name; that trivial, vanishing, superficial thing, that onely gilds the apprehension, and playes upon the surface of the Soul. It was not the meer crackling of thorns, a suddain blase of the Spirits, the exultation of a tickled fancy, or a pleased appetite. Joy was then a masculine and a severe thing: the recreation of the Judgement, the Jubilee of reason: it was the result of a real good sutably applied. It commenced upon the solidities of Truth, and the substance of fruition. It did not run out in voice, or undecent

> Eruptions; but filled the Soul, as God does the Universe, silently and without noise. It was refreshing, but composed; like the pleasantnesse of youth tempered with the gravity of age; or the mirth of a festival *managed* with the silence of contemplation" (Robert South, *A Sermon Preached at the Cathedral Church of St. Paul, Novemb. 9. 1662* [London, 1663], p. 26).

So that "meaning" here—the weight of the argument as much as its cogency—comprises the total analogical disposition: the tight gathering inwards of this local passion, so that "the Jubilee of reason" strikes with startling power *from an achieved centre*. And what could it "mean" without the constant appeal to analogy. "The mirth of a festival *managed* with the silence of contemplation" will yield nothing to a literal insistence. "manage," to train, handle, control a horse, with movements of the hand, carries full syntactic responsibility for achieving this paradox, which South well knew, putting the word into italics for a distinct purpose. The purpose whereby "silently and without noise" is neither tautologous nor a mere musicality, but the analogy possible within the shape of words, inherent.

Which even Mill would allow, as a proper basis for proceeding, though with caution. Reality, they say, cannot bear very much mankind: Mill at least knew that well enough.

> "It is in this last respect [analogy as guide-post] that considerations of analogy have the highest scientific value. The cases in which analogical evidence affords in itself any very high degree of probability, are, as we have observed, only those in which the resemblance is very close and extensive; but there is no analogy, however faint, which may not be of the utmost value in suggesting experiments or observations that may lead to more positive conclusions. When the agents and their effects are out of the reach of further observation and experiment, as in the speculations already alluded to respecting the moon and planets, such slight probabilities are no more than an interesting theme for the pleasant exercise of imagination; but any suspicion, however slight, that sets an ingenious person at work to contrive an experiment, or that affords a reason for trying one experiment rather than another, may be of the greatest benefit to science" (John Stuart Mill, *A System of Logic, Ratiocinative and Inductive, Being a Connected View of the Principles of Evidence, and the Methods of Scientific Investigation* [2 vols, London, 1843; 3rd revised ed., London, 1851], Book III, Chap. XX [Vol II, p. 91]).

So that now I find myself very much to regret what your man Cook said, since it was this summer that I did want to come. I suppose all the strings are finally tied. And have your own plans become more fixed yet, are you to be there for some time longer? I have a young chap here, Andrew Crozier, who will apply to come to Buffalo from this summer, so as to climb out of happie England. He reads carefully, and he too can manage, so that I hope it may be possible to take him.[3]

My very best, since tonight I feel that here,
Jeremy

> If to every thing and notion there were assigned a distinct Mark, together with some provision to express Grammatical Derivations and Inflexions; this might suffice as to one great end of a Real Character, namely, the expression of our Conceptions by Marks which should signifie things, and not words. And so likewise if several distinct words were assigned for the names of such things, with certain invariable Rules for all such Grammatical Derivations and Inflexions, and such onely, as are natural and necessary; this would make a much more easie and convenient Language then is yet in being. But now if these Marks or Notes could be so contrived, as to have such a dependance upon, and relation to, one another, as might be sutable to the nature of the things and notions which they represented; and so likewise, if the Names of things could be so ordered, as to contain such a kind of affinity or opposition in their letters and sounds, as might be some way answerable to the nature of the things which they signified; This would be yet a farther advantage superadded: by which, besides the best way of helping the Memory by natural Method, the Understanding likewise would be highly improved; and we should, by learning the Character and the Names of things, be instructed likewise in their Natures, the knowledge of both which ought to be conjoyned. For the accurate effecting of this, it would be necessary, that the Theory it self, upon which such a design were to be founded, should be exactly suted to the nature of things. But, upon supposal that this Theory is defective, either as to the Fulness or the Order of it, this must needs add much perplexity to any such Attempt, and render it imperfect. And that this is the case with that common Theory already received, need not much be doubted.

John Wilkins, D.D., F.R.S., An Essay Towards a Real Character, And a Philosophical Language (London, 1668), p. 21. This nominalistic attempt to construct an ideal language which in its structure and classification should exactly reflect

3. Andrew Crozier (1943–2008), English poet, critic and publisher, and notably a student of both Prynne and Olson. He attended Buffalo from 1964 to 1965.

"the nature of things" derives its main impetus from Bacon; the debt to the *De Augmentis Scientiarum*, Lib. 6 Cap. 1, is acknowledged marginally on p. 13 and is apparent throughout. "Certainly then," he argues in connection with his plea for a corporate effort to improve his classifications, "the Design here proposed, ought not to be thought unworthy of such assistance; it being as much to be preferred before that, as *things* are better then *words*, as *real knowledge* is beyond elegancy of speech, as the *general good of mankind*, is beyond that of any *particular Countrey* or *Nation*" (*The Epistle Dedicatory*). See further D. Stimson, "Dr. Wilkins and the Royal Society," *Journal of Modern History*, III (1931), and R. F. Jones, *Ancients and Moderns; A Study of the Rise of the Scientific Movement in Seventeenth-Century England* (2nd ed., St. Louis, 1961), p. 49. On the hostility of many new scientists to language in general, see R. F. Jones, "Science and Language in England of the Mid-Seventeenth Century," *Journal of English and Germanic Philology*, XXXI (1932), 315–331. On the "Real Character" and its connections with proposed language reforms, see George Williamson, *The Senecan Amble: A Study in Prose Form from Bacon to Collier* (London, 1951), pp. 279–298.

Gonville and Caius College
Cambridge
February 1, 1964

Dear Charles,

Postscriptum to a much earlier letter, when I remember to have written about English *like* and cognate forms. There is lively dispute about the roots and derivations involved here, with reference in particular to the conjectured tie between "corpse, body" and "similar, related." I myself am almost never convinced that there's no tie between homophones, even when they're semantically discrete, or seem to be. The sounded aspect makes them a pun on the voice, so that the act of speech must relate each to the other via the common factor of human utterance. Not that the pun need involve a close tie of meaning or function; separation in the linguistic dimension played off against identity or near-identity of sounded form seems to me a pleasure we may have experienced right from the beginning. Such a system of stress-patterns in the dynamics of a language would place certain very subtle powers at the disposal of a feeling speaker. And such stress is still of major value, force which can be released from the almost pun between the written and spoken word. Which may operate in either direction: *convert*, I say, perhaps as an imperative, perhaps not; the print-form releases a stress which only the whole field can resolve. Thus, *it serves to tie an utterance down into that field*; the sacrament of speech.

So that in this matter of like I would see it as a consubstantial pattern of significance, with ultimately no body-mind separation except as basic pun. This may all be unscientific: it's sparked out by a paper by J. A. Walker, "Gothic -leik- and Germanic *lik- in the Light of Gothic Translations of Greek Originals," Philological Quarterly, XXVIII (1949), 274–293. I enclose a photographic print of his conclusions, the last two pages of his piece. Much more depends from this than he ever knew.

The very best, as ever,
Jeremy

P.P.S. Prospect is now again alive (yes) since I have managed the cash for it, and due at the printers in ten days. I hope "Going Right Out of the Century" is still all right by you.

P.P.P.S. To make the weight and earn the second stamp. See how I can get through to the young, disguised as an "exercise," even at the bottom of the pit. Maybe you've already seen this: it's Ed Dorn's and fine sterling silver. Which, with prompting, they will come to see.[4]

Wyoming, New York
February 5, 1964

My dear Jeremy
Altogether thanks for notes on lic- [Had used the thing + wonder now how much 'error' I did have, on making it body as well as corpse or cormorant's flesh in Grammar A Book which is part of the Proprioception book now ready for press (except for Duncan's preface); and ever since you asked I have been trying to lay may hands on a Xerox copy of the whole book, to send you; it isn't a matter, probably, of more than 18pp—or 30.]

Also the correction to the typist adorns our mantel-piece, + our son [8] spotted it the other day—and liked it very much.

Hope all goes well + regret that yr semester
here wasn't possible.
Yrs, Charles

---

4. Prynne includes another copy of his Practical Criticism exercise on Dorn's "On the Debt My Mother Owed to Sears Roebuck." At the top of the page he writes: "Consider the sense of breadth and expanse that gets into the following poem, and the authority of the experience recounted; how far does this seem an essentially American experience? How effective do you consider the low key in which the poem proceeds?"

February 19, 1964

My dear Jeremy, I have just been going over again your own notes & letters as well as Jarvis in particular writing to you from H. M. Customs—Excise THE LIBRARY on the Original "Gloucester" merchant SAID MORRIS TOMSON Billingsgate WARD conspicuous person

The Civil War tore up so much of Gloucester's earliest years (John White's correspondence & papers, according to Rose-Troup, by a raid in Dorchester of Royal House)

The composite though, even if one takes it that the land was so small, and a barrel, on such a landscape—Turner, the arm of a poor sailor torn off by a shark—counts

Hope all is going wonderfully with you, and was extremely pleased to learn that Prospect was to appear, and that the item (on the contract etc) was to have made it, there. Please write, and will my own self. Yours out here in the lovely country side.

Charles

Gonville and Caius College
Cambridge
February 29, 1964

Dear Charles,

Many thanks for the card. I thought I would try the Fishmongers' company, just to see if T[h]om[p]son was one of them, since fish was so evidently his living (Billingsgate is still the premier London Fish Market). But no luck, as you can see; I enclose the letters, which take us no further on than before.[5] If I weren't such a hopeless amateur in these matters I should know where to go from here, but I confess myself baffled for the moment. And it's little use asking the professional because he just hasn't the push through to a possible answer. On second thoughts that Guildhall Librarian was still with me, and as soon as I can find the time I'll see if he has anything further to propose. Meanwhile poor T[h]om[p]son hops about with his four brackets, trying to keep four places open at once in the alphabetical lists which might tell us who he was.

Anyway, I am now thinking already about the next Prospect after this one now on the stocks. Would you have any use for a good swathe of space there, for a whole run of something? Perhaps ten or fifteen pages of the new Maximus, or

5. Prynne wrote to J. S. Barclay at Fishmongers' Hall in London on February 22, 1964 to inquire about whether Thompson was a member of the Fishmongers' Company. Barclay responded on February 26, 1964, saying that this was highly unlikely.

more, if you had it, and might wish to see it go out in that way? Creeley tells me he's heard you read most of this new presentment, and it's hard to wait longer than one need. Let me know, and I'll pin down the space for sure.

In fact things are beginning to happen here. There's now a range of subversive interest amongst students I'm in contact with, and I am hopeful of what will follow. Incidentally, you will hear shortly from Thom Clark, who has just been elevated into the poetry cockpit at The Paris Review.[6] Came over to Caius College for two years from Michigan State, and is very, very young. Highly recommended by Donald Hall, and that makes him a less certain proposition as far as I'm concerned, since like Hall he's something of an operator and is pleased to flatter himself by keeping in touch. His own poems are pretty and he sells them where there's a ready market; I've not yet seen him write a real one. But he is extremely young, and anything can happen, and I think he does want to open that magazine out.

I'm sorry this is a dull letter. I have a raging sore throat at the moment, and probably a slight fever as well, which I'll now carry off to bed. Ironically, I was offered the other day the fare money for a summer trip this year to your summer school; I'd asked about it and then forgotten the whole thing. A wasted opportunity. Time will tell.

All best wishes,
Jeremy

Gonville and Caius College
Cambridge
March 6, 1964

Dear Charles,

Thomas Clark has just showed me that about the war god & Cabot, which is as exciting as you must know it would be. In fact, now, right out of it, I'll renew two requests. Firstly, if I could have a sequence of that for the next Prospect there are twenty pages to be had for the asking. The format is quite large and it's to be fine, careful printing; I have a young design typographer who takes his tasks with alert zeal. Number six (on the stocks) should be out in April, and if I have real cause, as a real passage from Maximus would be, I should hope to go to press with Prospect seven almost immediately thereafter. And also to print with it, perhaps, two things more: Projective Verse (entire), and, if you should wish to do so, a new comment on that topic showing how you would now think in that

6. Tom Clark (b. 1941), American poet, novelist and biographer.

area or at a tangent from those lines. A piece for consideration, maybe to explore the grounds of that derivation idea, the root simile of where we can prove to have come from. Would you do this, or think of doing something similar? It would be very fine if, &c.

And secondly, if the Maximus is there in manuscript, how long do I wait to get a look at this? If you have a copy, of any kind, which you could send, I could photograph it and return it air mail and insured by return of post. Of course I'll wait if that is how it should be, for the Totem/Corinth print, but it's somewhat galling nevertheless. Or, if you sent it, I could have it typed up, quickly & with the accuracy of a Yale editor, and send back the fair typescript in two copies. The inducement, you see, to be useful so as to have access. Incidentally, if I haven't mentioned this before, you ought very much to read Maurice Merleau-Ponty, "L'Œil et L'Esprit," Art de France, I (1961), reprinted, Les Tempes Modernes, 184–185 (1961), 193–227. It's a brilliant and marvellous article, the last before he died, and you will recognise at once what he is arguing for. I've just lent it to Thomas Clark; as you can see, I'm all enthusiasm tonight, and hope very much to hear how things are with you. Ed Dorn is all fixed up to come to England for a year in October 1965, if he should want it; if he does, I hope very much it works. Meanwhile it's snowing here, & you can picture me gazing out of the window, waiting for the postman and the spring.

Every good wish, as always,
Jeremy

Wyoming, New York
March 9, 1964

My dear Jeremy:

Don't feel bad—or come anyway (if the fare is there, + you can use it for holiday. That is, Creeley, and Dorn, and Kelly (who is a most attractive + intelligent fellow: did he send you Matter?),[7] and Leroi (who will surely be the political core of the summer if the filthy Feinberg Law continues to be applied by Al-bany[8]

and I hope I myself will be (with family) back in a luxurious house in Gloucester (which I am trying now to rent) And would rather have you there—could I hope anyway *[to]* have that visit the RR Station kept you from making sic (fly'in directly to address: Goose Car! or smelly

7. Robert Kelly started Matter Books in 1964. Olson is probably referring to *Matter/Fact/Sheet/1* (1964).
8. The Feinberg Law was set in motion throughout New York state in 1949 as part of a nationwide "Red hunt" to purge those without loyalty to the United States government, chiefly directed at present and past members of the Communist Party. The Supreme Court upheld the law in 1952 despite a number of appeals; it was later ruled against in 1967.

Any way
hope your cold is
better—and altogether
thanks for more
(or nothing) on
T[h]om[p]son
+ delighted on space for
later poems (the publisher just currently
mining contract by refusing Jonathan *[Williams]*,
some power, so maybe all will be fine!

I don't have my Rose-Troups by, but that Fishmonger List, at least as of a date like 1641—a hair late! [or better Mr. Barclay's indication a list is 1600 to (1650): if it weren't erroneous or at least it should be interesting [?]

Actually letter of Gloucester mariner to wife July 18 1639 shows T[h]om[p]son then in London.

PS Don't take this at all as hinting or asking or any of that simply thinking— + putting it down. Please. (At least not altogether urging you on!

Love yours Charles

Wyoming, New York
March 13, 1964

My dear Jeremy,
Very much moved by both offers + will respond directly

Yours,
Charles Olson

March 25, 1964[9]

My dear Jeremy,
I do hope you will not at all be put off by what now will arrive in your hands
via air mail from
a Southern State

9. Letter undated but likely March 25, 1964 considering Olson's mention of having just talked to Jonathan Williams, and Williams' mention, in a letter to Prynne written March 26, 1964, of having spoken to Olson "last evening." Williams also included a thermofax copy of what would later become *Maximus IV, V, VI*.

but I have just now talked to Jonathan Williams,
who has the manuscript of the book and apparently he no more than I
has the typist I wasn't this time
and linotype he tells me True
I learned this finally this late night
in America and New York City
where printing all over the United States
—this is America no more except in the dreams of youth
So I am hereby responsible for taking advantage of you
type copy 1, to Jonathan Williams
the whole to you for your selection
and I would gain from one free copy, to offer
Northwest Review
 air mail costs enclosed
the other matters are
the thirty dirty
pages I like them
my owne selfe
Which you shall see
are there: don't mind
and ask me please for
collection; also Gulf of Maine
Poetry magazine Chicago Golden Issue August
1962 missing (in middle of Section V approximately

Alright; and I hope
you will not be anything but satisfied!

Yrs
Charles

Gonville and Caius College
Cambridge
March 31, 1964

Dear Charles,

The parcel arrived today, this morning to be precise, and I have spent the day reading through. Not "through" it you understand, since this was a first attempt simply to square with it, come over the contours at speed so as to have some sense of the volume there within. Which is "the earth" I take it, now down to the centre, heart, convergence of each separate thing. And the persons who need this: not huddling beneath any sky, but dispersed, and away into the past. What a feeling of the passage back, how far distant those proper names are in their fit places. The names; the swift carving. And the shape of the history on the page seems a new line to re-count, broken more as a Chronicle would, less "breathed" with a local & passing involvement.

But for the moment this is strictly technical. Jonathan Williams asks if the complete copy can be ready and back with him by 5th April: which is not possible. I would want it fast, but also accurate to at least some degree; you can be sure I will push it. Meanwhile I have worked over it with the typist, and in brief there are two obvious problems. Firstly (& small), do you want all the signatures and dates at the foot of the various letters &c., even when in pencil? Secondly is more difficult. I have warned of the need for exact transcription, including spaces and margins; and with this caution in mind she is understandably chary about the hand-written pages. Even where she can guess most of the words, the placement on the page and in sequence would be sheer divination. Transcripts are therefore essential of pages 40, 41, 42, 43, 44, 45, 46, 47, 48, 53, 70, 83, 88, 89, 90, 104, 104A, 105, 106, 108, 109, 111, 112, 113, 114, 115, 116, 118, 119, 121, 122, 123, 124, 146, 147, 183, 186, 193, 194, 195, 196, 197; which is quite something. If you can't identify the pages in question by these numbers, let me know and I'll return the actual sheets. But write fast, so that I can get back from the typist and actually "read" what is there before the eyes. Incidentally, I surmise you already know the Hávamál; but if you don't there's a fine text with translation ed. by D. E. Martin Clarke (Cambridge, Eng., 1923) which I could lend if you liked. I even learned Icelandic, though corrosion set in fairly quickly.

My very best wishes, as ever,
Jeremy

I thought you might find the enclosed cutting an interesting start.[10]

Gonville and Caius College
Cambridge
April 2, 1964

"So that the Greek word κόσμος [cosmos] which signifies the world, signifies also dress and ornament; as if the world were nothing else but a great

10. Prynne encloses a photocopy of Michael Ridley, "The Seal of Aetea," the *Guardian*, March 31, 1964, 8.

union and collection of all beauties and perfections. The sun (the psalmist tells us) comes every day dressed and adorned, like a bridegroom, out of his chambers in the East. He casts abroad a lustre too glorious to behold: it is enough, that we can see it at a second hand, and by reflection. Nor can the night itself conceal the glories of heaven; but the moon and the stars, those deputed lights, then show forth their lesser beauties: yet even those so great, that when weariness, and the lateness of the night, has invited some eyes to sleep, in the mean time the lights of it have kept others awake, to view their exact motion and admirable order. While the labourer lies down for his rest, the astronomer sets up, and watches for his pleasure."

Robert South, Sermons Preached upon Several Occasions, Vol. VIII (London, 1744), Sermon III, pp. 64–65 [not cheap Augustan Deism; South's dates were 1634–1716].

Your letter has just reached me, and of course you know I'm pleased to do it—more than this. Only please write quickly regarding my earlier questions, and also to say where exactly the Gulf of Maine piece fits in (I can procure the text from the library & will mortise it into its rightful slot (no prizes for woodwork there) when I know where). And don't whatever else comes offer this grateful sound, I can't take it: it's false, anyway, since the commerce/passage is just. You know what I mean. "Yet even those so great . . ."

Best, very much,
Jeremy

Gonville and Caius College
Cambridge
April 9, 1964

Dear Charles,

I have just heard of it, from Jonathan.[11] A terrible thing. I do not presume to "say" anything, but the ensuing silence is all for yourself. Passengers, ex illo tempore.

As always,
Jeremy

---

11. On April 6, 1964, Jonathan Williams wrote to Prynne to inform him of the death of Olson's wife, Bette. She died in a car accident on the night of March 28, 1964. See Clark, *Charles Olson*, 308.

Gonville and Caius College
Cambridge
April 11, 1964

Dear Charles,

In view of everything I am holding the work on Maximus; Jonathan Williams told me of Robert Duncan's offer and perhaps this might be the best way. You know I'd be pleased to do it, this without saying. It's what would best suit you, and be assured I wouldn't mind, however it went. Let me know what to do when you can.

Yours ever,
Jeremy

Buffalo, New York
April 15, 1964

My dear Jeremy,

I haven't got the answer on these forty pages—and the <u>Northwest Review</u> chance seems, by the date, buried. So it is solely now you me and the printer. Perhaps the obvious thing is to return the copies your typist has made to Mr. Williams, minus these pages, and let me catch up with them as inserts as I can.

How are you—and if you have written (since around April 1st) I wouldn't yet have seen them, staying as I now am in Buffalo and not having been in Wyoming since a week ago.

Yours,
Charles

Puyricard
Aix en Provence
France
April 17, 1964

Dear Charles,

If you should have written, the note hasn't yet reached me; it's probably waiting back at Cambridge. I shall be back there in three days or so. This is just to explain what might seem a delay without point. It's late spring here, which has just arrived, so that the trees have opened almost before our eyes. Sometimes it seems that the quiet place is an artificial luxury, rather than a natural condition, thus far have we come into the present moment. All this stone and ochre, the evasiveness in the light, so that at the centre there is always a kind of passing vacancy. Perhaps it's like a coast really, extended an improbable distance inland, and made palpable by the scarcity of water. Which is where I am, now, though hardly of note. Better not to solicit what little privacy there is.

I have been reading Mircea Eliade's *Myths, Dreams and Mysteries*, which despite its massive repetitions and pretentious scholarly gestures is an interesting book nevertheless, reconsidering some of the themes from his two major works *The Myth of the Eternal Return* and *Patterns in Comparative Religion*. In his Preface to the more recent book he writes: "The myth defines itself by its own mode of being. It can only be grasped, as a myth, in so far as it *reveals* something as having been *fully manifested*, and this manifestation is at the same time *creative* and *exemplary*, since it is the foundation of a structure of reality as well as of a kind of human behaviour. A myth always narrates something as having *really happened*, as an event that took place, in the plain sense of the term—whether it deals with the creation of the World, or of the most insignificant animal or vegetable species, or of an institution. The very fact of *saying* what happened reveals *how* the thing in question was realised (and this *how* stands equally for *why*). For the act of coming to be is, at the same time, the emergence of a reality and the disclosure of its fundamental structures. When the cosmogonic myth tells us how the world was created, it is also revealing the emergence of that totality of the real which is the Cosmos, and its ontological laws: it shows in what sense the World *is*. Cosmogony is also ontophany, the plenary manifestation of Being. And since all myths participate in some sort in the cosmological type of myth—for every account of what came to pass in the holy era of the Beginning (*in illo tempore*) is but another variant of the archetypal history: how the world came to be—it follows that all mythology is ontophany. Myths reveal the structure of reality and the multiple modalities of being in the world" (*Myths, Dreams and Mysteries; the Encounter between Contemporary Faiths and Archaic Realities*, trans. P. Mairet [London, 1960], pp. 14–15). It's unusual to find a man with any sense at all of the foundational scope of the early mythic narratives, that they should afford a world and the rhythms for living in it; I can tolerate even his gaudy French intellect in exchange for that.

Well I hope that what you have there begins to pick up again, I do hope so. I don't begin to understand anything at all, when it comes to it; which, for you, it has. Maybe it's less difficult than it looks: that would indeed be the worst of all.

All best wishes,
Jeremy

Gonville and Caius College
Cambridge
May 10, 1964

Dear Charles,

Good progress has been made with the typing, and what there is of the possible should be finished in the next few days. If you can't find time to transcribe the difficult pieces, maybe I should send what I shall have without waiting. I have had the typist number the pages lightly in pencil, so that you can re-arrange and insert without any problem. And query: is that poem on Gravelly hill (as in Poetry, Oct–Nov 1963) to fit in with this batch? And where exactly does the Gulf of Maine come in Section V? Don't bother with this if you can't, or with the transcripts, since I will in any case do what is possible as far as it will reach. Top copy to Jonathan Williams, carbon to you and one for myself if it's to spare? Jonathan can then work on it from closer, to caulk all the seams. Meanwhile I've just been listening to Haydn's Symphony No 52 in C Minor in a sharp haze of delight: it was one of two records I brought to the States with me, emblematic of what I was temporarily to renounce. Of course it's private to me and that past, but the play of timbre is more profound and disturbing each time I hear it. As I often do.

I hope life is good with you, or beginning again to be, and would be pleased to hear word. By sea I am sending the latest section of my colleague and friend Joseph Needham's great work on China, which we talk about whenever our paths can be manoeuvred into crossing.[12] He's let me have a carbon in return for some slight help, and I'd like it back after not too much delay. Incidentally I wrote to Robert Kelly at the address given on Matter but saw and heard nothing, at least up to now. Set I am not entirely happy about, about the whole mythic aspersion: there seems to be a blunting or masterful elision entailed, which keeps me too stood off from what I do still wish to know.[13] Geomantic rites, and not enough known about language or even how to shut up.

Why don't more people listen to Haydn, I sometimes wonder, as the latest batch of wild books arrives from New York or wherever. In some ways he was fully Mozart's equal. I do not understand really what it is to be in Europe, but this must be part of it.

Yours again,
Jeremy

---

12. Joseph Needham (1900–1995), embryologist and sinologist, author and founder of the *Science and Civilization in China* series initiated in 1954, fellow and eventually Master of Gonville and Caius College. It is unclear to which section Prynne refers, though probably volume IV, part 2 entitled *Mechanical Engineering*, which was published the following year.

13. Gerrit Lansing (b. 1928), poet and editor, published two issues of the Gloucester poetry magazine *Set*. Here, Prynne is likely commenting on Lansing's "The Burden of SET (editorial" in number 2 (Winter 1963–1964), 38–44.

Gonville and Caius College
Cambridge
May 20, 1964

Dear Charles,

Typing is now complete (barring only the indecipherable pages), & is being checked through at this moment. Package when complete should I think be sent to you in the first instance, so that you can add in the missing pages before sending the entire MS to Signore J. W. I have not been able to check the Yale Poetry Review 1963 printing, as our Library doesn't have this. I have checked the Auerhahn Maximus, from Dogtown—I, however, there are differences [A. has "Jeremiah Millet's house" where your MS has "Joseph Winslow's house"; A. has no comma after "shame" which your MS has (top of p. 4); A. has "brave" where your MS has "bravo" (half way down p. 4); and perhaps other small things]. The title at the top of p. 173 also gave me some difficulty; and the song "o John Josselyn you" is in part given twice (typescript, p. 39, followed by holograph, pp. 40–42 which repeats typescript before continuing with the remainder of the song). So that in just a few days I'll send off two copies to yourself: one to be checked, the Gulf of Maine section put into correct position, missing pages added, and the whole clutch thereupon dispatched to Highlands or wherever he now is. Hope this will be the right thing.

that the mountains of
Tempe had
been separated by an
earthquake[14]

he has the trumpet known
as the horn Gjöll,
and its blast can be heard
all over the worlds[15]

rises up from
those sleepings
where it all
comes from

Jeremy

---

14. John Lempriere, "Peloria," *A Classical Dictionary* [1788]. See *Maximus* II, 87 and Butterick, *Guide*, 368.
15. Snorri Sturluson, *The Prose Edda*, 54. See *Maximus* II, 154–55.

Gonville and Caius College
Cambridge
June 3, 1964

Dear Charles,

Here at last is the new typescript of the second series of Maximus letters. I am sorry it has been so long; the typists worked very hard at it, but there was a lot of checking to do and a number of corrections to be made. The whole thing is now as straight as I can make it from this end.

First things first. The following pages eventually proved to be not legible, or at least not so with sufficient confidence in the resulting transcript: 41, 42, 43, 44, 45, 46, 47, 48, 53, 70, 83, 88, 89, 104, 104A, 105, 106, 109, 111, 113, 118, 121, 122, 146, 147, 183, 186, 193, 194, 195, 196, 197 [these are the page numbers of the original MS]. That's a total of 32 pages which I've not been able to manage. I have included in the enclosed typescript a blank page for each of these, numbered like the rest in the top left-hand corner.

Secondly: I include also the following items. A photocopy of the Auerhahn printing of Maximus, from Dogtown—I, which as I have said differs in small details from pp. 2–6 of the MS. A typescript of "The Gulf of Maine" taken from Poetry, August 1962, pp. 85–88, which you have said belongs "in middle of Section V approximately." You will be able to slot this into its rightful place. A typescript of "Poem" [Gravelly Hill] taken from Poetry, October–November 1963, pp. 78–81, which differs in small details from pp. 155–160 of the MS.

I have not been able to check Maximus to Gloucester, Letter 27 as given in the MS against the version printed in the Yale Poetry Review, as our Library doesn't have this periodical. Also, is p. 110 the start of Section VI? If so, maybe you will want a sheet inserted bearing the mark "VI" between pp. 109 & 110. There is also the query about the song "o John Josselyn you" (p. 39 ff.) which I have already written to you about before.

I couldn't afford to send this by air mail. I hope it arrives safely. The carbon (which will be identical with the above) should I hope reach you just a few days later. Incidentally, there was no title-page to the MS as I had it.

Very best wishes,
Jeremy

Wyoming, New York
June 3, 1964

My dear Jeremy,

Now finally I can say hello—even if I am still plenty scared that I will face the next thing that happens. I am having a wonderful time living alone with my son (9 May 12th)—and expect my daughter (13) to join the two of us alone here the end of this week. But don't at all feel competent to keep even one of them going, so thereby the carnal fall of man (to talk like that fellow Eliade you put me on to) etc

Anyway each enclosure (+ sharpened, significantly the Needham) have come to hand, + *[a]* welcome "return" your letters all were [6 of the 9 weeks either Chas. Peter or myself were sick 3 each: built-in "Swedish" safety systems! Pure Irish the rest—+ reason!

Hope this reaches you (and ignorant of what your summer schedule is

Also (as of the book) I will still have to catch up on those 40 things + and seeking now (again) to do that

Please keep me informed on anything + all things—including such crazy matters [and I believe it was the last night or Two of Bet's life] that a razor blade fell out of one those two catalogues you sent me (a significance meant of all but it was a complete evidence of your own rate of speed—which I showed her—that you paid for the transport air mail to here of that Single Edge!

Yrs, altogether,
Chas

Gonville and Caius College
Cambridge
June 5, 1964

Dear Charles,

A rush note, to say that the top copy of your Maximus typescript was sent off today by insured post to the Wyoming address. With a full note inside, explaining some problems. The post office says the crossing takes eleven days; so that you'll know when to expect it. I hope it's OK and that publication plans are going all right. The second carbon copy will follow as soon as the stationers can supply me with another binder for it—they've temporarily run out but promise me one in two or three days. No more at this moment. I'd like to hear about anything from your strange & distant land, in the meantime.

Yours, as ever,
Jeremy

Gonville and Caius College
Cambridge
June 25, 1964

Dear Charles,

Here is the copy, then; I'm sorry it's taken so long.[16] End of term here, and the busiest time of the year. I wish sometimes I wasn't so entwined in this teaching thing, but if they're good it takes a fair certitude to abandon them. That's not self-esteem, but the fact, rather, that where else? As, with that razor edge, that the trumpets shall sound on the other side: forðon domgeorne drēorigne oft in hyra breostcofan bindað fæste [literally, thus those eager for renown often bind fast in their breasts a sadness of mind—from the Anglo-Saxon poem The Wanderer].[17] Well, this is short, to get this carbon to you, and to ask for a copy maybe of those difficult pages if you should be typing and have a carbon sheet to hand.

It's warm here, summer, and the proofs of Prospect have gone back to the printer. We had a big party a few days ago and drank champagne all night through, feeling like *[F.]* Scott Fitz*[gerald]* or some such. Emotionally how can anyone help being a near-Marxist (what with *[Barry]* Goldwater and that *[William]* Scranton man around); I thought that piece in Mainstream by Leroi J. was as good a punch as we're likely to see, a quick, knowing, passionate jab.[18] Thus it is, then: and how's this for the non-Hellenic range of it—hann sá fölskann er netit hafði brunnit [he saw the white ashes where the net had been burned].[19] Think of that pattern of ash, down by the shore, all ready for the wind if the water doesn't get to it first!

Yours as ever,
Jeremy

---

16. Prynne included a carbon copy of *Maximus IV, V, VI* with this letter, along with Henry Moore, *Studio* 167.653 (1964), 179.

17. Lines 17–18.

18. Arizona Senator Barry Goldwater and Pennsylvania Governor William Scranton were then competing for nomination as the Republican presidential candidate. Prynne refers to the article in *Midstream*: "What Does Non-Violence Mean?" (1963) later collected in *Home: Social Essays* (1966).

19. Prynne quotes from the *Gylfaginning* in the *Prose Edda*, likely in response to Olson's poem in the typescript for *Maximus IV, V, VI*, "Gylfaginning VI." See *Maximus* II, 325.

Gonville and Caius College
Cambridge
July 20, 1964

Dear Charles,

Having now some few days to myself, I've typed out these notes & references which may be of interest; no harm in using their machinery, even if they'd die rather than help (if they knew). In case you get to looking for such leads, or might wish to. What they all make towards is to say the least not clear, but Anatolia does seem pretty much of a hub whichever way you come at it. To know the linkage, however, and carry some kind of synoptic impress into the mind, this looks dauntingly out of reach? Or maybe there are other ways of holding a garden together than by learning the names of the plants; looking up at the stars, perhaps, or not voting for Senator Goldwater (who in concert with *[Charles]* de Gaulle and Lord *[Alec-Douglas]* Home constitute my most lurid nightmare). Any word, as it comes.

Yours,
Jeremy

E. Benveniste, Hittite et Indo-Européen; Études Comparatives (Bibl. d'Archéol. et Hist. de l'Inst. Français d'Istanbul; Paris, 1962)

H. Diller, Die dichterische Form von Hesiode Erga (Akad. d. Wiss. u. d. Literature, Abh. d. Geistessozialwiss. Kl.; Wiesbaden, 1962)

J. Duchemin, La Houlette et la Lyre: Recherche sur les Origines Pastorales de la Poési, Vol. I: Hermès et Apollon (Paris, 1960)

"The same kind of a dual character can be traced in the case of Pan or a hero like Heracles or, on the human level, Hesiod, for among primitive peoples the same person is shepherd and poet and fashions his gods in his own image. Duchemin draws on Indian and Sumerian mythology, and on the Bible to support her thesis that Hermes and Apollo were originally gods, both probably from Asia, who led the flocks as they migrated in search of new pastures, and showed the way with song. . . . The order and discipline which hold the flocks together reappear in settled communities. The idea of rule and law is common to both types of society, and this explains why Apollo becomes connected with the foundation of cities. An examination of υομός law or melody and υομός place of pasturage convinces Duchemin that the pastoral significance is fundamental" (P. Walcot, review of Duchemin, Journ. of Hellenic Studies, LXXXII [1962], pp. 154–155).

R. Dussaud, chapters in La Religion de Babylonie et d'Assyrie; la Religion des Hittites et des Hurrites des Phéniciens et des Syriens (Paris, 1945)

R. Dussaud, Prélydiens, Hittites et Achéens (Paris, 1953)

J. Garstang and O. R. Gurney, The Geography of the Hittite Empire (Occas. Publ. of the Brit. Inst. of Archaeol. in Ankara, 5; London, 1959)

I. J. Gelb, Hurrians and Subarians (Chicago, 1944)
Albrecht Goetze, "Warfare in Asia Minor," Iraq, XXV (1963), 124–130 [Hittite period, 1800–1200 B.C.]

"What is important for us here is the role played in the Dark Age [the 'middle part' of the Hittite period] by the Hurrians and by the thin layer of Indians which revitalised them from about 1650 on. For to them can be traced a fundamental change in the technique of warfare which is recognizable everywhere in the Near East at that time and characterizes the period as nothing else. It is the introduction of the light horse-drawn chariot. The impact of the new machine—this it may be called with full right—on warfare generally and also on the structure of society can be observed nowhere better than among the Hittites. Chariots in action are vividly known to us in the Egyptian cycles depicting the battle of Qadeš, the culmination of the war between Ramesses II and Muwatalliš" (pp. 124–125).

O. R. Gurney, The Hittites (Harmondsworth, Middlesex, 2nd ed., revised, 1962) [with full bibliography]

H. G. Güterbrock, "The Hittite Version of the Hurrian Kumarbi Myths; Oriental Forerunners of Hesiod," Amer. Journ. of Archaeology, LII (1948), 123–134 [see also F. Dornsieff, "Altorientalisches in Hesiods Theogonie," L'Antiquité Classique, 6 (1937), reprinted in his Antike und alter Orient; Interprationen (Leipzig, 2nd revised ed., 1959), esp. pp. 54 ff]

H. G. Güterbrock, "The Hurrian Element in the Hittite Empire," Cahiers d'Histoire Mondiale, II (1954)

R. Hacmann, G. Kossack and H. Kuhn, Völker zwischen Germanen und Kelten; Schriftquellen, Bodenfunde und Namengut zur Geschichte des nördischen Westdeutschlands um Christi Geburt (Neumünster, 1962)

E. Laroche, "Divinités Lunaires d'Anatolie," Revue de l'Histoire des Religions, 148 (1955)

E. Laroche, Les Hiéroglyphes Hittites (Vol. I, Paris, 1960)

P. Merlat, Jupiter Dolichenus (Paris, 1960)

Georges Roux, Ancient Iraq (London, 1964)

J. Simpson, "Mímir: Two Myths or One?" Saga-Book, XVI (1962), 41–53

> "The major function of Mímir is of course to be both the source and guardian of wisdom, especially magical, chthonic and prophetic wisdom; his name is cognate with memor, and the waters of his well . . . give knowledge, not healing" (p. 51).

Jan de Vries, Altgermanische Religionsgeschichte (2nd revised ed., 2 vols, Berlin, 1956–1957)

Jan de Vries, Kelten und Germanen (Bern and München, 1960)

Jan de Vries, Keltische Religion (Die Religionen d. Menschheit, 18; Stuttgart, 1961)

Jan de Vries, "Germanic and Celtic Heroic Traditions," Saga-Book, XVI (1962), 22–40

> " . . . We shall be compelled to conclude that the lines of the Scandinavian story [the battle of Brávellir] and the Indian epic [the Mahābhrārata] must be traced back to a common starting-point in an Indo-European tale, already elaborated in such a way that we may compare it with the legends we possess from historic times. Then we may safely conclude that alongside a mythical literature there also existing heroic legends" (p. 39).

Jan de Vries (trans. B. J. Timmer) Heroic Song and Heroic Legend (Oxford, 1963)

D. Harden, The Phoenicians (Ancient People and Places, 26; London, 1962) [reviewed favourably by John Boardman, Journ. of Hellenic Studies, LXXXIII (1963), 200]

E. O. G. Turville-Petre, Myth and Religion of the North; The Religion of Ancient Scandinavia (London, 1964)

"Since the hearing of Heimdall was so precious, we may suspect that this was the object hidden at the base of the holy tree. It may be conceived in concrete form, as one of Heimdall's ears. Óðinn was gifted with exceptional vision and, from his seat Hliðskjálf, he could see throughout all worlds. But Óðinn had only one eye; the other lay in the well of Mímir, beneath the World Tree, because, according to Snorri, he had pledged it in exchange for knowledge. Thus, the two gods, Óðinn and Heimdall, seem each to have pledged or pawned one of their most precious gifts" (pp. 149–150; see also p. 153 on the etymology of Heimdallr).

G. Dumézil, Les Dieux des Germains (2nd ed., Paris, 1959)
Jan de Vries, Forschungsgeschichte der Mythologie (Freiburg and München, 1961)

Gonville and Caius College
Cambridge
July 24, 1964

Dear Charles,

As a footnote I enclose this catalogue of an exhibition I've just been to see; you might find the introductions interesting.[20] There wasn't enough range or scope of objects on show to establish much, visually speaking, and the (inevitable) deficiency of truly monumental carving & reliefs didn't help much. But the organisers had evidently not really tried, since there were virtually no seals and seal-impressions either, and few examples of Hittite hieroglyphs.

That ramshackle kingdom (or "empire") must have been a mass of contradictions. Yet there's an image which comes through which is both moist and assertive. The upper parts of the drinking vessels have long angular spouts or lips, protrusive from the belly; in the jugs and pitchers there may be a pierced strainer at the base of the spout. A considerable confidence would be needed to guard the waters in such unstable shapes. The god-like figures where they appear on seals or reliefs usually have the tall (& typical) Hittite headdress, a conical cap (exhibits 174, 194) sometimes with curled flanges; but the apex is usually rounded and not wounding.

20. Prynne enclosed *Hittite Art & the Antiquities of Anatolia* (London: Royal Academy of Arts, 1964), for an exhibition held at the Diploma Gallery from July 23 to September 6, 1964.

The body is softer, less fierce than the Assyrian idiom and less rigid than the Egyptian. The early cult-figurines have swelling bellies, but they are often keeled. The jugs flare out to a fullness below the beak, but the shape may be ridged, or angular in some way. The glyphs themselves seem often to come from Vessalius, and suggest the cervix or the lobes of the lung. Yet the shoes curl up at the toe, the bull is sacred to the weather-god, the glyph meaning "king" would plough its own furrow (I illustrate this glyph as best I can, but Laroche is the unquestioned authority). Incidentally, all the Egyptian representations of what happened at the Battle of Qadĕs (Kadesh) are reproduced by W. Wreszinski, Atlas zur Altägyptischen Kulturgeschichte, II (Leipzig, 1935), plates 16–24 (Abydos), 56a, 68–70 (Karnak), 63–64 (Luxor), 100–106 (Rameseum, Thebes), 169–178 (Abu Simbel). The Egyptians persuaded themselves that they were the victors, though I suppose the outcome wasn't completely decisive in favour of the Hittites. So.

Best,
Jeremy

P.S. E. A. Speiser, "The Hurrian Participation in the Civilisations of Mesopotamia, Syria and Palestine," Cahiers d'Histoire Mondiale, I (1953)

---

28 Fort Square
Gloucester, MA
July 31, 1964

My dear Jeremy:

A Huxley, at Oxford, is presently arguing—via the Luwians + previously the "Pre-Achaeans"—a case for the Anatolians.[21] It is a last ditch in the face of the break-through, December, 1962, in Linear A.[22]

I am altogether obliged for your notes + references of the 20th, last intact, because the other truth is that anything which throws light on the common history of the Indo-European, such as those Saga-Book references is too much.

Hope all goes well. Am myself at last compo- + grateful for that. Please write always.

Yrs.
Charles

---

21. Olson refers to the work of the English philologist G. L. Huxley (b. 1932) here, probably *Crete and the Luwians* (Oxford, 1961), which Olson owned and annotated. See Maud, *Charles Olson's Reading*, 174.

22. Probably a reference to Gregory Nagy, "Greek-like Elements in Linear A," *Greek, Roman and Byzantine Studies* 4 (December 1963), 181–211.

Gloucester, MA
September 1, 1964 [postmarked]

Olson sent a signed copy of Charles Olson, The Maximus Poems / 1–10 *(Jargon ; 7 series) (Stuttgart: Auerhahn Press, 1953). The inscription reads "for Jeremy, August 31st 1964 Charles Olson."*

Gloucester, MA
September 5, 1964 [postmarked]

Olson sent Prynne a copy of his A Bibliography on America for Ed Dorn *(San Francisco: Four Seasons, 1964).*

Gonville and Caius College
Cambridge
September 25, 1964

A Draft Bibliography On
England For Charles Olson

Jeremy Prynne

Completed and dispatched, 25th September 1964

A continent which splits at the root, back into pre-Columbian and to the gentle English, has the leading edge. That is, the shape has a proper span, and can involve all the other beginnings by a natural congruence. And with the distraction to other people caused either by the manufacturer of need or the insistence on a colonial intellect, the field is open for a pure attention. Focus, keep the lines clear, and you are in; the work takes or finds a knowledge that also persists, but it reveals itself progressively, in the justness that opens out. It can look like exaction, or the single take of change, the incursion of how it could be made to fall out. And it is.

From the earlier beginning the premises must be more adroit, it's the singleness which above all must count. So that to start, it needs this singleness, an isolate certainty that will shave off much of the clutter. This is emphatically not to line up as showing the individual at the helm; singleness belongs first of all to what else there is, with the result that you attain the working stance by joining to it, taking the compactness which allows only partial overlap. In a word, the noun will do it, and give the placement that holds each one of us down. Take this, despite the insistence in the rest of this island that the pronoun starts it and that all the nouns are dependent (which is how we try to keep our puny "destiny" ticking over).

> Texts, to this end, as a working exclusion (though they will look to the contrary): The Cloud of Unknowing and The Book of Privy Counseling (circa A. D. 1370), and to keep the line clear to accuracy, the single care, all the poems by Sir Walter Raleigh. Don't be put off, no one has yet read these, from the inside.

So the singleness, with the noun that gives us the place to work from, which leads to a cutback of most of the public events that are cultured by diplomacy. This will set a marginal enhancement, of place just as such. The local is yours but must, from free choice, stay in the margin. Since otherwise it will illustrate, and subserve, and we're back in diplomacy again. Thus no bargain with nostalgia for where you are or were; it's a casual gift only, or an obsession, but not to be taken on any kind of middle ground. Minor Victorian clergy and the pre-Picturesque antiquary (i.e., seventeenth-century) would make a start, so long as the nouns govern themselves, and can be read as a transcription of facts in scope. From this via geology to the botany in consequence, with the stone always to grind back to. All nouns are single. That they subsist is how they are, are there.

After that, it's passage that will turn true, which is not quite to say process, nor yet how it passes. It takes the natural career of what's gained, that you know and move out, etc. Often to be carried is the major gist, that the continuity (or displacement) is felt in small. Don't be taken in by the large arcs of "motive" and "decision" and suchlike; these are diplomacy, which is only trade hypostasized and then purporting to make its own way. That you, I, he, will shift, take up, move, antedating the entire causal myth. That is, if you ask me I will construct the reason, to satisfy the "logic." At the level of passage it's not true, it's a vast European fantasy. For the proof, read *[Jonathan]* Swift, or Francis Ponge (especially Le Carnet du Bois de Pins and Le Verre d'Eau). Or anything.

> Digression: to regret being an island—Tolstoy and Dostoevsky; to be grateful at least for that—Proust, Thomas Mann, more or less the others. "Finis erat orbis ora Gallici litoris: nisi Britãnia insula nõ qualibet amplitudine, nomen penè orbis alterius mereretur" (Julius Solinus, Collectanea Rerum Memorabilium, Cap. XXV).[23]

23. "The Sea coast of Gallia had beene the ende of the worlde, but that the Ile of Brytaine for the

There's so much, that only the detailed presentments of time will show it, with perhaps travel as an incitement (essentially doesn't matter where), and the time of day, in purity. Again, almost no one has. The verbal outline of this passage is of relevance, but as a large part of it is sheer persistence, this feature may be misunderstood. For the verbs are by which we transact, in wish, recall, or in fact; yet total immersion in this continuum is to yield to the social anæsthetic called history. So that it's the gerund will contain it, as a brief turning or pivot upon the single noun, making the pastoral fiction within its own field. English journeys are short, not a way of life, so that the gerundial is an aggregate. A good route into how this can be understood is the history of optics, right up to the present; other places to start would be J. Daujat, Origines et Formation de la Théorie des Phénomènes Electriques et Magnétiques (Paris, 1945), or Letronne's study of "Des Opinions Cosmographiques des Pères" in the Révue des Deux Mondes for 1834. But the start must be personal, and must be sub-diplomatic. London is quite feasible, as it's by nature a landscape with nouns: a simple gerund with a period of recurrence smaller than you might believe. Weather is another way, microclimate, leading to the nearest coastline.

To understand the value of this for a beginning in the English setting, the poignancy of this crux as increasingly non-European needs to be grasped. It's the local here that holds it, protecting us from the fabulist who colonises the verb as a constructive agent, e.g., Kafka or Válery, or Husserl. To slow it without fully stopping: the object here is music. This can, and must in some aspects, be European: Haydn is essential, say, and Rameau, and Schubert. Again no one has got this right; Bergson and Mrs Langer falsify again and again, how the nodes will assemble as sheer (mere) sound.[24] "Literary" figuration makes up the diplomatic of musicology, which the human voice will refute. Verdi's Otello as not what it might seem, being an extension of passage by virtualising the narrative, not the sound.

> Texts: the middle symphonies of Haydn, the quartets of Schubert, and just to be specific, *[Thomas]* Campion's songs on Archive *[sic]* (Deutsche Grammophon Gesellschaft), ARC 3004 (mono), which will tell you more about Shakespeare than ever Coleridge or the helpless theatre. It's the intonation, of how the language shapes the feeling, that comes over: as if there could

---

largenesse therof euery way, deserueth the name almost of an other Worlde" in the translation by Arthur Golding, *The excellent and pleasant worke, Collectanea rerum memorabilium of Caius Julius Solinus* [1587] (Gainesville, FL: Scholars' Facsimiles & Reprints, 1955).

24. Prynne refers to Susanne Langer (1895–1985), American philosopher and educator and author of *Philosophy in a New Key* (1942).

be imagined a stage setting for Antony and Cleopatra or The Winter's Tale apart from the gerundial sounding!

So that, to recommence, the field is set by singleness and by passage (which may be the ecology of a river bank, or the Pennine Chain). This will bring in the local, but that implication mustn't be forced. And from here the beginnings can be reached out for. The Anglo-Saxons are the purest articulation of what may be meant by predicament, how the singleness crosses with passage. The Exeter Book has the range (including the riddles), and has been translated, but doesn't include The Wanderer or Exodus or The Battle of Maldon. The local is here and not coy, the Chronicle is a full periplum of its extent, and about the last time the regional scarps and river basins were visible from the written word. Except again, at the margins (& the sea—a special case as always). The Icelandic sagas point the fact, that for the most part English is therefore courtly, upper middle class, or knockabout (Defoe and the Bunyan of Grace Abounding are honorable exceptions). Hence the danger of relying on the local: no great plains in England, just what Solinus calls "magna & multa flumina." The moorlands have been colonised by gents shooting grouse or by too much passion (Emily Brontë). That is, the crowding makes completely necessary a tactic of survival. There was more coast in the mind of Anglo-Saxon (Germanic) England; but we have recently fought two irrelevant wars over them, which is a distraction. Certain private access to microcontexts is possible, but this can't be predicted, of course, so that only the more impersonal morpho-geology will keep the demotic/diplomatic pressure back (not single persons or their aggregate, but "denizens" or suchlike).

These two, singleness and passage, will finally, perhaps, trigger off the sense of volume that is required and from which we derive who we are—or could be. The slab or cut out of the extent, which is in part a quantity but also a persistence within the field. Near-monotony of the sound, of traffic as steady hum rather than an urgent grasp forward. Or thinned down almost to silence, i.e., from Richard Wilson to John Sell Cotman; texts here would be the songs of *[William]* Blake, or Christopher Smart's Hymns.

The geographic must be come at obliquely, either through the local already gained or by routes at a tangent. Since otherwise the folds in the crust are so particular, and so previous to any survey, they expound themselves (Cotman's very pure imagine the Norwich museum, The Marl Pit). From the beginning would be: Snorri's Edda (the Icelandic Prose Edda), which has recently been translated by Jean Young, leaving out parts of the Skáldskaparmál, for which *[Arthur Gilchrist]* Brodeur's version remains important. Also translations of the Poetic Edda by H. A. Bellows, and in part by D. E. Martin Clarke (in her edition with translation of The

Hávamál). And since Tacitus and Jordanes the best single introduction, *[Gabriel]* Turville-Petre's Myth and Religion of the North, London, 1964.

That would be the geographic of the origin, taking in the equivalent of Hesiod's two poems. For the lie of it on the land surface, H. C. Darby's Domesday Geography, now through to its fourth volume with more to come. Meadow, pasture, ploughland, woodland, settlements: that's the network of habitable partition which grew along the contours and by no rectangular survey, inviting a comparison with, e.g., J. W. Powell's Report on the Lands of the Arid Region of The United States. "After this, the king had much thought and very deep discussion with his council about this country—how it was occupied or with what sort of people [hu hit wære gesett. Oððe mid hwylcon mannon]. Then he sent his men over all England into every shire and had them find out how many hundred hides there were in the shire, or what land and cattle the king himself had in the country" (The Anglo-Saxon Chronicle, translated and edited by Dorothy Whitelock, entry for A. D. 1085). Also refer to Bede's De Mundi Coelestis Terraeque Constitutione as a cautious account of the prevailing cosmography.

And to discover what this established placement (very much an island) could support in outward movement, and by retroinference the nature of the land from which), any and all of the Hakluyt Society's publications, giving logs, descriptions and reports from the Elizabethan voyages as well as a very complete account of the spans and maritime ventures of that age. The major document is still Hakluyt's own collection, The Principal Navigations, Voiages, Traffiques and Discoveries of the English Nation, made by Sea or over-land, to the remote and farthest distant quarters of the Earth, at any time within the compasse of these 1500. Yeeres (edited by Sir Walter Raleigh, Glasgow, 1903–1905, in twelve volumes).

Which is where you came in, and where the rich, pure language took on its new (and maybe only) life into this century. It's difficult, with a Socialist government about to happen here, to separate this from an urban "concern" for a just present and a better future, with the US Air Force brooding over the land. The purest shaft of memory is via Skeat's Etymological Dictionary back to Julius Pokorny's Indogermanisches Etymologisches Wörterbuch: that's the geographic of the language and perhaps therefore the grammar of which all else is syntax. Thus, and still, only the persistent noun.

As ever,
Jeremy

P.S.

"Our land has two extremities; the tops of the mountains, on the one hand,

> and the sea-shores, on the other: It is the intermediate space between these two, that forms the habitation of plants and animals. While there is a sea-shore and a higher ground, there is that which is required in the system of the world: Take these away, and there would remain an aqueous globe, in which the world would perish. But, in the natural operations of the world, the land is perishing continually; and this is that which now we want to understand" (James Hutton, "Theory of the Earth; or an Investigation of the Laws observable in the Composition, Dissolution, and Restoration of Land upon the Globe," *Transactions of the Royal Society of Edinburgh*, I, [1788], p. 296).

The paper was read to the Society on 7th March and 4th April 1785; it was re-issued in expanded form as *Theory of the Earth, with Proofs and Illustrations* (2 vols, Edinburgh, 1795). To this theory of the continuous shaping of landforms by fluvial erosion, sedimentation and upheaval, the whole range of U. S. geology (Powell, Newberry, etc.) owes its remote but traceable origin.

And a year earlier: "In such an island as this of Great Britain, situated in a region of variable winds and temperate heat, more or less influenced on the one side, with the most extensive continent of the earth; on the other, with the Atlantic ocean, there is reason to conclude, that showers will often happen, without extreme quantities of rain falling at any one time; and that the climate of this country with respect to drought and moisture, will incline towards the latter. This is also found to be the case, comparing Britain with the drier regions of the continent" (James Hutton, "The Theory of Rain," *Trans. Roy. Soc. Edin.*, I [1788], p. 71). The paper was read to the Society on 2nd February 1784; in it Hutton observes that "The climate which we inhabit has, for character, temperance in extreme" (p. 82), which is apt in almost every other respect as well. Hutton's influence in this field can be followed in George Greenwood's *Rain and Rivers* (London, 1857), who re-argues the fluvialist case with great vehemence. And so the "soft inland murmur" of river waters is thus determinative as a structural agent; the land swerves and accrues to its measure. Fluent substance, once more, or the fresh and running gerund; which is how, continually, the land comes to lie.

SUNYAB
Main Street
Buffalo, New York
October 1, 1964 [postmarked]

Rec'd—and already *appreciated* (+ Yrs. O.

Gonville and Caius College
Cambridge
October 5, 1964

Dear Charles,

I've just had another letter from your man Cook at Buffalo, asking if I might come over for the Summer, 28th June to 6th August this year. Hugh Kenner and Guy Davenport "have already agreed to come." This is just a note to ask, is there a chance that anything of value might be possible in that way, to make the prospect worthwhile? Ed Dorn told me that his time there was a mechanical contrivance, and that they broke open the possible effect of that contact by staging it all simultaneously, so that each cancelled the others out. And that the whole place was bland and extortionate, and so on. But my point is, would anyone be there, within range and to talk to? Cook offers no more than $2500, which would not carry me round much. Does there plan to be any imminent gathering for next summer, which I could (or might) come closer to? Again I do want to come and for all the same reasons increased more than before; but I'm wary of what could be a didactic cage. I'd really want the south-west for preference, or something more open and tenuous than the eastern clot (which I "know" from last time); but above all the chance of a true process with half a handful of found persons. Otherwise no one thing to be gained.

If you could write with some notion of what might be perhaps about to happen, a meeting of any kind, I would know better how to answer this man Cook; whether to come on those terms and make what I could of that. He asks for a quick response.

Yours ever,
Jeremy

Buffalo, New York
October 12, 1964

Dear Jeremy

I'm so discouraged myself tonight (with a heavy cold, and only this silly motel room to have turned around in now for a month) that I may not be your best adviser, but your letter (as of Cook's offer to you for next summer) came in tonight, and I am anxious at least to get off a reply, your letter having traveled off course by Gloucester. (Off course? Wld that I were there, in my house—except, as I was thinking just now in the nearest restaurant, a delicatessen, I'd be no better off in Gloucester, actually, when it comes to eating out, as they call it here.

Alright. I was the one who reminded Cook that you had preferred a summer spot when you turned him down as of a full year last year.—And thought you might, for reasons of your own, have a use for a trip etc next summer. But on the basis of what you are saying I'd assuredly suggest you pass it up; that is, that it would only be interesting if you thought you could do a job exactly within the appointment (which has been my own experience, and why I came back) but not at all on any of those grounds of expectation, which seem, dreadfully, to have screwed Ed and Leroi here.

In fact it's perfectly apparent that there isn't any such sort of jamboree in the present time between the old City and the Old in fact University (? Nor does Trocchi's sigma U, or the Bang-up Youth Pop and Art City seem to, dither.[25]— My own sense is Research, and that learning ought rapidly, or had ought some time ago, been in our hands; but that our own exchanges would seem what we do have yet. I dare say I thought Buffalo might—and still do, but I have not been able to go through executive walls, and assume anyway that the largeness of all (not even the problem of the "State" of New York) forbids it.

It wld, as indeed private work, require patronage and that world, as you'd know probably there—and here by the same man Allen Pryce-Jones—has been captured by advertising men (the journalists of this time.)[26]

Anyway, my own pleasures (which are now exclusively formal) are those of the classroom, and such persons as say the presence of Crozier (plus several like editors and poets who came from other places)—in fact exactly "Research" likelihoods, but the system I don't believe can financially etc see these small increments (?)

Printing, too—though even there—even here—the time factor is poor ((equipment, and the natural offices which make go are equally spread—or as you have it there from Ed bland and exploitative, was it?

(That by the way I don't think cases the joint: Buffalo is 75 years off the pace; and therefore, even if it seems stupid, and ignorant of uses, which it is, isn't for the comparative which I take it Ed is making:

as you yourself say "southwest" (doubt it altogether!) etc

Anyway, please keep me on, on those matters which are ours. And maybe the wisest course of all, wld be to acknowledge Cook's invitation, report it as soon as possible for you the coming summer and yet by so doing hold open that older original idea of his of asking you for a year—[27]

25. Alex Trocchi (1925–1984), Scottish novelist, publisher and member of the Situationist International who worked on Project Sigma throughout the 1960s. Here, Olson refers to Trocchi's concept of sigma as a spontaneous university in "Sigma: A Tactical Blueprint" *City Lights Journal* 2 (1964).

26. Probably Alan Pryce-Jones (1908–2000), British author and editor of the *Times Literary Supplement* and later the *New York Herald Tribune*.

27. Prynne sent Cook a telegram on October 24 to accept an offer for a summer teaching position the following year, and followed up with a letter on November 3rd.

and give me the chance that, in the coming winter and it will be clear by spring, whether any institute or research program can break those departmental—Englishy organization

YES, no? For if all there was any off tackle hole, and independent conduct could be brought into future, I'd be very pleased if you were (as you wld have been!) now doing the same seminar I am instead of you—right now.

Like that is, still, too much, is it not? And betokens Cook. (The only thing I can tell you privately though is, that when I broached all my intentions to him purposely out for a weekend with his family in Wyoming exactly a year ago, he said 20 years too far ahead!

But I never have been led by those projections: my own irritation, in a sense, with both the Niagara Frontier Review and the "poets" the past summer is that they don't recognize the other possibility, that only us convocators are etc.—well,

here I always was happiness, and clearly can better stay at my own blast

Good luck; and please let me hear; for I haven't given up quite yet—with a bad cold, and no place to call my own!

Best, yours,
Charles Olson

Ultimate Note: I am applying myself for a renewal of my Guggenheim; and would be pleased if you could write for me, to bring them up to date. Will let you know, if you wld let me know may I use your name?

Last of all note: One good guess is Europe, now—catching up 15 plus years—will be more open, + active, than the States (inc. this old hole) Buffalo!

[written last] In fact—[FINAL PS]—there would seem to be more room here, for a program at least, than in more established, if previously tolerable, + flexible, places [city, + university],—I'll at least take a shot at it before I do—if I do—decamp. A promise!

Buffalo, New York
December 18, 1964

Dear Jeremy:

Only actually to be again in touch—+ hope your own silence is better than my own. But for the enclosed 5 clams if you wld check yr Univ. Press for

[John] Chadwick's fascicle Cambridge Anc. History (1962?) on Early Greek Language (? (75¢)

+ Chronology pamphlet (same): 'Egypt; Western Asia; + Aegean Bronze Age' (2.25)

Anyway; they're very useful—+ if you were so minded shoot 'em to me air mail?

Anyway still using (yr own fascicle); + still intend to send you Lines Written for Jeremy Prynne 1963 on the Gerundive

Hope ya look forward to what I hear ya have
gone + done!
Charles

Buffalo, New York
December 20, 1964

My dear Jeremy,

Greetings, at least, for the season; and will you get me out of a sticky hold-up? Tom Maschler, at Jonathan Cape (30 Bedford Square WC1, L) has taken an option on both the Distances and Ishmael (and the latter for American publishing as well)—and I have held him up a month or more simply because he asked me to get him a copy of Ishmael! And I have not done it: could you (simply to relieve me) see that he gets even your own copy! or perhaps Tom Clark has one; or Anselm Hollo direct, there in London?

It wld get me off a bad hook, and wld help unleash my forces—on all sides (I *[am]* also in bad water because I haven't equally advised new publisher Berkeley, to go ahead on what sounds like a fine edition (Auerhahn doing the printing) of the HUMAN UNIVERSE and other essays (which collects those from 1945–1960).

Also in fact Proprioception (a small book of those different 'essays' since—1960–1963) is hung somewhere between Dublin and London—and of all things the MAXIMUS—which you did give me a reading copy of!—is still undelivered to Williams-Wilentz (mainly because Wilentz makes one nervous he doesn't want a typographer other than his own to do it.[28]

So that about catches me up—if you'll give that one there a nose. Also (by the way) have you still intact the original Maximus I had Jonathan send you air mail? (If so, and you could ship it to me here, I could proof this bloody volume once and for all, and get rid of it. (Again—and please accept it—I enclose a check for $10.00 to cover air mailing that to me, here: this month is my only chance in the year to get to that work.

28. Eli Wilentz (1918–1995), cofounder of Corinth Books, which published Olson's *The Maximus Poems* in 1960.

Apologizing for this being only and all business—and, fearing I'll catch you at home away from Cambridge, and equally coming in on you at this season—yours,

Charles

Gonville and Caius College
Cambridge
December 22, 1964

Dear Charles,

Just a very quick note at the end of the year, to send you the print you asked for.[29] I'm swallowed up at the moment by obligations I can't hope to keep pace with—and thus feeling rather forlorn about the immediate outcome. It's too much, and I damn well wish it weren't, but perhaps it may come clear in a few months. Or years. As if there weren't other and better things to do, being blocked off by this choking clutter. Well, sing for it I suppose, and let it flow as it may. Meanwhile a brief review note by Paul-Henri Michel, "Renaissance Cosmologies," in Diogenes, 18 (1957), 93–107, and a much tougher piece by M. T. d'Alverny, "Le Cosmos Symbolique de XIIe Siècle," in Archives d'Histoire Doctrinale, XX (1953), 31–81, remain no more than glanced at. Time, and the Houre, runs through the roughest Day. I will write when I can, and be glad to.

Until then,
Jeremy

Bramble Wood
The Glen
Farmborough Park
Kent
December 29, 1964

Dear Charles,

Your letter dated 20th December has just reached me here at home this morning. As you guess, I'm away from Cambridge at the moment and thus not able to work as fast as could be hoped. However I'll be back in College on the Friday or Saturday (1st or 2nd), and shall send then Tom Maschler my copy (the Grove

29. Prynne enclosed John Chadwick, *The Prehistory of the Greek Language* (vol. II, chap. XXXIX of the revised *Cambridge Ancient History*, issued as Fascicle 15) (Cambridge, UK: Cambridge University Press, 1963); and W. C. Hayes, M. B. Rowbon, F. H. Stubbings, *Chronology: Egypt—to End of Twentieth Dynasty; Ancient Western Asia; The Aegean Bronze Age* (vol. I, chap. VI of the revised *Cambridge Ancient History*, issued as Fascicle 4, Cambridge, UK: Cambridge University Press, 1964).

paperback only, alas) of Ishmael, and also post to you at Buffalo by air mail the photocopied typescript and manuscript of Maximus, onwards from letter 23. This as soon as I reach Cambridge, by the first mail and willingly as you know. I will telephone Maschler at Cape to tell him that *Ishmael* will shortly arrive, and ask also if he would like to see anything else I can show him. I had heard he was starting something, but the literary gossip just wears me out, when it's all from the fringe to whom it costs so little. Instead of just reading or looking, getting on with all the human business and not anxious to seem to know all the other timetables.

You should have the Cam. Anc. Hist. fascicles by now I hope. I haven't written properly for some time, partly because I'm bullied out of having space to think and also in part because I have less sense now that I know the ground on which the thing might proceed. It is just a fact that I (being European) do not know one word of Greek, and I don't think I am willing to take this on except as an issue in confirmation. That is, to get at the coming to know, by weighing the language against its ethical and physical substance, you do need to be very close. Or I would need it.

So that I prefer (not that any man's knowledge is much his choice) to work it from other grounds, perhaps more local and less historistic. Probably less "millennial" as well, since I am uncertain about ever knowing (for myself) the real thrust of such a span without more Assyriology, or more rock. That's why it's difficult to write with substantial relevance, to make it carry the trust, and I'll not do it on a last week for the first time basis. Don't misunderstand me, I know the shape of your thing quite closely, but it's not mine as it joins to what I know myself. The gap is too large, physically, maybe we are simply waiting to talk. I respect that too much to make some fake adjustment, since the parallel is interesting as near, not as a nudged convergence. And I really don't accurately have the feel of it, from here now; the passages are clogged with gossip and I'm damned if I'll have my eyes silted up with another person's local finds, without all the evidence.

I don't know, this is a floating letter and not much to be trusted perhaps. Except that I do mean all the respect and interest to say this, take the thing as real rather than dutiful. And the shared footing is a strange thought, a physical ambiguity since no two men quite stand on the same rock. The reckoning is what can come to hold—I just think so this evening and feel too far off to have more than the work, and a half invested semaphore. What the hell, anyway, I'll see everything gets done, and do now send my especial love, across all of it.

Jeremy

CHAPTER 5
1965

Gonville and Caius College
Cambridge
January 4, 1965

Prynne returned the manuscript of the second volume of the Maximus poems to Olson in Buffalo.

The Tavern
Gloucester, MA
January 6, 1965

Greetings of + for the New Year

Lord, Jeremy, I don't know Greek myself. And I agree with you, one has no basis of experience of poems or anything of that sort in a language unless that language is your own or one equally (is it possible?) known. But—+ this has been the crazy part of it (+ in a minute I'll tell you the jewel of that all)—I have been at it for years, the other way around: roots roots roots [which then is a sort of archeology for sure, etymology that way is.

But here's what happened: I hope I as I wholly assume I did send you The Niagara Frontier Review. Well anyway in it I reviewed Preface to Plato Harvard-Belknap Press 1963 by Eric Havelock.[1] And argued here for the 1st time was a real basis of literary criticism relevant to writing of the past 50 and even 150 years (since Keats). And who should come to Buffalo last month to lecture but Havelock? And what did he say to me [he is of course Chairman of Classics Yale this year + was Director of such Studies Harvard last year + for some years] "What do you make of Hesiod's diction, Olson?" I thought for the life of me I never made it so well! / had it so good! Love + Thanks for

1 fascicles

1. See Olson, *Collected Prose*, 355–58.

2 letter accompany
3 letter from home

all in, + here. + for the chore(s) with Maschler he now wants to see Maximus, he wrote today but it seems promising altogether.

The Tavern
Gloucester, MA
January 15, 1965

Dear Jeremy,

Just to write you, and thank you, and to signal you that these New York foundations may, at my request, be asking you to stand in for me on a chance I may be able to get back via them to my own natural way of life here in my own 'woods.' I so find the world able to be going its way, and that I do prefer to be 'home.'

(Actually, I don't know whether these Rockefeller people, who this past week suddenly came in with a nomination that I apply for one of their a-wards; but I had, as I told you, already sought a renewal of my Guggenheim fellowship [granted originally for Call Me Ishmael and renewed, once before some 15 years ago, for another matter], and they will, I'm sure, ask you to give them your measure of myself,

who is,
yours,
Charles—or as my wife called me,
Charles o

Hope all is well; and think of you often.

Gonville and Caius College
Cambridge
March 3, 1965

Dear Charles,

I'm scattered all over the place at the moment & have been so in fact since October, being pulled into shreds by the work and attention demanded of me here. So that this note is contrived as an island in chaos. It's writing this ungainly knowledge, into capsules that I don't believe in, for long sequences of hourly doses; and administering the young into trim slots for life; the whole succession of trying to keep up and make a responsibly accurate job of it, reading the sources and trying to make some sort of a guide through the confusion; I'm just so attentive & tuned to what I can now no longer at this rate even more or less manage, it attenuates me. I'm just thinned down to nervous, anxious pecking. I've not read a book through in proper quiet, following the line and taking a sequent bearing on the surrounding evidence, for months and months.

So I can say nothing of use. I'm just frayed to bits & can feel it all slipping by, blast it. Or I would have written, and would have parts to contribute to the argument, to the discussion and the work that needs to be done. But without a care for precision, the whole tangle becomes worse. Thus, Robt Creeley wrote back in the Black Mountain Review that he had been told of an "essay by an Elizabethan, Samuel Putman, On Proportion, where he speaks of numbers and measure as being arythmus; and of that rhythm which we find in poems, as rhythmus" (this was in Vol. 1, No. 4, page 55).[2] So that now one of my students tells me he has searched the Library for this Samuel Putman and his essay, which is of course actually the Second Booke ("Of Proportion Poetical") of George Puttenham's treatise, The Arte of English Poesie. Contriued into three Bookes: The first of Poets and Poesie, the second of Proportion, the third of Ornament (London, 1589). Such misdirection is a small price to pay, for a spark of life out of the ashes of European pedantry, the whole grinding machinery for crushing the contour of the written word. But does it then follow that even a temporary & patchwork accuracy, knowing where things are (for example), need damage what it still holds as prime concern? So I'm on a knife-edge in this context, and doubt the whole set-up, because to be allowed to know little more than the large outlines costs so very much. Look at it, hardly a free moment to keep the work breathing and in flow; so it is now six o'clock in the morning and I have to be at work by ten again, that's why I've not written & am so exhausted as to complain at such length. And wonder of it whether this particular effort (vis, the knife-edge) is worth it, to out away at Professor Rosemond Tuve and Professor Susanne Langer and Professor Doctor Jan de Vries from inside the walls. Listen to this, from Vries's book Heroic Song and Heroic Legend (trans. B. J. Timmer, London, 1963): "Homer's Iliad and Odyssey surpass any of the other epic poems in the world. He is the first poet of Greece and directly or indirectly the paragon of most epic poetry and certainly of the main epics of Europe. The fascinating contents, the beautiful form, the grand style and the richness of images of his language lend these poems the great charm which, after so many centuries, is still felt

2. See Creeley, *Collected Essays*, 36.

by anyone who reads them" (page 1). Or this by Dr I. L. Gordon in his edition of the Anglo-Saxon Seafarer (London, 1960), in a series supervised by the Quain Professor of English at University College, London, and the Professor of German at King's College, London: "But the main intention of the seafaring theme is not the conveying of this abstract moral idea in concrete terms. The poetic genre to which the poem belongs is one in which the meaning of human situations is developed and exploited in the form of reflective dramatic monologue, and the most plausible explanation of the form and theme of The Seafarer is that it is an imaginative evocation of physical and emotional experiences that are used to illuminate a symbolic spiritual truth" (page 10). So it's a great snarled jungle, a complete home industry trading on the fact that there's enough past in the kitty for the present to get to work with its tweezers and tropic catalogues, without worrying how it may contrive to keep its own miserable self in workable human condition. "The Mind of Europe": It's a journalist's card catalogue; and all those museums, exacting their polite dues from those who are only too thankful that the doors close at six and the animals locked in for the night.

This isn't a thinking letter at all, but a kind of shout to say that I am just still here and that the air may clear a little over Easter. I've not been able to do what I should in another respect, too, which has put me off writing. My own copy of Call Me Ishmael has it seems been borrowed and not returned; I asked more or less all of my pupils (!) and everyone else, but can't track it down (much safer to be a bibliophile); so I asked Tom Clark and several others, who wrote round, but without success, and then a friend who was to have borrowed the copy in the York University Library. I wrote to him four or five times, and also rang him up, but so far he's too vague to have done anything; so that I have had no note as yet from Rockefeller or Guggenheim; but you may be sure that when I do the best headed notepaper will come out and I'll write them the most judiciously approving endorsement I can manage. That's at least one advantage of being inside. About the Plato thing I can't even begin to cope at the moment, being as I say pulled about & quite hopelessly all over the place. I'd be pleased to hear, a note which might hold things down for a bit, if you had time, out into any damn open field you can happen to see in front of you. And if you'd like any of the latest fascicles of the Cam. Anc. Hist. sent over, just let me know.[3]

As ever,
Jeremy

---

3. Prynne enclosed two copies of *Prospect* 6, along with a list of fascicles 25–36.

SUNYAB
Buffalo, New York
March 25, 1965

My dear Jeremy:

Please, very seriously, consider such a 'Methods' course—or at least (also?) a course such as you originally proposed "On Recent American Writing + the phenomenology of perception."

Yrs,
Charles

April 9, 1965

Prynne sent Olson a copy of Joseph Needham, Time and Eastern Man: The Henry Myers Lecture 1964 *(Royal Anthropological Institute Occasional Paper No. 21; London, 1965), with the inscription:*

for Charles
the fragrance, which
we leave,
coming out
of the place where,
the thyme, ago
Jeremy

SUNYAB
Buffalo, New York
April 17, 1965

Dear Jeremy,

Very useful to have Needham (even if he seems to have all the ideas, and at those terrible moments shows he hasn't experienced any one of them. It is one of the crazy states of knowledge now, that we have the advantage of an eranos of historiography, where men such as Needham and Eliade and a few others can bring all the ideas to bear. But it has now for a very few years been evident, hasn't it, that they are hung up on the corpus?

I say all that but you also know I can use every bit they do bring together—and this particular one, is useful. (One happy instance of the difference was Ed Sanders, who was here last week and read with John (Wieners) and myself, to the undergraduates, mostly 340 girls; and he turns out to be perfectly capable of spending the rest of his life, as he said, reading and doing editions of Herodotus and Hesiod.[4] In fact I believe the Frontier Press will publish his translation of the Theogony.

I guess what I am proposing is that <u>their</u> historiography is now "ours"!

Love, and looking forward to
"Tansy, fu'them" seeing you somehow soon,
either
here—or there! Yrs,
Charles

Please write as often as you can, even as I know you are this year any way encumbered

Holy Saturday

Plus Ed, plus <u>Ed</u>
Dorn: his mind
is the
<u>WIMPLE</u>

one curious thing Needham [+ Eliade??] doesn't seem to know Israeli Muslim thought of the early + 13th century—or at least mention it as a part of post-Christian time; and in fact hooked actually to Indo-Greek, + if Arabs were progenitors of modern <u>science</u>.

Gonville and Caius College
Cambridge
April 21, 1965

Dear Charles,

Your note just came through this morning; which I was pleased to have and will write back, now, despite the crush (new term started yesterday). There's so much worth having even if the others do only half command it and with such lack of grace: as, the common extent linking <u>tempestas</u>, <u>tempus</u>, & <u>templum</u> (from *<u>temp</u>-, extend, stretch, compare English "time & tide"). Eliade has this in view but won't allow a shape belonging to the words, as a contour of spoken conduct. He pushes it into a metaphysical excitement about "religion," when it's just a space marked out in whatever continuity, & then dedicated to a form of knowing (see Pokorny, pp.

4. Edward Sanders (b. 1939), American poet, translator, activist, and musician; and John Wieners (1934–2002), American poet who studied at Black Mountain College with Olson.

1064–1065). Originally, of course, a field in the heavens mapped out by the augur. According to Herodotus the Persians had no temples; he would not think of looking upwards. As for time, this is the pure weather of being (tempestas first meant time, then season, then [bad] weather). The point & contour of what has or may become, as it can be determined and thus be a place of special awareness.

Joe Needham doesn't deal much with Arabic sources, and is away, so that I can't yet remind him; I will, as if the marshalling is unhelpful it's at least there. But see Paul Kraus, "Dschābir ibn Hajjān und die Ismā'īlijja," Dritter Jaresbericht des Forschungsinstituts für Geschichte der Naturwissenschaften (Berlin, 1930). George Sarton has much of it, despite his painfully stupid protagonist worry about "progress"; try his Introduction to the History of Science, I (Washington, 1927), especially pp. 583–584 on the beginnings (A. D. 864 ff), also pp. 593, 660–661. Vol II of this work (Washington, 1931) has an extended outline of Nāsir al-dīn al-Tūsī, whose sheer achievement looks to be a coherence of remarkable density; Sarton's skeleton is on pp. 1001–1013. His knowledge of much before him (including Greek as well) could make his compactness into another example of held extent (into the past, as a form of knowledge, like the lesser but admirable Johannes Eriugena).

It's a great inducement: time & tide.

Will write later, when
there's weather for it
Jeremy

Gonville and Caius College
Cambridge
April 29, 1965

Dear Charles,

Joe Needham is back and "knows" quite an amount about the Ikhwān al-Safā (the Brethren of Sincerity), which he refers to in his Science and Civilisation in China, Vol 2: History of Scientific Thought (Cambridge, 1956), pp. 95–97. He has a very generous mind, even if it's mostly assemblage; I respect him like few others here. This is really to say that I've at last found a copy of Call Me Ishmael and sent it to Maschler at Jonathan Cape, who has very promptly acknowledged its arrival.[5] I've also made a Xerox photocopy [more correctly electrostat, I suppose] of the Mayan Letters, which I've sent in good hope. Something should come of it, at this highest time. I've even lent some magazines to our Library here, in connection outward from some lectures (readings, actually) I'm giving on the sound of words that

5. Prynne enclosed a copy of a letter to Tom Maschler dated April 19, 1965.

can actually be heard. Read plenty of Whitman "Song of the Rolling Earth" and more, Ginsberg's "Death to Van Gogh's Ear!" and the Supermarket poem, Duncan's "Propositions" (from The Opening of the Field); and some passages from Thoreau and John Wesley Powell. It just breaks open, with a neat click. Have you anything on tape read by yourself, that you could send, by air mail? Just an idea.

I have not yet seen, though I have the note by me, Hugh Hencken's "Indo-European Languages and Archaeology," American Anthropological Association LVIII No 6 Part 3 Memoir 84 (December 1955). And also P. Bosch-Gimpers, El Problema Indoeuropeo (Mexico, Universidad Nacional, 1960), though I don't really read Spanish with more than guesswork. No more now; there is a very certain quiet tonight, in the air, and nothing else: at all.

Yours again
Jeremy

What about that project, to come to London, or perhaps with one of those big grants? Don't forget, I'd be pleased to write, before myself coming on out. . . .

Gonville and Caius College
Cambridge
May 17, 1965

Dear Charles,

My "course" of readings and suchlike (i.e., salutary admonishment about the Cartesian palisade) is now finished, and still seems to have been a worthwhile experiment; as an "official" course of lectures in an ancient European university it must be something of a starting-point. For those who listened, I mean, to have an occasion for that kind & degree of provocation. Well, we over-rate what can be done; but maybe at some single point it could lodge, more or less reading the whole of "Bartleby" out loud, or *[George]* Oppen's Materials or the opening of *[William Carlos Williams's]* Paterson. I'm sending the list of what they now do have to read and work from, which I have loaned for this purpose and despite some degree of objection.[6] And also a broadsheet with some sheer verbal

6. Prynne's list of "American Publications Deposited in the Anderson Room, Cambridge University Library" includes the following: Olson, *Mayan Letters* (1953), *The Distances* (1960), and *A Bibliography on America for Ed Dorn* (1964); Robert Duncan, *The Opening of the Field* (1960); Robert Creeley, *For Love: Poems 1950–1960* (1962); Paul Blackburn, *Proensa* (1953) and *The Dissolving Fabric* (1955); Michael Rumaker, "Exit 3," "The Pipe," "The Truck," and "The Desert" in *Short Story 2* (1959); [Charles Bukowski], "Manifesto" in *Nomad* 5–6 (1960); Denise Levertov, *Here and Now* (1957); Gary Snyder, *Riprap* (1959); Robert Kelly, *Armed Descent* (1961); Jack Spicer, *The Heads of the Town up to the Aether* (1962); LeRoi Jones, *The Moderns: An Anthology of New Writing in America* (1963); Fielding Dawson,

sequence, prose as writing, which could not happen here, as a part "history" of another contour.[7] Names, dates of no relevance (being protective apparatus); just a hallucinating awareness of the placed word, tracing the inflections, what it is like to stand where each phonemic particle comes from. That's not English at all.

Nor is the other clipping, of your pieces, which I hope you won't mind being given to those who came.[8] I read these to them and finished with "In Cold Hell," which seemed to get some distinct kind of grip there. PV they have in the Allen anthology.[9]

Or could have taken from the extraordinary example of Hölderlin, about whom Heidegger writes: "Dichtung ist worthafte Stiftung des Seins. Was bleibt, wird daher nie aus dem Vergänglichen geschöpft. Das Einfache lässt sich nie im Masslosen. Den Grund finden wir nie im Abgrund. Das Sein ist niemals ein Seiendes. Weil aber Sein und Wesen der Dinge nie errechnet und aus dem Vorhandenen abgeleitet werden können, müssen sie frei geschaffen, gesetzt und geschenkt werden. Solche freie Schenkung ist Stiftung. Indem aber die Götter ursprünglich genannt werden und das Wesen der Dinge zu Wort kommt, damit die Dinge erst aufglänzen, indem solches geschieht, wird das Dasein des Menschen in einen festen Bezug gebracht und auf einen Grund gestellt. Das Sagen des Dichters ist Stiftung nicht nu rim Sinne der freien Schenkung, sondern zugleich im Sinne der festen Gründung des menschlichen Daseins auf seinen Grund. Wenn wir dieses Wesen der Dichtung begreifen, dass sie ist die worthafte Stiftung des Seins, dann können wir etwas ahnen von der Wahrheit jenes Wortes, das Hölderlin gesprochen, als er längst in den Schutz der Nacht des Wahnsinns hinweggenommen war ("Hölderlin und das Wesen der Dichtung" [1936], in Erläuterungen zu Hölderlins Dichtung [2nd ed., 1951], pp. 38–39).[10]

Elizabeth Constantine (1955) and *Thread* (1964); David Ossman, *The Sullen Art* (1963); Joel Oppenheimer, *The Dutiful Son* (1956/1961) and *The Love Bit and Other Poems* (1962); William Stafford, *West of Your City* (1960) and *Traveling through the Dark* (1962); Gilbert Sorrentino, *The Darkness Surrounds Us* (1960); Ron Loewinsohn, *The World of the Lie* (1963); Edward Dorn, *The Newly Fallen* (1961) and *Hands Up!* (1964); and William Bronk, *The World, the Worldless* (1964).

7. Six blocks of prose without bibliographical information in the style of a Practical Criticism exercise. They are taken from Nathaniel Hawthorne, *The Marble Faun: Or, The Romance of Monte Beni* (1860); John Wesley Powell, *Report on the Lands of the Arid Region of the United States* (1879); Ernest Hemingway, *A Farewell to Arms* (1929); Robert Creeley, "Jardou" (1952); Douglas Woolf, "The Cat" (1962); Ed Dorn, *Rites of Passage* (1965).

8. Prynne enclosed a pamphlet of Olson's poems containing "Other Than" [1953] (*Collected Poems*, 165); "Maximus to Gloucester, Letter 27" (*Maximus* II, 184–85), "Of the Parsonses" (*Maximus* II, 233–34), and "Proem" (*Maximus* II, 306–7).

9. "PV" refers to Olson's essay "Projective Verse."

10. "Poetry is the founding of being in the word. What endures is never drawn from the transient. What is simple can never be directly derived from the complex. We never find the ground in the abyss. Being is never a being. But because being and the essence of things can never be calculated and derived from what is present at hand, they must be freely created, posited, and bestowed. Such

This isn't easy to translate, without using abstract names (like "simplicity") for what are ascribed and located qualities, mapped into the world, by being founded back upon an unnamed substance (thus "the simple thing," or "the simple" as a way of pointing into the world, at what is thus aptly discovered there). I'll try to make some English versions soon, if I can make the time, including the later part of Hölderlin's letter to his brother, dated 1st January 1799. The poems themselves would be a much more stringent challenge, and anyway the birds are now screeching at what appears to be dawn. The opening of the sky, to what insulting sequence of glances one hardly wishes to consider.

I hope all goes well
even so
Jeremy

And if there should
be a tape I
could use it over
here

Buffalo, New York
May/June 1965 [undated]

Jeremy:

To greet you—and to regret enormously it should work out we pass each other [instead of one of us at least being in our usual place[11]

Very good luck here, and don't mind any faulting: put them in the way of your thought, and be sure they can use your tried discipline.

All best—and again deepest
regrets, to miss you—
Charles

Buffalo, Thursday Night

---

free bestowal is a founding. But when the gods are originally named and the essence of things comes to expression so that the things first shine forth, when this occurs, man's existence is brought into a firm relation and placed on a ground. The poet's saying is not only foundation in the sense of a free bestowal, but also in the sense of the firm grounding of human existence on its ground. If we comprehend this essence of poetry, that it is the founding of being in the word, then we can divine something of the truth of that verse which Hölderlin spoke long after he had been taken away into the protection of the night of madness." See "Hölderlin and the Essence of Poetry" in Heidegger, *Elucidations of Hölderlin's Poetry*, 59.

11. Prynne taught as a Visiting Lecturer in the Department of English at SUNY Buffalo from June 28 through August 6, 1965. He did not meet Olson during this time.

SUNY
Buffalo, New York
August 5, 1965

Dear Charles,

A brief note, mainly on a technical matter. A young ex-student of mine, currently in his first year of graduate work at the University of New Mexico, has written to tell me that he wants very much to come to Buffalo this fall, to take your courses &c. He has applied for a Teaching Fellowship, and has been warmly recommended by Robt Creeley. However, I have just a day or two ago spoken to *[Gale]* Carrithers here (who seems to have all the hirings & firings in his hand), and he gave me some archly slithery tale about not having any more room for Teaching Fellows (closing dates and all that). The man's name is John Temple, and clearly Carrithers didn't like him, didn't like his having a letter from Creeley, didn't like my speaking for him and not being able (or willing) to shout his virtues as a competent scholar.[12] In fact he's no scholar at all, being all shot up in various ways: nervous, disorganized, fragmentary, vulnerable and so on. I know for sure that he has real potential, but it may be some way down; he'll have to resolve himself and aim at something before much can happen. I would like him to come here if that were in any way possible: could anything be done? Could he work in the Library, or something? He needs some kind of support, as he has nothing of his own. I shall be at Cambridge Mass within the next few days and will drive out hopefully to see you if you're at home.

Best wishes: Jeremy

Gloucester, MA
August 12, 1965

Looked in this afternoon but everything seemed locked up, and no workable information from the environs. I'll call back this evening in case anything has happened. Leave a note if there's a number I can call or suchlike.[13]

Jeremy

Gloucester, MA
August 13, 1965

Gloucester: Friday 13th August, being about to depart (tomorrow) for another place

12. John Temple (b. 1942), poet, critic and teacher who studied with Prynne at Gonville and Caius College and with Olson at Buffalo.
13. Jack Clarke, one of Olson's former students, left a note for Prynne asking him to call that evening.

no one thing
to say, leaving
nothing but
all that smell of
the sea
(private
& the gulls, squawking
in the knowledge
of time of nothing
at all, here
on the rim.
Viz, the shelf out
as a pillar to fortune
the shoals a
quick draw
or longer, which is
a width to be gauged
by the most
specific &
hopeful
eye[14]

otherwise it is not very interesting, any more than some other instance, where the sentiment either droops round the postcard stands or resides in the hardest rock. Someone would have to take (the) charge, on a sprit such as this is: thus, tomorrow I shall aim across to Ed at Idaho.

Tell me if there's anything I can (or should)
do, & meanwhile
may all the lights
be equal outside this, your window
0355, Fri 13 Aug
JP

PRA054 BA073 1965 AUG 28 PM 6 06
B LLW161 NL PD=TDB GLOUCESTER MASS 28=

14. This is a draft of Prynne's poem, "Fri 13," *Poems*, 50.

EDWARD AND HELENE DORN AND JEREMY PRYNNE=
842 EAST CLARK ST POCATELLO IDA=

PLEASE BOOK ME WILL FLY BACK LOVE=
CHARLES=

Gonville and Caius College
Cambridge
October 9, 1965

Prynne sent Olson Glotta: Zeitschrift fur griechische et lateinische Sprache *41.3/4 (1963), ed. Harmut Erbse, Hansjakob Seiler, and Bruno Snell.*

---

28 Fort Square
Gloucester, MA
November 5, 1965

My dear Jeremy: It was such a pleasure to receive in today's mail the Mycenaean-Greek list—and thereby have word from you.[15]—I miss very much our old line of activity.

I wrote for you a poem[16]

Maximus of Gloucester

Only my written word

I've sacrificed every thing, including sex and woman
-or lost them—to this attempt to acquire complete
concentration. (The con-
ventual.) "robe and bread"
not worry or have to worry about
either

Half Moon beach ("the arms of her")

15. Olson refers to J. Chadwick and L. Baumbach, "The Mycenaean Greek Vocabulary," published in the issue of *Glotta*.
16. See *Maximus* III, 473. Prynne produced a typescript version and sent 2 copies back to Olson in his letter of November 8, 1965.

my balls rich as Buddha's
sitting in her like the Padma
and Gloucester, foreshortened
in front of me. It is not I,
even if the life appeared
biographical. The only interesting thing
is if one can be
an image
of man. "The nobleness, and the arête."

(Later: my self, a shadow on the rock.)

Friday November 5th
1965

(Later: myself (like my father, in the picture, a shadow
on the rock[17]

Gonville and Caius College
Cambridge
November 8, 1965

Dear Charles,

I've wanted so much to write. I am hedged damnably by cares too tedious to recount, again, & as much as before. And now, along a meridian across the forehead (of the World), I am struck. Transfixed by it: as a pledge, offered into the cosmos as a hostage. "Violence shall no more be heard in thy land, wasting nor destruction within thy borders; but thou shalt call thy walls Salvation, and thy gates Praise" (Isaiah LX). That's the other city, of course, and forced by a hateful spiraling out of our own hated demeanour. But I wish you it, & into it, as a hope and necessity (but O ever less than reliance). Really I could weep, and force this down in scatter because I daren't trust an intermission: to wait or to be thrust aside, by some pusillanimous conceit. It is a nearer thing than any other shaft of history, issuing from a cleft within the earth on which we stand. I'm not yet at such a spritted (or even broken) actus, not knowing whether to trust that it might break open & not just into helpless fragments. But I do know the sound of the occasion & am now moved to weeping by it.

17. This second version of the closing lines appears on the back of the envelope containing this letter. Prynne chose this last one for his typescript version, and it is also the version published in *Maximus Poems: Volume Three* (1975). See *Maximus* III, 473.

I will
always, as ever, write
willingly and
from need (love
again
absolutely always

[At once, so as not to delay, now to you ——→ Jeremy

Gonville and Caius College
Cambridge
November 9, 1965

Dear Charles: again it's too far, and too much; the whole aiming of such a thing gathers a directness it is hardly possible to believe, across the distance. The great powers for me are still released by the mediate conditions, so that I'm easily ruined by the other shore (looking out, that is, to our shared sea). And want to be, want it so much I could run on the sword, what is it now really & as a fix that you have there, with you. With a range of stupendous forms, like the wildness & exile of a sandy topsoil, not supporting life but postponing all its images. Simply and from the deepest point this is to say, I know from the sound of your voice that you must, but: the cost, the damned whole misery and then ultimately to be taken amiss. I don't know how to say any of it

I can't do it. No exaggeration I am weak from the fact, that poem is a wound, you must have the whole substructure of the English island beneath you, I bestow this trivial gift, and what could come of it must be raised up, now, it's not possible for me to get this held to the page. Since I crossed the sea just like a ballad, with the one guarded hope, to give you this as a totally specific gesture: a respect which runs out into time like light. Instant by instant the past builds up, the whole becomes more violently sacred & no pattern for rest. The Holy War—this is love & a wretched affection, you must hear that and I can't do more than hedge it across the page. Not magnanimous, nor honest, but a physiological necessity; your standing in the world is a true theoretic anguish. So that the weather must always be watched, for constant treachery, which is a piece of puny advice I offer in complete seriousness.

This sounds like a missionary tract, but the real sound must be there & to be traced somehow, as otherwise we are truly lost, I can't control it anymore: Oh Hellicanus, strike me honored sir, giue mee a / gash, put me to present paine, least this great sea of ioyes ru- / shing vpon me, ore-beare the shores of my mortalitie, and / drowne me with their sweetnesse: Oh come hither, / thou that begets him that did thee beget, / Thou that wast borne at sea, buried at Tharsus, /

And found at sea agen, O Hellicanus, / Downe on thy knees, thanke the holie Gods as loud / as thunder threatens vs; this is Marina.[18] Pericles: the wisdom & utter necessity of excess, but to keep to the land or even lashed to the mast.[19]

Thus you have everything, at this
moment, that I could ever
command or (the quaint word)
dispose; rising now
in the east or wherever
damn well else
it's yours but the old
weather must be (must still
be watched, thunder
is a natural phenomenon
the entire sequence
is holy, inviting no
sympathy: who should dare
let that out, towards
what there is
anyway
love the set, tight, the life
the land lie & fall, between
also the teeth, love the
forgetfulness of man which
is our prime notion of praise
the whole need is a due thing
a light, I say this in
danger aboard our dauncing boat
hope is a stern purpose &
no play save the final lightness
the needful things are a sacral
convergence, the grove on
a hill we know too much of—
this with no name & place
is us / you, I, the whole other
image of man

18. William Shakespeare, *Pericles*, V.i.11.192–201.
19. What follows is a draft of Prynne's poem "Lashed to the Mast." See *Poems*, 49.

So that now you must write, directly, with the complete knowledge of where you are. I mean, literally, for what you depend & the whole range of it. I can no longer bear the gossip and can't do without it now. Surely you as of certainty had to leave Buffalo; the nest of enticement nearly did for me, even. And I do wish you would come, by any invented means, I would have waited longer in Gloucester if I could have stood there unprotected (i.e., any damn place, twitching before my eyes into a real fact: I couldn't take that or wish to, but as demesne in a very old sense). Would you come, and could this be fixed, very literally. I must know exactly how things lie and the books and outlooks, or I shall go crazy. Rebuff this if you must, as it's another piece of weather, but at this moment I am laid low with urgency: the chances for humankind could be fairly said to rest on it.

I live literally
in a portable basket
of hope, of love
the written word

Jeremy

> "As I have mentioned how the people were brought into a condition to despair of life and abandon themselves, so this very thing had a strange effect among us for three or four weeks; that is, made them bold and venturous, they were no more shy of one another, or restrained within doors, but went anywhere and everywhere, and began to converse. One would say to another, 'I do not ask you how you are, or say how I am; it is certain we shall all go; so 'tis no matter who is sick or who is sound'; and so they ran desperately into any place or any company" (Daniel Defoe, A Journal of the Plague Year).[20]

Gonville and Caius College
Cambridge
November 16, 1965

Dear Charles,

The Language Lab voice-doctors at Berkeley tell me that they can't (won't) release tapes of your recent lecture and reading there without a "personal

20. See *The Works of Daniel Defoe*, II, 60.

release" as they call it. I enclose a note to this effect; if you can see your way to this, could you sign it and send it back to me?[21] I am used to this kind of intricately administered warfare & shall get through to it by sheer pressure of hope.

Thus, quickly,
Jeremy

> "That the terrestrial Matter, which is thus carried by Rivers down into the Sea, is sustained therein, partly by the greater Crassitude and Gravity of the Sea-water, and partly by its constant Agitation, occasioned by the Tides, and by its other Motions, and is not permitted to sink to the bottom; or, if any of it do, 'tis raised up again by the next Storm, and being supported in the Mass of Water, together with the rest, 'tis by degrees exhaled, mounted up with the Rain that rises thence, and returned back again to the Earth in fruitful Showers. That by this perpetual Circulation a vast many things in the System of Nature are transacted: and two main Intentions of Providence constantly promoted; the one a Dispensation of Water promiscuously and indifferently to all parts of the Earth; this being the immediate Agent that both bears the constituent Matter to all formed Bodies, and, when brought to them, insinuates it in, and distributes it unto the several parts of those Bodies, for their Preservation and Growth: the other, the keeping a just Æquilibrium (if I may so say) betwixt the Sea and Land; the Water, that was raised out of the Sea, for a Vehicle to this Matter, being by this means refunded back again into it: and the Matter itself restored to its original Fund and Promptuary, the Earth; whereby each is restrained, and kept to due Bounds; so that the Sea may not encroach upon the Earth, nor the Earth gain ground of the Sea" (John Woodward, An Essay toward a Natural History of the Earth: and Terrestrial Bodies, Especially Minerals: As also of the Sea, Rivers, and Springs. With an Account of the Universal Deluge: And of the Effects that it had upon the Earth (London, 1695), pp. 48–50).

Just a postscriptum to add that we now have a xerographic copying machine installed here in College (about 10 yards distant from my room). Quick, easy to use, and I have unlimited access without charge or favour. If you have parts of the Written Word that you'd like in facsimile, just mail it to me and I'll gladly at any time do the rest.

Poor Woodward believed with too specific a literalness in the Great Deluge,

21. Prynne included a note addressed to Robert Krones at the Language Laboratory in Berkeley for Olson to sign. Prynne requested tapes P-128 and P-142, which contain Olson's lecture, "The Causal Mythology," and his poetry reading.

which has been held against him ever since that time (as it has against Thomas Burnet's The Sacred Theory of the Earth). Both of them knew a good deal more of where they stood, literally considered as an extension into the cosmos, than we do. Maybe Alex. von Humboldt was the last, in his Kosmos (published 1845–62, just before the world collapsed into notion & salesmanship).

---

28 Fort Square
Gloucester, MA
November 17, 1965

My dear Jeremy,

(Just finished another hitch-up [on this long thing I seem to be involved in, for the Wivenhoe Park Review, of the Vinland Map and Carpini Relacion, and you mustn't please mind that you shouldn't have right back acknowledgement for your response for that 'lay-up' of a poem I sent you.[22] (I've also been involved almost since receiving both your Special Deliveries by receiving Saturday, by friends' delivery, my automobile [left there at departure last July], with all those books + clothes and papers etc which had accumulated, or been carried, West.

It is happy, actually, to have what I have carried in, back in the house.

I shall write, and in the meantime, know how very much it does make it possible to have you there to write to and to enclose—and that always seems a poem of such order—such as to expect your concern and welcome.

Charles

---

28 Fort Square
Gloucester, MA
November 18, 1965

My dear Jeremy:

I have this dream, to have the cover of the new Maximus volume [IV, V VI] be the Wegener Map of the Earth in his theory where the continents were once all Hers—and She in her turn was surrounded by Ocean [I'm still persuaded Anaximander or whatever it was made that lovely one of 'Homer's World'—or in fact the equally like 'Norse' one of 1000 AD)!—have that—'Mercury'!

Anyway, not yet has one of these bloody American or Canadian new hot-shot

22. At the invitation of Andrew Crozier, Olson sent an essay/assemblage called "The Vinland Map Review" for publication in *The Wivenhoe Park Review* 1 (Winter 1965), which considered Father John of Plano Carpini's visit to Karakoram, the capital of Mongolia in 1247, among other events. See Olson, *Collected Prose*, 327–35. Carpini also appears in *Maximus* III, 536, 619.

oceanography labs [Tuzo Wilson's, Toronto—or Ewing's, yet, Columbia] put in my hands [to pass to Wilentz—or to Jonathan, if he'd stop walking] a professional colored map of the *[Alfred]* Wegener picture in the state just as the seams [of the future] are showing.

Without (yet at least, for I have some strings and still, with above laboratories, and am now trying Harvard) engaging yourself but as always rather to tell things to you, if Cambridge should include any geographer who has newly renewed attention to the Wegener theory, and shld by chance possess such a map, do let me know.

Quickly, + just having opened your generous suggestion on Xerox—plus

Will write shortly,
Charles

By the way I open this up to enclose back your request to those people and do send it. But I have in fact since signed all their fussy documents.

Gonville and Caius College
Cambridge
November 23, 1965

Prynne sent a typescript of Sir Orfeo, *ed. A. J. Bliss (Oxford: Oxford University Press, 1954), Auchinleck text, lines 227–77; and Geoffrey Chaucer,* The Pardoner's Tale, *lines 720–38, in* Works, *ed. F. N. Robinson (Oxford: Oxford University Press, 1957).*

C. A. M. King, Beaches and Coasts (London, 1959), Chapter 12:[23]

Clearly this account, while it alludes to many of the features, would have to be subject to a radical transformation for its terms to assemble into a true image of the coastal zone. His whole view is a genetic aetiology offered as explicative device, so that for example waves "will the more readily be able to turn the coastline to face their direction of approach by moving the material" (p. 372). Thus the sequence of reactive process requires agents, and a whole willed dynamics of exertion. Like all bourgeois sensibilities, his image of the sea surrounds and conditions his knowledge of land; the shore-line is intelligible only through the quick language of wave motion.

The first stage might be to reverse this position, so that the inertia of position became the salient fact: the tenacity of place whereby for example an erosive sequence is countermanded by protective silt in drift along the coastal shelf. And as this fortunately sounds an absurd projection of humanist heroics, the

23. Prynne enclosed a complete photocopy of chapter 12 in addition to these notes.

whole dynamic image of a future entropy (the last flatness or entropic doom) can be abandoned. The coast, that is, being contradistinguished as the primary resistance of history, in its substantive aspect (accretions of "the time when" rather than "before and after which"). And once set up like this, the two myths of process can be left fighting on their own conceptual level (in the text-books), so that the sheer continuity of change is the coastal name, the geographic, the time-point as where we are, linear randomness crossed with the extent of the known place (since sequence is much more local than time and emphatically not reducible to the vulgar anxiety of "causes").

As in whatever case, how is a "'low energy' coast" (p. 383) caused, if not by entropic purpose? The cliffs too are ontogenetically determined, and thus weather is another part of the intentional cosmos (the "cycle"). Yet the bays "open" to the sea, which "laps upon" the land—which is certainly more true if persistence is not to be genetically shifted over into resistance. To have place we would need "sistence," which is held at least as steadfast, again where a man is now, keeping his ground but in no sense a victim of fortitude (cf. Battle of Maldon, 1.127). Under foot, not pressure or ground as adequacy of support, but place whether it will anyway. We hope for too much, are too unwilling to forget.

Gonville and Caius College
Cambridge
November 25, 1965

On behalf of Her Majesty Queen Elizabeth II, Her
Ministers and Government for the time being, and
of Her loyal subjects and the Nation over which
Her reign extends,

I herewith offer a complete set of unconditional
apologies for the enclosed wisdom purveyed to
said Nation by the Press upon whose every Word
we depend for the fullness and life of the Spirit.

In the name of the whole rotting complacency,
and that the whole extent of it may shortly explode, I hereto affix my mark:[24]

24. Prynne enclosed two recent reviews: "Guru of the Western World" [Review of Charles Olson, *Human Universe*, ed. Donald Allen (San Francisco: The Auerhahn Society, 1965); Charles Olson, *Proprioception*; Charles Olson, *A Bibliography on American for Ed Dorn* (Four Seasons, 1964)], the *Times*

Gonville and Caius College
Cambridge
November 27, 1965

Prynne sent a small pamphlet of poems with the quotation from Gilbert and the illustration, "Comes Litoris per Britaniam: Notitia dignitatum," as a coversheet. The poems are: "Lashed to the Mast" (Poems *49), "A Figure of Mercy, of Speech"* (Poems *39), "Living in History"* (Poems *41), "Airport Poem: Ethics of Survival"* (Poems *38), "The Stranger, Instantly"* (Poems *40), "On the Anvil"* (Poems *42), "The Holy City"* (Poems *43), "How It's Done"* (Poems *44), "If There is a Stationmaster at Stamford S. D. Hardly So"* (Poems *45); all of which were collected in* The White Stones *(1969).*

"When, therefore, one views a slope from which an
ancient lake has been withdrawn he recognizes its
shore trace in a series of features which embody
a horizontal line. Here the line is the meeting
of a terrace and a cliff, there it is the crest
of an embankment, and elsewhere it is the brow of
a delta plain; its manifestations are diverse,
but it is never wanting. To an eye placed at the
proper height and distance all its elements blend
together and it stands forth as a continuous, horizontal, undubitable shoreline."

G. K. Gilbert, "Contributions to the History of
Lake Bonneville," U. S. Geol. Surv., 2nd Ann. Rept
(1880–1881)

COMES LITORIS PER BRITANIAM: Notitia dignitatum,
page relating to the Count of the Saxon shore,
with outline of Britain, showing forts from Bran-
caster (Branoduno), Norfolk, to Porchester (Port-
um Adurni), Hants. A copy made in 1436 from a
Carolingian copy of a 4th or 5th century original.
Bodleian Library, Oxford: MS. Canon. misc. 378,
fol. 153^{v}.

Literary Supplement, November 25, 1965; and "Westward Who?" [Review of R. A. Skelton, Thomas E. Marston, and George D. Painter, *The Vinland Map and The Tartar Relation* (New Haven, CT: Yale University Press)] in the *Times Literary Supplement*, November 25, 1965.

November 28, 1965

I doubt Mr. Woodward cld possibly have caught any of that Matter he is at such pains to worry about crowding up the sea. What is so moving though (and his piece is another example) is the loss [as you say yourself, in feeding me Thomas Burnet's beautiful title, is the loss to 17th century man [and currently for most English and Americans, and worst for them as Protestants, Melville only the re-corrective of That [The Protestant] one, of Alchemy. How its loss stole from our peoples the Sacred—and I begin to think [except for Descartes, + after all he was a Catholic and had chewed up the Counter-Reformation Jebbies by the time he made it as his own Chick] it is, by inversion, the same worse thing the 2nd half of the 13th century was. (I'm altogether 'led' by the several 'pieces' you have sent in the past few days. This is simply to jot down this.

Charles (Sunday November 28th)

PS. I learned yesterday [from one of my Buffalo men, Charles Doria—Catholic, from Cleveland][25] that Dante was a member of *[St.]* Francis's Third Order. Enough, even considering that it is he. It starts me figuring: was Giotto? How does one find out such uncoded things (AA—after Alchemy—and BN: Before Needham) Is there even a Needham of the West?

PS 2. Is it only now that the Twin Thing [with Blake a sort of Hiatus] the queer state of After Faith and After Alchemy is seen at all?[26]

December 9, 1965

My dear Jeremy—If anything, particularly the Ill. London News, shld come under your notice, of Spyridon Marinatos' reported discovery of wine cups, a diadem and other gold which he is claiming as datable early 16th century BC, from a site 20 miles north of *[Carl]* Blegen's "Pylos," it wld be very useful to have copy of anything which digs into the matter at all. (As it is I have a Wesleyan Post—Buffalo Courier Express story only, from Athens—+ though undated I'd imagine it's 10 days ago.

I've been somewhat dropped off my purpose and course by sudden destruction of houses here which I cldn't let pass [I asked Dorn to forward to you one

25. Charles Doria, American poet, translator, teacher, student of Olson's at Buffalo, and notably recipient of Olson's "The Advantage of Literacy Is That Words Can Be on the Page: A Bibliography on the State of Knowledge for Charles Doria" (1963) in *Collected Prose*, 353–54.

26. Olson also included a photocopy of his poem "An 'enthusiasm,'" published in *The Gloucester Times* on October 16, 1965. See *Collected Poems*, 629–30.

spread, in the Gloucester Times]. Also been distracted continuing to get heat into my house—or also keep what heat there is more useful, finding that any plans for travel admit seen yet as useful as trying to keep with + at work either at hand or piled up from the past. If I can feel well [though this dead pass of the year at least, which I realized yesterday, for the first time, as I was mopping my 4 square yard of linoleum here on the kitchen floor, was a series of shocks in childhood—I had always actually taken it, not that I don't continue to, being a Capricorn, as Saturnine anyhow! and that the shortness of the day does squeeze the heart in these Northern [or at least New England] Climes—Nearctic anyway. And I so abhor the continuance of breaking the year by that wretched post-Christ invention of his Birth as having to happen now—or I so think they are bad Greeks, and Jews! Hip hip hoorah going to Florida—or the more assured, or comfortable, or pitiful, going to Nassau. And like a factory clock I so prefer to go right along until it has passed. Then open one's eyes to the new sun

Mine right now: 4 PM? is just as I write smoking red as smokey red wonderful blue red vase now 7/8ths of itself now 3/4s two trees against it smoke from the Magnolia dump directly where she now sets SW now less than 1/2 a *[sic]* done now 1/3rd Here to see now less in a slow winding of this amount of phrase going now a little 'nail' of his self there slips almost away is a line only . . . want Is gone [time—by my clock—4:14PM ow

[just checked today's newspaper—Sunset 4:13
(Friday, that is, so today's
must have been—how much is
Each day's loss—?
have already thrown out
yesterdays

But, + will be back to you on all recent matters,
Charles

Gonville & Caius College
Cambridge
December 11, 1965

Dear Charles,

Another brief note, thus to have some of the words for it, in the start of a possible order. All from the two vols I happen to have here, now, as the whole area is contested as if the roots were dragon's teeth indeed.[27] I don't know exactly how much support Tucker would have at this time, especially since sīdus as a component of consīdero seems somewhat back in favour. The entire spread looks augural to me in any case, even the Egyptian field, so that the heavens could hardly not be there overhead. As, indeed, they are.

Jeremy

Gonville and Caius College
Cambridge
December 13, 1965

Dear Charles,

Briefly, to note then that the sun did sink as accounted for, and to enclose the Illustrated London News report on the discoveries at Peristeria. On the way back from Colchester to Cambridge with Ed last Friday, crossing all that slightly undular farmland in Essex and Suffolk during the late afternoon, the sun was again one of those heavy & almost reluctant globes low down on the horizon. There was mist in the wrinklings of the ground, which gathered into clumps of trees and the dips as the road followed the surface. The whole thing was an effect of almost palpable folding, being encased by the smallest shifts of that contour, with gradations of vibrant greyness holding the bulks of the landscape into place. So that to pass some men going home on bicycles, and pumping themselves heavily up an incline in the road, swaying a little from side to side as they transferred the weight of their bodies from this pedal to that, was to get the whole mess of it into the eye, as confirmed by the pendular sun: we could have been in Finnish Lapland.

Whereas now outside, 3·20 p.m. & barometer at 29.74, there's one of those calm winter afternoons holding a great deal of energy latent and apparently nothing much happening. The sky open & fluent, and blue so as to transfer this to the stonework and small distances visible within the courtyards. In fact there's more light in precipitation than is visible from any one level—I can feel it in the quick successions of small sound coming in at the window, the whole being an instance of that mobility & crispness of air which has always been one of our principal forms of alertness (here in England, as for instance with all that subtle

27. Prynne's note includes photocopied dictionary excerpts from two sources: "Aírþa," S. Feist, Vergleichendes wörterbuch der gotischen sprache (1939), pp. 125–26, trans. annotated by A. S. C. Ross, Etymology, with Especial Reference to English (London, 1958), pp. 55–56; "saeculum," "diēs," "deus," "tempero," "tempestās," "templum," "tempus," "consīdero," "deus" from T. G. Tucker, A Concise Etymological Dictionary of Latin (Halle [Saale], 1931), pp. 64, 78–79, 211, 239.

weather in Keats's letters). As to be drawn off into that, his to *[John Hamilton]* Reynolds dated Sunday 3 May 1818, "that like the Gull I may dip," which leads him into the famous Mansion of Many Apartments: "We no sooner get into the second Chamber, which I shall call the Chamber of Maiden-Thought, than we become intoxicated with the light and the atmosphere, we see nothing but pleasant wonders, and think of delaying there for ever in delight: However among the effects this breathing is father of is that tremendous one of sharpening one's vision into the heart and nature of Man—of convincing one's nerves that the world is full of Misery and Heartbreak, Pain, Sickness and oppression—whereby this Chamber of Maiden Thought becomes gradually darken'd and at the same time on all sides of it many doors are set open—but all dark—all leading to dark passages—We see not the balance of good and evil. We are in a Mist. We are now in that state—We feel the 'burden of the Mystery,' To this Point was Wordsworth come, as far as I can conceive when he wrote 'Tintern Abbey' and it seems to me that his Genius is explorative of those dark Passages" (Letters, ed. Forman, 4th ed., Oxford, 1952, pp. 142–143). Or the beautiful quickness of weather in his note again to Reynolds of Tuesday 21 Sept. 1819, prompting, as he says, the ode "To Autumn."

Or the very beautiful patience of the Cambridge naturalist Leonard Jenyns (later Blomefield), whose interest in the fluent supersession of weather never blunted into that theoretic concern with the genetics of change as above all to be accounted for. The nineteen years of his attentions are everywhere in evidence, so that when he writes "settled" or "changeable" the language has the authority of being out there but also accumulated—as in a rain gauge or those shifting banks of cloud. "The whole body of the lower atmosphere" he writes (on p. 306), and shares with Keats the honour of that knowledge. I've just Xeroxed a clutch of pages from his Observations in Meteorology, which I also enclose.[28]

Nearly five o'clock, and completely dark—has been since a quarter past four or so: still full of sounds but damper now & closed down into our northern privateness.

And so: and ever,
Jeremy

---

28. Prynne includes Rev. Leonard Jenyns, *Observations in Meteorology: Relating to Temperature, the Winds, Atmospheric Pressure, the Aqueous Phenomena of the Atmosphere, Weather-Changes, etc., being chiefly the results of a meteorological journal kept for nineteen years at Swaffham Bulbeck, in Cambridgeshire, and Serving as a Guide to the Climate of that Part of England* (London: John van Voorst, 1858), ch. 6, "General Observations on the Weather," 303–12.

Gonville and Caius College
Cambridge
December 14, 1965

Post Scriptum:

> "A cosmical history of the universe, resting upon facts as its basis, has, from the nature and limitations of its sphere, necessarily no connection with the obscure domain embraced by a history of organisms, if we understand the word history in its broadest sense. It must, however, be remembered, that the inorganic crust of the Earth contains within it the same elements that enter into the structure of animal and vegetable organs. A physical cosmography would therefore be incomplete, if it were to omit a consideration of these forces, and of the substances which enter into solid and fluid combinations in organic tissues, under conditions which, from our ignorance of their actual nature, we designate by the vague term of vital forces, and group into various systems, in accordance with more or less perfectly conceived analogies. The natural tendency of the human mind, involuntarily prompts us to follow the physical phenomena of the Earth, through all their varied series, until we reach the final stage of the morphological evolution of vegetable forms, and the self-determining powers of motion in animal organisms. And it is by these links that the geography of organic beings—of plants and animals—is connected with the delineation of the inorganic phenomena of our terrestrial globe."
>
> Alexander Von Humboldt, Cosmos: A Sketch of a Physical Description of the Universe, trans. E. C. Otté (5 vols, London, 1848–1858), Vol. I, pp. 348–349. The original German publication of Kosmos began in 1845.

I was going to propose a number of specific instances from Humboldt's Introduction to this work, but the piece is so dense & intricate that you ought to have the whole thing (in case you don't already own it). I'll Xerox this & send it along with this note, so that apart from everything else you can grab up the footnote starting on page 51. . . . [29]

December 15, 1965

Prynne sent the complete issue of Past & Present *12 (November 1957).*

29. Prynne enclosed a photocopy of the complete introduction, pages 1–61.

December 16, 1965

Prynne sent the following materials:

Sonia Cole, *The Neolithic Revolution* (London: Trustees of the British Museum [Natural History], 1965).

G. S. Kirk, ed., *Heraclitus: The Cosmic Fragments* (Cambridge, UK: Cambridge University Press, 1954), pp. 306–24.

W. K. C. Guthrie, *A History of Greek Philosophy*, I: The Earlier Presocratics and the Pythagoreans (Cambridge, UK: Cambridge University Press, 1962), 205–12.

December 17, 1965

Prynne sent James Mellaart, Earliest Civilizations of the Near East *(London: Thames and Hudson, 1965) along with its review in the* Times Literary Supplement.

December 18, 1965

Prynne typed sections from Walt Whitman's "Kosmos" (pp. 431–32) and "Walt Whitman" (p. 50) from Leaves of Grass *and adds the line:* Walt Whitman, an American, one of the roughs, a kosmos.

---

28 Fort Square
Gloucester, MA
December 18, 1965

Jeremy,

Excusing like they say the goddamned boring Marxian "Commie" crap I am very happy to have Past + Present in today [Saturday December 18th, and already, happily have been in to both Crossland and of course Childe + a sweeping single not even radar swoop on Lat-ti-more-lat-ti-more [whom I was a younger younker of, date 1943, + spring zing "44" if the Federal Govt—or as I think it was we used to say [some name for processing]—had been 24 hours sooner [they sent me the telegram that short a time after I had had to take another job] I'd have been in China and I shd think long since another one of the former China [America persons (!) "hands"!) if the Japs hadn't decided I was the Original Mountain Goat[30]

30. Owen Lattimore (1900–1989), American scholar of China, was accused of being a "China Hand" by Senator Joseph McCarthy during the Red Scare.

Point to get anyway all messages to you—+ that all has come through including your own handsome volume + I shall be more with everything [even if I am unreasonably long through

this particular part of the "natural" year—so love + let me (+ keep me continuing)

your friend Charles
Olson

What pictures the stars
teach us or offers us
they form or lesson vies
they whatever perform for
aren't they—or this night this
hemisphere this North degree the
date tonight is my[31]

31. This poem appears on the rear side of the envelope.

CHAPTER 6
1966

Gonville and Caius College
Cambridge
January 1, 1966

Prynne sent a typescript of his poem, "Song in Sight of the World" with the dedication:

Jeremy Prynne, for Charles Olson,
Cambridge, New Year's Day, 1966.

Gonville and Caius College
Cambridge
January 5, 1966

"The homonyms that do exist in English have arisen for various historical and phonological reasons and not at all for lack of possible alternatives, the phonological forms of which would not conflict with those of words already in the language. Nothing illustrates better the historical nature of language than the existence of homonyms."

M. W. Bloomfield & L. Newmark, A Linguistic Introduction to the History of English (New York, 1964), p. 90.

"Celts and other peoples of western Europe shared this natural fear; the sea must one day get the upper hand."

E. O. G. Turville-Petre, Myth and Religion of the North; the Religion of Ancient Scandinavia (London, 1964), p. 284.

AND: M. H. Wuttke, Cosmographia Aethici Istrici ab Hieronymo ex Græco in Latinum breularium redacta (Lipsiae, 1854)

Gonville and Caius College
Cambridge
January 11, 1966

A good new year to you Charles, since I haven't written in a talkative way since that began. Over here it's pretty cold at the moment, trying to snow outside though earlier it's been too cold even for this. And raw, with very chill & cruel winds—how I know what that word means—which curl in over the fenland from the North Sea and feel like the Baltic. I've spent a lot of time before & after Christmas with Ed and Helene and the beautiful kids at Colchester; centrally heated there (which is an unusual luxury for England) and with fine warm stoves as well. He is a man of great splendor, though I suppose he still doesn't realize that; I've just written to the Guggenheim to tell them so and hope they will agree. It would keep him free for next year, at any rate, which is what he wants and of course should have.

But this is about something else, and must be brief at this stage as term has just to-day begun. Up to this moment I haven't had a single chance (i.e., the time involved) to ask about Wegener and the map you wrote about. But now I see a very exciting symposium run by the Royal Society of London on Continental Drift, which is in effect a re-examination of the Wegener theory corrected in some instances but essentially now and after the heated rejections held to be very close to the facts. Palaeomagnetism seems to be the decisive new evidence. I enclose a list of contents for the whole volume and prints of the first & second papers, so that you can see what's going on.[1] The whole thing is expensive and also heavy, so that it would be best to see it over there in some library if it could be obtained. The most directly exciting paper is perhaps IV, by Sir Edward Bullard (a member of this College, of course), which has maps in colour I can't reproduce. But I'm trying at this moment to get offprints, and will send you one as soon as I can: his Figure 8 might even make a right-up-to-the-moment cover for Maximus!

The whole collection refers to Wegener unceasingly. W. B. Harland (another Caius man) has two discussions touching on that earlier synthesis, and if you want that map of his I'm quite certain that this could be brought off without difficulty. Your U.S. & Canadian hot-shots certainly seem somewhat behind with this information. Incidentally, if you do decide you'd want to have the entire

1. Prynne refers to *Philosophical Transactions of the Royal Society of London, Series A. Mathematical and Physical Sciences* 258.1088 (October 28, 1965) [A Symposium on Continental Drift]. The first two papers were S. K. Runcorn's "Palaeomagnetic Comparisons between Europe and North America" (1–11) and T. S. Westoll, "Geologic Evidence Bearing upon Continental Drift" (12–26).

volume, just tell me and of course I'll send it at once. I must stop, as I'm frantically occupied, trying to be humane as a positive and direct assertion (that sounds stupid, but having tried yourself to work it for students inside some other thing, you must know too well what that means).

All my best,
Jeremy

Gloucester, MA
January 11, 1966

Jeremy,

Here is one which really would seem to open up a problem:

my Master [in English History] when I were a freshman, George Matthew Dutcher, a few years ago I had occasion to notice said almost all persons who migrated to the colonies, had not, in England, had surnames; and chiefly took them from trades or such, when they reached, as independent creatures, this side. (!)

Which raises this question: I believe the man who principally, possibly, bossed the Harbor Front at least of Gloucester in its settlement [as the 15th or something "Churiel" + turn, 1642] had his surname before he came—originally to Boston—from Stepney: William Stevens or—Stephens (?). Can you, in this world, tell me what, in 'Englese,' "Stevens" might specifically be?

I mean, other than—what it may of course come from, a plural of "Stephen"(s)??—or is there a 'steve' like reeve any chance?

Why curiously it does involve me in asking you is (of course): 1. that I cannot find a "history" of surnames any way [despite my "Master"!]

Who WAS a SOUR + BEAUTIFUL GIANT [he "flunked" me on my Honors bibliography, so that I lost High Distinction!—and ONE YEAR LATER on my MA was the kind of a man to say he complimented me on my bibliography

—+ 2. wow: has anyone [like, inc.—Tucker!—or POKORNY—anyone—done, among Proper Nouns, derivations on—like—Proper SUR-NAMES?

? ?

? ? ?

as of having an intolerable visit [for you, alone] of 6 days—permitted
by me, so I CAN'T
- like - COM-PLAIN—
fr. JOHN TEMPLE [all last week—+[for me] a
CRITICAL WEEK God help me]——trying to enlist

(over)
to him the
recent "Swedish" underneath nominates(curious adjective Hawkes + wife +
Biddy Ellis-Davidson, in
Antiquity abt march the past year
"Kew?" discoveries out of the English earth
Long Man of Islington (?) [Hawkes]

* * *

I hope this is also [again] a-n-o-ther way for you to know I both have rec'd + have begun to use the several things you both have copied written + sent during these precious weeks, love your friend

Charles Olson Gloucester

Gloucester, MA
January 14, 1966

Oh Lord, Jeremy, your people slipped me right in the middle of Magmatism! Page 21 was dropped!

I can't tell you how useful striking this symposium has been to me. And you are basically right that my Canadian-US sources [Wilson, Heegen, and of all that lousy Ewing, at Columbia—typical of that University—hasn't even yet replied—and I tried him two solid years ago.

I shall be most obliged for that color job of Bullard's—or, in fact, if he or anyone has a colored Wegener just when the jig-saw splitting shows of the original single Earth. Which, as you know, has been my purpose, for the cover of the volume, since Wyoming.

Up to now I have thought—for such a cover—the old Round-Earth project in [Wegener's] would be greater + slip more in on the Innocent On-Lookers! But what you say of Bullard's Figure 8 might also be it. Isn't Westoff marvelous on Carboniferous (and Permian! Wow

And now that I have seen the pitifully pedestrian page-proofs sad Wilentz has come up with (cheap man) my cover at least will have to cheer the poor reader up!

The Poor Reader

I shall be most aided by anything you can do—could a visit by you to Sir Edward be within bounds of courtesy, and possibility? (My own experience—as I sd in Letter 23 (even as of my man Master Merk is that [we] as literary persons are—or they are never comfortable, like business people and athletes as Pythagoras sd (!) with us on-lookers.[2] However there is one perfect statement of something now at best least guessed (over) in Westoll's paper here [in today Friday January 14th]: stating on uniformitarianism and the listing as limitation where individuals can hope to study only a small part of the evidence

Isn't that lovely?

And doesn't it betoken the end of both ends of art and reason as it has been cooked and served since Plato + Socrates started ignorance + false satisfaction "ignoratim" to use my greatest of all Cambridge masters' word for it

on its path. Humanism certainly has worked itself into a ne'er do well finally thank God.

I so admire present American youth anyway for choosing at least to have 1) its own experience; + 2) to get it, so for as they can, straight. That at least is a beginning on the level of satisfaction [again the Cambridge Master's word—though, happily, I did have that dream, reported in one of the two Pastoral letters, long before I had done anything but be asked one night to a dinner at Hester Pickman's, to meet the Master (surrounded, as all such precious men seem to be, finally, by admiring, + interfering, females!) Not that I right now wldn't want one or more just such love & loving females!

You wld know of course I think the other side of it—reason, has only just begun again!

Love, + greetings to you too
now that it is (66)

55 Himself

What is interesting is how,
at the end of the eyes, he
resembles my Indian chief of his own [Note the Roman
day: from signalling, "Non-Roman" Condition
using the sun!] or the sculpture of the "Founder"
of this "Country" on the reverse side][3]

---

2. "Letter 23" in *Maximus* I.104 mentions Frederick Merk (1887–1977), an American historian who taught Olson at Harvard.

3. Olson refers to the five cent postage stamp on the front side of the envelope that depicts a sculpted head of George Washington.

187 Lexden Road,
Colchester,
Essex
January 16, 1966

Dear Charles,

Today Ed & I have been to see the site of the Maldon battle—the causeway is still there and it looked fine in the snow.[4] We've been talking for a long while, and with constant but somehow baffled hopefulness, that you might come over here, and soon. Across all those puny barriers and intermissions: as if the mere Atlantic was ever much of a shot anyway. And with news from John Temple, and suchlike, it has just now struck us ALL THREE that you should come and that we should cut right through all this possible and probable and provisional notion.

We thought we would all go to Italy in the Spring vacation (when we're all out of school), which would be very beautiful. You must take it all in both hands and come. Ed and I want very much want *[sic]* to split the fare, so that none of us shall be potential victims of some slipped adjustment. We have steady and ill-gotten incomes, so that's no less than possible—and no talk about that.

Now, the proposition is really this: we want you to come and it's quite suddenly come to a head—there is no possible reason why not, as we see it. I have spoken to BOAC in London over the telephone, and they have a special excursion fare BOSTON—LONDON—BOSTON, which we would so like to get for you as you cannot begin to guess. This operates on weekdays except Friday (& except Saturday and Sunday), and to get the special round trip rate you would need to stay at least two weeks. You could stay more than three if you liked it, so we'd have no problem covering the small extra on it's running over the three week period.

* Planes leave Boston for London direct on Mondays & Thursdays. *

Let us know by return, to satisfy this quite specific feeling that the whole thing would simply be RIGHT, when you could come. For the trip in April (we aimed to start about 7th April), or at once and stay for just as long as you were able, or come at any point in between. But you must feel the cable stretched to snapping-point, as I most certainly do. Just write with a date, and the entire project could just drop off the tree.

Love, as ever
Jeremy[5]

---

4. Prynne's poem, "Song in Sight of the World," mentions "the battle of Maldon," which occurred in August of 991 CE near Maldon in Essex between the Anglo-Saxons and Vikings.
5. There are several lines after Jeremy's signature written by Edward Dorn that reinforce Prynne's imploration to Olson.

Gonville and Caius College
Cambridge
January 18, 1966

Prynne sent eight pages of photocopied excerpts regarding the etymology of Stevens as well as the advertisement for The Cambridge Ancient History, *volumes I and II, revised edition, edited by I. E. S. Edwards, C. J. Gadd and N. G. L. Hammond, listing fascicles 40–52.*

"steeve" in *New English Dictionary*, XI.I (Oxford, 1919), 906

"Stephen" et al., in P. H. Reaney, *A Dictionary of British Surnames* (London, 1958). "See also his The Origin of English Place-Names (London, 1960)]"

"Stephen" et al., in C. W. Bardsley, *A Dictionary of English and Welsh Surnames with Special American Instances* (London, 1901). "See also C. L. Ewen, History of Surnames (1931) and Guide to the Origin of British Surnames (1938), discussed critically in the "Introduction" to Reaney's *Dictionary* (his bibliography includes a full survey of the earlier literature)."

Pages 665–674 of Catalogue 802 (European Philology—1965) from B. H. Blackwell Limited, Broad Street, Oxford, England.

"Steeve" in Joseph Wright, *The English Dialect Dictionary*, V (London, 1904), 748

"Stevenage" in J. E. B. Glover, Allen Mawer, F. M. Stenton, *The Place-Names of Hertfordshire* (Cambridge, 1938; English Place-Name Society, Vol. XV)

"Stevenage" in Eilert Ekwall (ed.), *The Concise Oxford Dictionary of English Place-Names* (Oxford, 2nd rev. ed., 1940) [There is now a 4th ed.]

Title pages to A. H. Smith, *English Place-Name Elements*, 2 vols. (Cambridge, At the University Press, 1956) [English Place-Name Society, Volumes XXV-XXVI].

Map of "British Names" from Smith, *English Place-Name Elements*, Part I

Map of "The Scandinavian Settlement" from Smith, *English Place-Name Elements*, Part I

Map of "Distribution of Place-Names in *-ing*" from Smith, *English Place-Name Elements*, Part II (see Part I, pp. 282–298 for the discussion of -ing).

January 19, 1966

Without an accompanying letter, Prynne sent an offprint of a map showing the reconstruction of how the continents once fitted together prior to their expansion. Source is unspecified, but it appears to be a version of Alfred Wegener's theoretical reconstruction per Olson's request.

January 20, 1966

Prynne encloses a letter and timetable from the British Overseas Airways Corporation (BOAC) that he had requested on January 16. He notes in the margins:

> Or to hell with that intricate postponement—why not just write & say you'll come now & I'll fix everything. Name the day.

January 21, 1966

Prynne sent an offprint of Edward C. Bullard's paper from the aforementioned Symposium on Continental Drift, "The Fit of the Continents around the Atlantic" (41–51), as well as Bullard's brief accompanying note.

Gonville and Caius College
Cambridge
January 22, 1966

Charles—further to my notes from Tucker &c, to reach beyond that.[6] De Vries states most emphatically that he regards the myth of Týr, and the loss of his right hand to the Fenris wolf as part of the ruse to bind the wolf, as extremely early; he puts it right back in to the Indogermanic period (i.e., before the European dispersion). I would prefer de Vries here (Vol II, pp. 23–24) to Turville-Petre who calls Týr a "faded god" (Myth and Religion, p. 180), which seems a quite misplaced satisfaction on his part. Týr played an important part in rune magic & gave his name to the rune ↑. He was less prominent in later Scandinavian myth only, it seems, because by then he had ceded his place to more specific figures. A god of the skies & heavens is too much with us: in our later wisdom we require more private and disposable appeals.

Also you might like to know of H. B. Woolf, The Old Germanic Principles of Name-Giving (Baltimore, 1939).

Quickly & with love,
Jeremy

---

6. Prynne includes 3 large photocopied pages of clips from "dei-" et al. in Pokorny, *Indogermanisches Etymologisches Wörterbuch*, 183–87; as well as the beginning of section 360 regarding Týr from de Vries, *Altgermanische Religionsgeschichte*, book II, 25–26.

January 25, 1966

Jeremy (Friday—+ please shoot right down to Ed

At the moment the billows are surging. So obviously it wld be not wise to come. But what your invitation, and Ed's, has done of course is to make it perfectly clear that the way to do it is simply to go to Boston some night and fly over to see you.

For that alone (without speaking of all I know I'm already missing, + will, if you go off to Italy without me) I owe you both a million francs your own Over Here

Uncle Sam—Whoever

Charged the Tables

Gonville and Caius College

Cambridge

January 31, 1966

Dear Charles,

Just a note, as of a new (and rubricated) scholasticism: the stratigraphy of current language. Remember to come when you can. When will there be some more work to see, as the West poem for example, or are you back in the East with Maximus?

(compare *[Thomas]* Traherne:
"The East was once my joy; & so the Skies
And Stars at first I thought; the West was mine:
Then Praises from the Mountains did arise
As well as Vapors: Every Vine
Did bear me Fruit; the Fields my Gardens were;
My larger Store-house all the Hemisphere.")[7]

I hope everything goes swimming forward & will hope to see anything you've got. I enclose a bit of mine, since talk is difficult so far in other terms.[8]

Keep well,

Jeremy

Prynne's structural gloss on Olson's poem "The Twist" (Maximus I, *82–86)*

7. "An Infant-Ey" in Thomas Traherne, *Traherne's Poems of Felicity*, ed. H. I. Bell (Oxford: Clarendon Press, 1910), 12.

8. Prynne includes his poem "The Numbers," *Poems*, 10–12.

transcribed below, also includes a photocopied clipping of the entry for corpus (-oris) *from Tucker,* Concise Etymological Dictionary of Latin, *66–67.*

The Twist

BODY the thing itself in this veracity
STRUCTURE the house / was
a dobostorte
FRAME Trolley-cars are my/
inland waters
SUBSTANCE the tide the air / sea ground the
same, tossed / ice wind snow
CORPOREAL } my wife has
FLESHLY } a new baby the outer-land
FAT }

BIND UP } the figures / shoveling the mass / drives on, / the whole
MAKE COMPACT } of it / coming, / to this pin-point

CLOSE, THICK in the wet soil an apartment house
was like a cake
FORM, BEAUTY as dreams are, when the flowers blackberry
the day / encompasses blossom
MAKE/WORK/BUILD I plant flowers for him the ditch that Blynman made
What we are doing
JOIN those couples I'd have gladly gone where it goes out & in
did go to to bed with
BELLY the French dress, cut / on the bias
APPEARANCE through which I looked like an oven– a paper
door village
TWIST, WHIRL as they go after she the river / exactly calyx and corolla
around the left me there at the bridge by the dog
fills itself, at its tides bend to turn
POETRY letting the song lie

Gonville and Caius College
Cambridge
February 1, 1966

Dear Charles—Ed showed me your piece on the Vinland map, and as you'll see

I passed over the Brooks Adams words to an "eminent" historian of medieval European trade—a fanatic literalist of the spirit, anxious not to give much away.[9] But it does slip through: (a) trade & money flow on land "clogged up by tolls" (proto-capitalist self-strangulation on a continental scale); and (b) as we should have guessed would be the corollary to that: INSURANCES.

With the Shah of Persia's *compliments*

P.S. E. Roukema, "Some Remarks on the la Cosa Map," Imago Mundi [cartographic journal], XIV (1959), 38–54.

February 2, 1966

My dear Jeremy—

Like SIR R. CLARKE sayeth a Marxian—STEW: I don't believe I had acknowledged PREVIOUSLY receipt of P + P (Past + Present):

X DOBB Trinity

X JONES—?

+ of course [ROSS LAND]—wow humour:

inc. SIR BULLARD—very veri- [+ thus to ack-] nowledge as received TO DATE

Charles

February 4, 1966

I tell you Prynne,
from across the Atlantic you
give me, Latin

love,
O.

Gonville and Caius College
Cambridge
February 9, 1966

Dear Charles,

Some self-explaining letters &c enclosed, together with the monochrome

9. In addition to a photocopy of Edzer Roukema's article, Prynne also includes his exchange with a scholar at Cambridge regarding Brooks Adams's *The New Empire* and its discussion of thirteenth-century Flanders and the rise of maritime trade.

illustration from Wegener's book.[10] Can you give me any more information about the coloured version? Harland really should know this material well, despite his silly "pride" and so on (and despite his policeman's interest to know my interest). Can you tell me where you saw the map; whether it hung on a wall or was an insert to some book or journal, etc., etc. Any lead, to get started again.

In haste, but
no less for that
Jeremy

Gonville and Caius College
Cambridge
February 11, 1966

O Charles look at these
words / I am in mortal
danger from beatitude

the text was edited
by A. E. Housman & was
a life's work

the English (there being
none) I have had
made, for this

for the owl in
the dark, of our heads

et quoniam caeolo descendit carmen ab alto
et uenit in terras fatorum conditus ordo,
ipsa mihi primum naturae forma canenda est
ponendusque sua totus sub imagine mundus.

10. On January 25, 1966, Prynne wrote to W. B. Harland, a geologist in the university's Department of Earth Sciences, about whether a more recent version of Alfred Wegener's map of the reconstructed continents in the latter's book *Die Entstehung der Kontinente und Ozeane* (1920), was available. Harland could not provide any information.

[And since it is from high heaven that poetry descends and fate's established order comes to earth, the very pattern of nature must be my verse's first theme and I must set out the whole universe in its proper guise.]

Manilius, Astronomicon, I. 118–121

hoc opus immensi constructum corpore mundi
membraque naturae diuersa condita forma
aeris atque ignis, terrae pelagique iacentis,
uis animae diuina regit, sacroque meatu
conspirat deus et tacita ratione gubernat
mutuaque in cunctas dispensat foedera partes,
altera ut alterius uires faciatque feratque
summaque per uarias maneat cognata figuras.

[This great fabric fashioned from the vast frame of the universe, and nature's components in their diverse forms of air, fire, earth, and level sea are ruled by a divine force, a soul; God's holy breath blends throughout. Silently he governs, dispensing the covenants that bind each part with each, so that one exerts influence upon another and is influenced in turn, and in variety of aspects the sum remains the same, one family.]

Manilius, Astronomicon, I. 247–254[11]

February 12, 1966

Prynne sent a photocopy of John Dowland, The First Booke of Songes or Ayres of Fowre Partes with Tableture for the Lute *(London, 1597).*

Gonville and Caius College
Cambridge
February 14, 1966

Dear Charles:

Both Ed and I have gone halves towards getting this to you, presuming after this small delay that you could not do without a political document of

11. Prynne refers to the English poet and philologist A. E. Housman (1859–1936), who edited and published an edition of the Roman poet Marcus Manilius's *Astronomicon* in five volumes (1903–1930). D. R. Shackleton Bailey (1917–2005), a Latinist then teaching at Cambridge, translated these lines for Prynne.

such current relevance.[12] With both our love, & we hope you'll come over soon.

And for this short time
Jeremy

---

28 Fort Square
Gloucester, MA
February 16, 1966

A Valentine "present" for Cambridge University

My dear Jeremy:

I hope—for my own pleasure, that Massachusetts owes her existence, and the distinction of her "sons," occasionally, to show a different command of experience I reasonably think [being a Fellow myself of John Winthrop "House," Harvard University, in the earlier years 1937–1939] can follow from a direct line + transference of knowable differences of thought + feeling and I do mean those two rational functions

I do hope, on St. Valentine's Day [who probably himself was, wherever he is, also a graduate of both Cambridge + Harvard, feeling being so much the pleasure of his Name Day anyway, and, in my own "book" of both experience and thought, the one important "holiday" of the year—

I am hoping no person of your University is one of such anonymous reviewers in the London Times Literary Supplements recently, particularly issues November 25th, 1965, and January 27, 1966, for this critical + Important reason:

that though there is no let-up, on the contrary that the use for and the evidence of historical scholarship, and thought, and science, or scholarship of the historical, and applied, and experimental or theoretical, at this date confirms uninterrupted and in some cases improved,

that what singularly + happily has specifically for a certain date in the 19th century been most obviously long overdue + required—unquestionably since

12. Prynne refers to a copy of *A Symposium on Continental Drift*, eds. P. M. S. Blackett, Sir Edward Bullard, and S. K. Runcorn (London: The Royal Society, 1965), which included two inscriptions: an untitled poem from Dorn and "The Wound, Day and Night" (*Poems*, 64) from Prynne. The latter's dedicatory epigraph reads:

For Charles, the shades of Manilius,
Henry Howard, Earl of Surrey, & the
Department of Geology and Geophysics in
the University of Cambridge [England] [.]

at least a date very close to the founding of Cambridge University herself—say, imagine, 1224—(which I happily think probably was on February 14th Old Style corrected)

is a Single World View of man + creation. Her most distinguished Philosopher, has, as recently as 1927–28, done this, in all candor;[13]

in the same breath, though, and with a like candor, there does seem one additional matter needed to make sure that no such error as the England of the Times—at least those instances of it, referred to above [and themselves conforming to American thought itself, and poetry] shall by any means be let pass—or hopefully shall not occur again, flying as they so do in the face of the very gains made, + in such a matter of concern to man on the earth any where—and either in abeyance since 1224, or, struggled for again ever since by the mind + feeling of man, to bring matter + means once more to the love + service of God as well as of man, a man, one American physicist, mathematician and logician, from Cambridge, Massachusetts 1839, needs—and be only, to be added to celebrate, This Valentine Day, 1966, what a union has occurred: Popular Science Monthly January issue 1878[14]

Hurrying off—at the moment—to: Now False-Cambridge I will send quotation left out within as soon as I am back.

The enclosed 3 poems
written for
Jeremy Prynne
February 16th
1966 (A.D.)
Charles Olson
dixit et[15]

Pytheas 2
Flamborough Head,
Tarbat Ness

—and the northern nest

13. Probably a reference to Alfred North Whitehead (1861–1947), whose Gifford lectures during 1927–1928 were later published as *Process and Reality*.

14. Probably a reference to Charles Sanders Peirce (1839–1914) who published "How to Make Our Ideas Clear," in *Popular Science Monthly* 12 (January 1878), 286–302.

15. The subsequent three poems do not appear to have been published before.

Shetlands: 61° N

Then—as Ottar told Alfred—
bore north and turned eastward
And a light northwest wind for four days
where the land curved south and he had to wait
—Tanais!
Here the Bjarmians—and he did not tell Alfred
how many walrus. Nor how much ship rope

Even astronomically more interesting than Stonehenge
And traversed
walked all over it on foot, 333 B.C.

Britain and found her
periodus as

4000 geographical miles (all her coasts,
and Europe's as far as the Tanais:

and afterwards,
to the east [Phoenician, and then Norse

secrets

[the 'Dvina!]

Gothic 1
in large covered barns because
of the want of sun and abundance
of rain

Those who came to America

Sir Edward H. Bunbury
History of Ancient Geography
vol. i. ch. xv. ¶ 2 (London,
1883; also

H. F. Tozer, [same title],
pp. 152–164 (Cambridge,
1897

---

28 Fort Square
Gloucester, MA
February 20, 1966

I mean—+ it's like [I have to,
as you may know] take it I am/are their Valentine [+ I do not mean
Santa Claus! Valentinus—not that recent ('Copt?—?]

My dear Jeremy
I mean that St.
Valentine, you wld of course know—otherwise,
Valentine the
Lord, you'd not have done it
what we call in the Tarot
what a 'present' that is
Man of Hearts, the King of the CUPS.
I wrote already (to Ed, on CUPS—receiving it [yesterday]—and asked him
to send you on my 'cable'!
King of Hearts
Delightful [also will manage to type out for you to you—(and yours? the
end of my own Valentine
Actually you
I discover now it was 24 he came (When did Lawrence, first?)[16]
An aside, to my self
And thus he wrote those lectures, say,—in fact the date I think he puts in
[to the text, as of a RR timetable—+ floods—is
1927 itself

Have [in the past week] realized (as well) that—did it have to wait for all of
them until Alfy (also obviously probably a "Saint" [of our new Comic Strip
Order

16. Olson refers to Alfred North Whitehead, who came to Cambridge University in 1884. The reference to "Lawrence" remains obscure to me.

ORDO SECULORUM (as you will note it reads
on the back of the enclosed
FAMOUS DOLLAR-BILL
fr the other side:

they make me mad too these Adams brothers [not Charles Francis, that is if their oldest brother [I think]—by the way he has a beautiful piece on his father—their father—dedicating a statue to Lincoln as the Emancipator in Manchester (who, if I have it right—and

My point [read every other line] was anyway how accidental
[Richard] Cobden, the guy who stitched them up? Manchester did keep England from
—+ busy and careless (traveling all the time
supporting the South, despite the loss of home, + pay from
+ rushing back, to live as close as
the loss of cotton?) It is this realism—activism—and
possible in the shadow of, the White
the lack of its 'thought' which has made me this last
House only their father decently
week turn with such vexation and
had to do with—those dirty little Times
Brooks as well as my old suspicion
LS Americans Henry and Brooks Adams
of Henry: they were a couple of ghosts [LTLS ghosts!]
—so were
because they wldn't look hard enough to see what pulley
to have picked up so much on Lord
was up, in American thought. It took Alfy
Kelvin etc. instead like their own
—or Alfie—to write: "my obligations to the English and the American Realists is obvious"[17]
best, and better consequences [or → over
born 1861—only 13 years after Brooks [+ Yeats is born 1865]!
predecessors—and I don't mean Wm James (or for that matter Henry Either

I do have, in a poem I don't see how you cld have seen—A Po-sy A Po-sy—written back before 1950 [+ back to back to another, one of the 1st poems I sent

17. See Whitehead, *Process and Reality*, xii. Olson has written two separate trains of thought in the even and odd lines in the section beginning "—+ busy and careless," but "instead like their own" above appears to match with "predecessors" four lines below. Whitehead was born in 1861.

Creeley in the batch to him when W. C. W. told me there was such a man up in Littern, New Hampshire, who proposed to edit a little magazine, and if I had any thing I considered immortal!—imperishable!—The Morning News] in Posy I quote

as Mrs Henry Adams sd
of Mr Henry James, Henry
doesn't bite off more than he can chew, he
chews on more than he has bitten off[18]

The Cambridge Ancient History fascicle 51. The Anarxa Letters from Palestine; Syria the Philistines and Phoenicians, by W. F. Albright
later: with the enclosed—so as not to waste it!—buy me [when you are downtown, will you? from the list you sent me recently

Sunday February 20th
It SEEMS so elementary but
can you put me on to an
Anglo-Saxon-English dictionary—I mean
as natural a one as a Webster?

Gonville and Caius College
Cambridge
February 21, 1966

Dear Charles,

To thank you for the poems most especially, and to recognize with whatever twist to it that we are, post Pythias, the starting-point for so much else outward from here. The chimney sweep brushing the soot out of Ed's chimney this morning, with jointed rods still made of Malacca cane, said he not uncommonly found the upper throats jammed with seagull's nest remains & suchlike. Like those storks nesting on the roofs in Scandinavia or the Russian fairy-tale hero [Ilya the Cossack] curled up on the kitchen stove: you have the world image right there in the hearth. Lares, which are not domestic, as we now complacently would think, but the specific knowledge of position as a divine component—augural again, as I persist in thinking.

18. See Olson, *Collected Poems*, 110.

And in any case, this is more than a ring of ports & creeks on a very indented coastline. One of the consequences of never being at great distance from the shore is that I am not tempted (as very much so in the mid-West) to fantasy surrogate images of embarcation—or how in Ohio to be sure to catch the tide. Often the water is an abrupt thing; an optional extension, into some newer clarity of knowledge. When the more frequent alternative was the hunt within a royal forest, the pastoral excursion into the country, what we call field sports (picnic in the stadium). I can't give you much of this sense of it, but the terrain is much more densely land-locked; the journey is either hope, merchandise, or exile, and now since our derisive claim to a role east of Aden not any of these things. You should really come and see, for yourself.

I enclose typescripts and also a few conjectures about detail. Also some mid-fourteenth (no, I mean mid-fifteenth) century carols from a MS in the Caius library.[19] The sea there is extravagance, to go out of your way, temporary shift in truth. The Norsemen were clearly over-adequate to their sense of value, and as their privacy was so attenuated they took up with ambition & the "high seas." As we did, later, though active only at the fringe and holding the profit very still at the centre. So, well, this is nothing: I'll write again, and meanwhile thanks for the poems and the last letter (still down in my mind). I am suddenly very interested in the English, and Crozier I have a hope for (even Temple, but not that forlorn Thomas Clark—ingenious drift-wood washed up on nobody's beach, which perfidious mobility I now detest at full power). Not of course even to bother with the Times Lit. Sup. as that's too dull even to think of.

Coasts must be kept clean:
Yr. coastguard friend
Jeremy

Gonville and Caius College
Cambridge
February 25, 1966

Dear Charles,

Right back and at once, in no sense prejudging and clipping any other thing: the Anglo-Saxon word-lists—

1. J. Bosworth & T. N. Toller, An Anglo-Saxon Dictionary (enlarged ed., Oxford, 1898), plus Supplement (Oxford, 1921)

19. Prynne sent typescript versions of Olson's three poems sent in his previous letter, along with a few marginal queries about spelling. He also included one typescript of two fifteenth-century carols, "Hos is to hoth at hom" and "Were it undo that is ydo."

The major lexicographic corpus, inadequate in many respects but chief & necessary authority

2. J. R. Clark Hall, Concise Anglo-Saxon Dictionary (4th ed., with Supplement by H. D. Meritt, London, 1961)

   Brief with respect to illustrative citation; i.e. (of Course) a much curtailed scope

3. F. Holthausen, Altenglisches Etymologisches Wörterbuch (zweite, bis auf das Literaturverzeichnis unveränderte Auflage, Heidelberg, 1963)

   Skimpy & unintelligent etymologies, making few divisions of sense & usage

4. Fr. Klaeber (ed.), Beowulf and the Fight at Finnsburg, with Introduction, Bibliography, Notes, Glossary, and Appendices (3rd ed., with 1st and 2nd Supplements, Boston, 1950)

   This glossary is intricate & a primal sequence of definition linked into the poem

Which is some place to start from, or from which to oversee the ground across which the other histories have gone. And to show just how beautifully articulate in an exact sense that all was, the enclosed piece of what is already the special pleading of woman: passive sufferance, the hope & language too warm for its occasion.[20] Or as otherwise could be said, again:

VALENTINE
Jeremy

Gonville and Caius College
Cambridge
March 3, 1966

Thinking of you tonight Charles, and of the strange figures which do sometimes come in also. In fact a whole number of things, like that beautiful temple there in Gloucester with one wall knocked away, and like the frozen pond I was taken out to, somewhere on a New England farm (Christmas 1960), to skate or rather to watch the family do so. Each point makes a perfect circle and the arcs of our competence describe (in that geometric sense) the human ground. This kind of astrology is total and is possessed of great powers, though I suppose any fool could call it "the future" & begin to explain how we don't know what it is. Or don't we, I would say, since the trust we do (or I do, now) feel in this matter is more than the simple lack of alternatives. Forms of knowing: "Tutti li

20. Prynne includes a copy of the Anglo-Saxon poem "The Wife's Complaint."

miei penser parlan d'Amore; / e hanno in lor sì gran varietate"—all my thoughts speak of love, containing in themselves such great diversity—in the Vita Nuova, XIII. Well, perhaps that's another perfect circle, except that we are very accurate people and the politics of such a condition are quite strict. I don't much like to think about that war, but I do, and it's clear to me that it is in no sense being fought. The argument is about superior presence, and in almost every sense this rests on who has it at night: this is always the test, of who will most commandingly recognise what he can't see. Whites of anyone's eyes.

Tonight it feels like warm rain, though in fact it's not yet warm out so as to be counted on. I think again it may well be the astrology of projection: tears of the muses, real saline drops. "E perché piangi tu sì coralmente, / che fai di te pietà venire altrui?"—and why do you weep so from the heart, making pity for you come to all other men? (Vita Nuova, XXII). There are no answers but that this is a single arrow aimed to that house which I do remember up on Fort Square, and indeed climbing up those steps. Here's a piece I wrote yesterday, out of an even greater quiet of spirit & desire.[21] What we most truly have we should keep, or try to.

In every way,
Jeremy

March 3, 1966

My dear Jeremy:

I'm missing three books, and for the life of me I can't find them in this house. They just have suddenly got vital to my work (as they indeed have been) and by that very token, + just because they are the sort of real + formed-up stuff you + I both know are what do make it, and that you might well have had that use of them, to use them yourself, can you help me, as the last person in the house before my return? I've checked with everyone (and *[Jack]* Clarke, who was here this summer, + righted up the books in the living room—not at all, as I keep telling him, was that helpful!). The three are:

The Fisherman's Own Book (Proctor Bros. Gloucester circa 1875)
The Siege of Fort Lowell—a pamphlet actually, an address abt. 1890 say?
to an historical society Portland, Maine (and the one item which solidly
places the Gloucesterman who opened "Portland" for successful occupation
[against the French and the Indians]

21. Prynne includes a typescript of his poem "Moon Poem" (*Poems*, 53–54).

—and Willis's History of Portland, [this one is published Portland too, date? 1860??] which was given to me some years ago by Gerrit Lansing when that same they the Lowell [above] had to do with, was so much in my Time

If you should, by any chance—± as you know from my point of view quite logically—have borrowed them—or indeed have any memory of seeing or looking at them, when you were here, it wld settle my mind, which for 10 days now has been rattling around the house—and my son even got going on the problem, + dangerously (the dope) because from the tallest bookcase he fishes out one book I had for years been missing

Ok—simply to ask in hopes + prayers you
do have them + that will end the search, yrs,
Charles

All things sent rec'd, + only reason I've been slow to respond solely some disorder these last 10 days.

Gonville and Caius College
Cambridge
March 7, 1966

Dear Charles,

Your letter arrived this morning & alas I am no rescuing angel: I am quite sure I didn't even set eyes on the three books you mention. Possibly they were there, but I would surely remember if I had seen them. In fact the only thing I read (& do recall) was Frances Rose-Troup, Roger Conant and the Early Settlement of the North Shore of Massachusetts. The rest is silence and I am myself quite sure that I would know if anything else had lodged in my attention. I brought nothing away but the street map I bought in the main street, & which is so intricately ambiguous about what is sea and what land.

So that this is a comfortless letter, which nearly I don't write (not wishing to dash what hope there may be). I will look to see whether the Lowell pamphlet is in our main Library and if so will have it xerographed; but it does seem unlikely to be there. Thus I don't well see what I can do, which must sound heartless but assuredly is not so. I have been trying to set hands on a copy of The Phoenix Nest for a month now—it has been stolen from our Library—and that line of advance has stopped dead; similarly a volume of Wordsworth from which I in fact want to send you one thing—all the other pieces are Xeroxed bar this, and again I can't even reflect on that whole matter without feeling dislocated by it.

I'll complete the gloom by quoting from a puritan divine of expert dismalness; he was said to be a singularly mild and saintly person (& of course I believe that entirely): "This embittering of sensual and carnal delights is a thing of the greatest concernment, and therefore must be necessary and all must be concerned in the Vertuous enterprize; the greatest blessings, (the want of which make a Man perfectly miserable) depend upon it, even God's love of complacency, and the Application of Christ's Merits, and the Benefits of his Death, and Passion; these belong not to the Soul, that is enamoured with sensual delights, no more than they appertain to Dogs or Swine; nay, they are useless, and insignificant to such a Soul, as much as the Mathematicks are to an ass, or idiot. There is a perfect anti-pathy betwixt these, and the comforts we speak of; for they are intended only for humble, broken, contrite Hearts, which temper a Person that's fond of sensual delights is not capable of" (Anthony Horneck, Delight and Judgement *[sic]*: Or, a Prospect of the Great Day of Judgment, And its Power to damp, and imbitter Sensual Delights, Sports, and Recreations [London, 1683], pp. 116–117).

Well, anyway, I feel now quite immune to that separation, knowing that pleasure has a very keen projective bitterness, and in any case is a selection from the thicker tones, the real needs (what we know being so much prior to that flimsy regret). The stern facts are not pain (who wouldn't be "perfectly miserable" if there were such an option?) but generousness, probably, such for example as Whitman knew in those hospitals, redeeming nothing (as being never so vulgar) but still having more to carry than the line would easily hold. "Something veiled and abstracted is often a part of the manners of these beings" he says in Specimen Days. What we know is our most neutral sorrow: that we are grateful: how we do go on down.

Write whenever you can
Yrs
Jeremy

P.S. E. C. Kirkland, Charles Francis Adams, Jr.: The Patrician at Bay (Cambridge, Mass., 1966)

March 9, 1966

Prynne sent a photocopy of Maurice Pope, "The Origins of Writing in the Near East" Antiquity 40 (1966), pp. 17–23.

---

28 Fort Square
Gloucester, MA
March 11, 1966

Wow (Jeremy) am I excited: just opened [+ haven't opened yet your letter of the 8th] the mailing to me—of the 9th, of Pope's essay: very important (to me, to have that.—And I imagine, you mailed it Wednesday, + I am writing you Friday just past noon [no hour listed British Postal offices??]

Had awaked with strong desire to write + tell you how much I read your Moon Poem.[22] And liked it. And wanted [having so long ago shied from offering you—must be three years!—my 'poem' to you [for you, explicitly] on Mars, + Shakespeare, + the gerund in English poetry

—+ then (when you wrote for me the Draft of) A Bibliography on England etc, + yrself then sd gerund I am the more anxious not to counter your own proceeding.—What delights me here in your new poem (which you well yourself know, for the gravity as well of your recognition, in yr letter to me the next day, of the place the vocabulary has, in your hands, turned itself to the possession of, I wished only [as I had fumbled then, on the gerund, + won't now, on the 1st + 3rd person] to quite simply say that: that in fact your clear sign of the stile turned half way to let your body through is that 'I' of mid-poem, followed by 'We' then to bring it home.

Love + a thousand blessings [as well as my thanks, at the moment, for this sharp use Pope offers me

Charles

Will, be on, +—I hope—more constant + 'poor' two weeks or so but spring—thank God—seems here; + it is for me this year like the forge [or fuze?]—fire, was it?—blood in its sweet form of wine for me, this marvelous chance [Friday March 11th 2 PM

March 14, 1966

Prynne sent a copy of J. Kr. Tornöe, Norsemen before Columbus: Early American History *(London: George Allen & Unwin Ltd, 1966).*

---

22. Ralph Maud speculates that Olson probably refers to Prynne's "Moon Poem" in a filmed interview with Richard Moore that began on March 11, 1966. See "Filming in Gloucester," 214n12.

March 14, 1966

My dear Jeremy,

Many thanks for your swift reply on those 'Portland' + Gloucester books.

And please excuse me for asking: it was the last chance. Whoever did take just those particular books [and it seems as though it must therefore have been I—but for the life of me I can't find them, or figure out where I might have taken them to] must have been as intelligent then as you and I!

Will write directly again

yrs
Charles

Gonville and Caius College
Cambridge
March 15, 1966

Your letter arrived this morning, with the sun (which at that time I didn't see) & a cold day: spring holding out on us still, but due to fall, like rain, on those early mornings warm and the more splendid with surprise as one has spent the whole night talking and confident in the dark. That does happen, as if at the solstice one is re-instated in the movements of one's body, the eddies of sight and talking & to go down to the river to look at the water over the balustrade of a stone bridge. What does it is warmth, a changed idiom, and spring is indeed almost here with us too. The seasons are the motions of being, the world set at large in its own quality.

That moving with authority, through the air, the bearing of seasonal change, is what your letter brought with it and called to mind. I was very pleased to have it, if I should even need to say this any more, but I do so from mere pleasure. How euphuistic pleasure is, as a motion in which we reside; retaining the urgencies which keep our moral substance compact, but also generous & hopeful for the quicker tones and their interplay. What to do with this is another matter, arising perhaps only in a practical sense. But the quality of it is recognition, that in change we do not lose who we most nearly are. That's what I meant of course by the community of wish.

Which is a constancy also maintained in the language itself, and the disposition of quantity in speech. Noam Chomsky, for example, writes this in assessing priorities of structure in the grammar of transformation (he is talking about relatives): "Each major category has associated with it a 'designated element' as a member. This designated element may actually be realized (e.g., it for abstract Nouns, some (one, thing)), or it may be an abstract 'dummy element.' It is this designated representative of the category that must appear in the underlying strings for those transformations that do not preserve, in the transform, a specification of the actual terminal representative of the category in question. In other words, a transformation can delete an element only if this element is the designated representative of a category, or if the structural condition that defines this transformation states that the deleted element is structurally identical to another element of the transformed string. A deleted element is, therefore, always recoverable" (Current Issues in Linguistic Theory [The Hague, 1964], p. 41).

My sense of speaking and of being is thus more and more gerundial, as you recognise, and as I suppose slowly I recognise myself. If the language can keep its quantities intact, that recoverable element (which in the end is knowledge) will accrue despite all forms of apparent supersession. Whom we love, cease to love, or just grow strange towards, perhaps through distance: there could be a grammar of loyalty which would entail no formal clinging to the specific, but which would celebrate our instatement in the human body & the community of desire. By quantity of course I mean very locally the measures of poetry, and the syllable as a constant element in the transformations of speech or myth; here's a lovely example, from Herrick's Hesperides, addressed to Musick herself:

Charms, that call down the moon from out her sphere,
On this sick youth work your enchantments here:
Bind up his senses with your numbers, so,
As to entrance his paine, or cure his woe.
Fall gently, gently, and a while him keep
Lost in the civill Wildernesse of sleep;
That done, then let him, dispossest of paine,
Like to a slumbring Bride, awaken againe.[23]

The pace of this is exactly adequate to the innocence of wish sustaining it: that the sick youth should be rested. Of course it's a charm in the old incantatory sense, but that's just a specific directedness given to the power, of accurate recognition, all these words each given due meaning (the poised syllables of the first line, for instance) but held in equipoise. The 'needs' of syntax are dispersed: "As to entrance his paine, or cure his woe": so as to describes a fictitious purpose, since what is wished for is the complete relaxation of all that worry about which way to go. The "civill Wildernesse" is more than an emblem

23. Robert Herrick, "To Musick, To Becalme a Sweet-Sick-Youth," in *Hesperides*.

for repose, it describes the world we might live in as in effect a practical possibility, what we could actually afford to lose. The whole sense of innocence as *rest* is a beautiful play on *while* in the most profound way. For as a conjunction this usually fixes the hinge of anxiety, the limit of duration measured as critical to some *other* action. Thus the Duke in *Measure for Measure*, here almost casually: "See this be done, / And sent according to command, whiles I / Perswade this rude wretch willingly to die" (IV.iii). Time, in other words, as interim defined by intention. Yet for Herrick the inversion of order in the words offers *while* as the something which may keep the youth entranced, as also the word slips back to *charms* through the tacit pun on *wile*. The force of *keep* is in countermand of *while*, since it locks up the perspective & exilic force of the conjunction, and releases a much deeper sense. This *while* as a stretch of time, earlier a period of delay or idleness, reaching back to the same root as Latin *quiēs*, 'rest, quiet, sleep.' As a well-trained classical scholar Herrick would of course know that. The fall *is* gentle; in Chomsky's terms, a "deleted element is, therefore always recoverable." And what is recovered here is precisely that quantity of speech which is duration as repose, measure, the complete adequacy.

Not that this is in any entire sense an 'answer' to pain, where we do (I think too easily) project ourselves into tragic priviledge *[sic]* as a means of escape; but rather a complementary definition of *place*: where we are. The *so* in Herrick's poem reminds me of *The Winters Tale*, and especially where Florizel describes the displacement of purpose by action as festive within itself:

> What you do,
> Still betters what is done. When you speake (Sweet)
> I'ld haue you do it euer: When you sing,
> I'ld haue you buy, and sell so: so giue Almes,
> Pray so: and for the ord'ring your Affayres,
> To sing them too. When you do dance, I wish you
> A waue o'the Sea, that you might euer do
> Nothing but that: moue still, still so:
> And owne no other Function. Each your doing,
> (So singular in each particular)
> Crownes what you are doing, in the present deeds,
> That all your Actes, are Queenes. (IV.iv)

What more is there than this, the like play on *still* and maybe also *euer*, linked by *so*, the whole motion figuring the world not in some boring Platonic sense of the abstract, but exactly: as knowledge. *This* is who we are: he was, as you are, and I am, who and what the whole of it finally is. What Wegener could have done with the original unison of language.

Love, as euer so:
Jeremy

March 17, 1966

You didn't, Jeremy, use my green dollar bill to send me that latest CAH fascicle: won't you accept any of my own money?—It is such a pleasure to have all these exchanges [Turvo's book in to day[24]

Cld I inveigle you to spend the enclosed for me? I shd so much like to own *[G. S.]* Kirk's Heraclitus The Cosmic Fragments [University Press Cambridge, 1954] and because I hate businesses [maybe it's American presses even—Harvard, for example, today, vex me, sending me, on my order

[20 good American dollars enclosed]

[Gerald F.] Else's Aristotle's Poetics—vulgar book making (vulgar fellow too—my own old friend when Tutor—he Senior Tutor—John Winthrop House [sounds good now that JF Kennedy + I (!)

Also, if you'd enjoy—only—doing it: Mr Whitehead's The Philosophy of the Atom or something (just before Process + Reality—about, in fact, the date of his 'migration' to the U.S.[25]

These then are pleasures—+ it solely being you I ask if you wld care to

PS
You didn't
utter a word back
to what I thought [was
my happy
Valentine: did it not
hit you at least that way
at all? Yrs—Charles

Your biblio by the way on all that geomorphic stuff has struck at least Wah in Buffalo[26] with that neat + usable . . . what I then rewrote as:

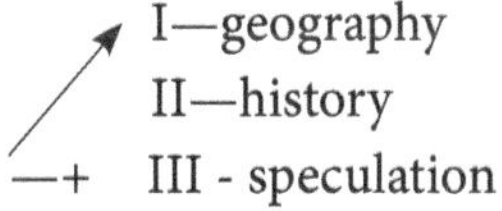

24. Olson refers to the volume by Tornöe sent to him by Prynne on March 14.
25. Olson probably refers here to Whitehead's *Principles of Relativity* (1922).
26. Fred Wah (b. 1939), a Canadian poet who studied at SUNY Buffalo.

to have struck a blow
yesterday [this am
in fact] to
eradicate eventually
That English Roman clerk's son
from the history of the human race
Thursday March 17th: am
happy [as an Irishman—one-half minus
my Mother's birth here]

Gonville and Caius College
Cambridge
March 18, 1966

Dear Charles:

A few odd things, as postscript.[27] As far as pleasure goes, it's interesting to see what dislocation it produces in the causal nexus; that is, "I did it for pleasure" is not really any answer at all to "Why did you do it?" The language with which we specify the tones of being will affix only to processive nouns, as in "with pleasure," "for pleasure." Otherwise we can only relate the matter elsewhere: "I did it for good reason, in spite of objection, out of very personal motives." What we should know is that "doing for its own sake" is specifically a form of being, and not part of the fiscal linkage of transfer. To do it "for love" or "for pleasure" is the partial & localized recognition of real continuance, the ground of feeling. Only formalism prevents us from doing it "for hope" and "for trust" as well as "for love." And if the tones ever could diversify and blend into a complete arc, the reason-and-motive dialect(ic) would simply melt into the ground. Even Aristotle sometimes seems to have recognized this: "Pleasures are not processes nor do they all involve process—they are activities and ends, nor do they arise when we are becoming something, but when we are exercising some faculty; and not all pleasures have an end different from themselves, but only the pleasures of persons who are being led to the perfecting of their nature. This is why it is not right to say that pleasure is perceptible

27. Prynne includes a photocopied excerpt from W. A. Ringler Jr. (ed.), *The Poems of Sir Philip Sidney* (Oxford: Oxford University Press, 1962), Commentary [on Poem II from *The Old Arcadia*], pp. 389–90; his own notes from Paul Schilder, *The Image and Appearance of the Human Body* (New York, 1950), 84–85, 98, 126, 273, made while at the Widener Library at Harvard on August 11, 1965; and a note from W. Heffer & Sons bookshop (dated March 14, 1966) stating that the Albright facsimile requested by Olson has not yet been published.

process, but it should rather be called activity of the natural state" (Nicomachean Ethics, 1153 a 9–15).

"The F[rench] Plaisir [= pleasure] is merely a substantive use of the O[ld] F[rench] infin. Plaisir, to please; just as F[rench] loisir (leisure) is properly an infinitive also" (Skeat, Etym. Dict., p. 450).

"My own heart let me more have pity on; let
Me live to my sad self hereafter kind,
Charitable . . ."[28]
(G. M. Hopkins)

Yours as always: Jeremy

Gonville and Caius College
Cambridge
March 27, 1966

Dear Charles,

I've just got back (from a trip with Ed to Newcastle to see Basil Bunting) & have found your two notes waiting for me. I really am sorry about the vanished books, but more pleased (and beyond all that) to see how the entire issue continues and is, to say the least, not always specifically painful. This must be a short letter, as I have too much to do and we all leave for Florence at the end of the week. Firstly: if by now you have had a note from Ralph Maud at Vancouver, making some proposal about a book or journal and adding my name in some more or less direct way, please completely disregard any part apparently assigned to me or use to which my name is put. I have today found Maud's letter in which he mentions, vaguely, some such idea, and it sounds quite loathsome to me. This I should make clear is the first I have heard of such an idea from him, and I have written back immediately, signing right out of the whole projected affair. Humdrum perversions of that order are quite usual, I suppose, but it might just possibly have stopped you in your tracks to find my name fluttering from such a flagpole. I have, and shall have, nothing to do with the idea, which nauseates me very much. So that you can feel absolutely free to say whatever you like about this, if indeed you haven't already done so.

Second: no, of course you can't send me cash and expect to get away with it. What you need or would like you quite properly mention, and if I can get it I can

28. Gerard Manley Hopkins, "My own heart let me have more have pity on; let." *Poems of Gerard Manley Hopkins*, ed. Robert Bridges (London: Humphrey Milford, 1918), 67.

and will. This is simply the commonalty at work, as it should be. If I were poor in any exact sense I should need to have the help of it; but this not being really so, I can just have the pleasure involved and enjoy the directness (of, for instance, not struggling with strange booksellers and all that). Thus your cheque wings its way back, not out of irritation in any way at all, but out of ease and affection. The Heraclitus will be on its way in a few days, and a French paleographic atlas is already en route. The Whitehead is, I think, out of print, but I have written to Oxford to inquire, and shall get hold of a secondhand copy if I can't find a new one. The Albright will come as soon as it's printed.

There are many other things, like the fine quality of Basil Bunting and his old man's coy lechery; a sort of leathery owlishness. But that must wait (not too long, I hope).

For the moment,
Jeremy

But if, for example, you could send me the new O'Ryan, I'd be delighted.[29]

Gonville and Caius College
Cambridge
March 27, 1966

Prynne sent Henri Termier et Genevieve Termier, Atlas de Paleogeographie *(Paris, Masson & C, 1960). He also ordered G. S. Kirk,* Heraclitus: The Cosmic Fragments *(Cambridge, UK: Cambridge University Press, 1957) and had it sent directly to Olson in Gloucester.*

Dover
Kent
April 2, 1966

Just setting out from the Other shore. If you'd like to join us, we'll be until 16th April at: Presso Pelligrini, Via XX Settembre 4–8, Firenze, Italy.[30]

All the best
Jeremy

---

29. See Olson, *O'Ryan 1, 2, 3, 4, 5, 6, 7, 8, 9, 10* (1965)
30. The photograph on the front of this postcard is a shot of the White Cliffs of Dover.

28 Fort Square
Gloucester, MA
April 24, 1966

[Sunday April 24th!

Jeremy Perhaps just to clear my head, hope by the way your own is now finally back on!

but: any way there [again, P.R.O.? to check vessels built before 1630: in particular the Royal Merchant, 600 tons by William Stevens (Stephens—+ I'm pretty sure for Stepney? date of building—? + if discernable any info on shipyard capable of such bldg?

Yrs—+ have been like 'Post' in the "Wilderness" [grey rain + fog—+ Sunday Daylight Saving Silence, enough to make one do feel off the like Earth

H H + H

isn't it alright?
what a
—world
And all of ya sayin
Enjoy
My Trip too
For ya

Emmanuel Downing reported [to an officer of the English date unknown—but clearly early 1630] that Mr Aldersey, the lord keepers brother in law + Mr Craddock, had told him on the Exchange last evening that [Wm] Stephens "hath built here [London] many ships of great burthen: he made the R. . MT a ship of 600 tonnes"[31]

Gonville and Caius College
Cambridge
April 29, 1966

Dear Charles,

I wanted to write while we were all in Italy, and since then, but I couldn't do it. I don't know how to explain, except to say that the condition was extremely

31. See Butterick, *Guide*, 319, who links this passage from John J. Babson's *History of the Town and City of Maximus* (1860) to *Maximus* II, 218.

vulnerable: nakedness almost, so that I was shaken by too much. I tried to get you a photograph of the little bronze statue by Bertoldo of Orpheus, but they had none. That figure was too much for me, anyway, again, to see it there as a figure of return (as if, having once seen it when first there, in 1959, it had even been far absent). And they are more powerful as one has left them, they accumulate the knowledge that one subsequently has; so that seeing such things again is a release of it all. And my friends from the first visit, and all the Dorns in a kind of catalepsy, running from one to the next with a little cry, and the jokes. At this moment I dare hardly use my ears, since listening to the voice is almost unbearable, even the days are beautiful and too much so. You shall have some of this, therefore, as the will of it here in these lines. The grace of some past accumulation, in the curve of an arch up from the one column to its neighbor, the felicity of it: it's a live and trembling quality: history turned on its axle. Round the hillsides the land is terraced in strips, curving along the contours and shored up by drystone walling. In April these strips are brilliant green, with the silver olives twisted like crumpled paper. And direct from Virgil's Georgics, What makes a plenteous harvest, when to turn / The fruitful soil, and when to sow the corn; / The care of sheep, of oxen, and of kine; / And how to raise on elms the teeming vine: Dante's guide to the underworld, put into couplets by the impatient Dryden.[32] It's too much, it really is. Edward and Helene are blossoming, putting out leaves and gracefully, with wit, and that's too much as well. How does one survive this, the pleasures by which we are assailed?

Do come, in the
summer maybe: an
Entrance

With love
Jeremy[33]

Gonville and Caius College
Cambridge
April 30, 1966

Dear Charles,

What I said in my last note was only part of it. The condition is engrossing, and because to me it's so strange and vehemently welcome, I've just written to

32. Prynne quotes directly from the first four lines of John Dryden's translation of Virgil's first *Georgic*. See Dryden, *Virgil's Husbandry*, 1.

33. Prynne included the typescript of his poem, "Break It, As I Am," which was published as "Break It." See *Poems*, 51.

Ed. This is not pride, you understand, but about the world: what it's like and what more certainly it also is. The enclosed is what I wrote to Ed, which I know he'll not mind my sending to you.[34] Because it is extraordinary, an entire condition, & nothing will ever be the same. I wish you were not so far off. So many degrees, the earth, the air. Hours resting on the sea. Put out in the worse storm for ten weeks, it was his nature they said. Was it hell—the sky rose all about him, he could hear the heart of the world, turning. His mind made of coral, his eyes a straight road; his legs the city which he had never seen. How she stood there as she slipped past the door, her hands like the glide of an approach. How the world is: literally, the towns that I don't need to name, the violence of political greed. 'Grow' should be an intransitive verb, even if we starve to death.

What is it all
about, Charles: that
is not a question
but, in its halting
way, the answer

Love,
Jeremy

Gonville and Caius College
Cambridge
May 4, 1966

who built Vulcan's palace and died from
the bite of a scorpion, the figure of
great rains : this is to thank you
for his book, the matching image now
slotted back : a great pleasure
and was not careful with les girls, but
who would not have traded that for a
quarter-section in the
ORION
ORION Elysian Fields?

JP[35]

34. Prynne included a photocopy of his letter to Dorn, dated April 30, 1966, and a poem, "Just So." See *Poems*, 59–60.
35. Olson had apparently sent his *O'Ryan 1, 2, 3, 4, 5, 6, 7, 8, 9, 10* (White Rabbit Press, 1965) with his previous letter.

Gonville and Caius College
Cambridge
May 5, 1966

Here are the cards which I would have sent, & had ready, to do so[36]

now with love
JP

> "With this kind of bodily sensibility to colour and form is intimately connected that higher sensibility which we revere as one of the chief attributes of all noble minds, and as the chief spring of real poetry. I believe this kind of sensibility may be entirely resolved into the acuteness of bodily sense of which I have been speaking, associated with love, love I mean in its infinite and holy functions, as it embraces divine and human and brutal intelligence, and hallows the physical perception of external objects by association, gratitude, veneration, and other pure feelings of our moral nature. And although the discovery of truth is in itself altogether intellectual, and dependent merely on our powers of physical perception and abstract intellect, wholly independent of our moral nature, yet these instruments (perception and judgement) are so sharpened and brightened, and so far more swiftly and effectively used, when they have the energy and passion of our moral nature to bring them into action—perception is so quickened by love, and judgment so tempered by veneration, that, practically, a man of deadened moral sensation is always dull in his perception of truth."
>
> John Ruskin, Modern Painters, I (1843), Pt. II Sec. I Ch. II; Works, ed. E. T. Cook and A. Wedderburn, III (1903), pp. 142–143.

Gonville and Caius College
Cambridge
May 8, 1966

Solomon in all his glory, defending his thousand vineyards within the form of a Divine City: pre-Revolutionary & thus not a state in any "national" sense, but to keep the shape of a belief. It must also have been intensely political, but maybe to preserve knowledge rather than power ("a wise and an understanding heart").

36. Probably a reference to the ORION card of the day previous. They may have been sent together along with the excerpt from Ruskin's *Modern Painters*.

Ed showed me your letter of 14th March, and I suppose it isn't just that Solomon knew enough to make the door posts for his temple out of olive tree wood (I Kings, VI.33) rather than expensive and weightless "ideas." But that must be part of it, even if the kingdom was shrewdly defended around the fringe. Anyway, this is just to send the piece over, for the tenuous projection of History.[37]

Gonville and Caius College
Cambridge
May 9, 1966

Prynne sent S. K. Runcorn, "Palaeowind Directions and Palaeomagnetic Latitudes," Problems in Palaeoclimatology, *ed. A. E. M. Nairn (London: Interscience, 1964), 409–19.*

May 14, 1966

Dear Jeremy,

Don't please mind that you have had no acknowledgement to all you have sent me, your own poems + letters, + the serial pamphlets + books [that is the Kirk Cosmic Fragments also came, in this time].

Truth is, a combination of my own worsening nerves and publishing pressures [proofs, etc] have kept me from enjoying, or feeling at all free literally to live at all, that my strings of life + attention—+ indeed any sense of poetry itself, or other pursuit of knowledge than the surprising pleasure of the local subject (!)—

And did you, by the way, ever receive that funny, almost querulous (?) request, as of a William Stephens, Stepney—+ his great ship the Royal Merchant (600 tuns *[sic]*? or 400?)?

All's well really—though very scowred?/scoured?/scouwered? + dour + to hear from you from all quarters is a joy,

Charles

May 15, 1966

Dear Jeremy—Sunday May 15th:

Wld you feel willing—+ I can hear all your objections but you cld risk it with

37. Prynne enclosed Mordechai Gichon, "The Defences of the Salomonic Kingdom," *Palestine Exploration Quarterly* (July–Dec. 1963): 113–26.

that device of mine which has so long covered all my deficiencies—"Notes" or better in this instance "Tentative Grammar of Runes with plates!! for the [Niagara] FRONTIER PRESS?

I as Editor ask. It wld be a bomber—+ curl the Northern edges of any way the lattice but as well now that the list slowly will inc. (by John Chadwick's agreement, *[Harvey]* Brown told me Thursday!) that Mycenaean Dictionary you so happily thought to send me—as well as Pope's Ambiguity piece [he also has given his permission]

Now what we need is you having De Vries plus, but it being a writer's handbook—+ in this case, though I am ignorant, I shld think, it need not be a big book [Though what you—+ to some extent as well Count Oxenstierna—have given me, is as well an impression of the depth here [ex. your note to me of Jan 22nd this year] is right back where those other items now possible on the Frontier list go.[38]

OK. Quickly. Happily—+
I hope to your
liking,
O

Gonville and Caius College
Cambridge
May 16, 1966

Marcel Destombes (ed.), Mappemondes, A.D. 1200–1500; Catalogue préparé pa la Commission des Cartes Anciennes de l'Union Géographique Internationale (Imago Mundi, Supplement IV: Monumenta Cartographica Vetustioris Aeri; Amsterdam, 1964). [There are reproductions in black & white.]

Jeremy

Gonville and Caius College
Cambridge
May 18, 1966

Dear Charles,

No one thing is ever wasted: you need be sure of that. I too am in a violently divided state, and it's mainly a question of time, that certain habits of mind cost too much to maintain & yet can't easily be thrown over. But by the end

38. Olson likely refers to Count Eric Oxenstierna, author of *The Norsemen* (1965).

of June I am about free of it, and then I hope you may even make that trip; if it doesn't happen soon there will start to be hallucinations somewhere in mid-Atlantic.

As you'll see I am inquiring about the shipping.[39] *[Ralph]* Davis used to be at Hull, and is reputed to be an expert on the actual detail & working of mercantile sea-borne traffic. I hope he may have some suggestions, though if not there are others whom I could ask about this. The difficulty is (as I found before) that the damn names are so frequent of occurrence, the vessels so often given common names which they share with dozens of others, that to trace the thread of it as one ship goes back and forth is very difficult. Where have you found the Royal Merchant mentioned, and at what date is William Stephens its owner? He's not in the Rose-Troup list of Adventurers, I see. Stepney is even now in the heart of the wharfland of London along the lower reaches of the Thames, so that the location is quite logical. But as soon as I have more I will indeed send it to you: no one thing is ever wasted.

Over the Western Wave:
Love,
Jeremy

Gonville and Caius College
Cambridge
May 20, 1966

Dear Charles,

It must be the Port Books: everything points to them, and only going right through them with the eagle eye & claw of need will get through to what there is.[40] Why, really, don't you come and do it? I know the microfilm isn't the same, since one is in no sense there with it, but sealed in some stupid crystal. I shall press on, but do let me know with as much accuracy as possible what you already have about the London Merchant and Our Man in Stepney.

39. Prynne wrote to Ralph Davis at the University of Leicester on May 12, 1966, referring to Davis's paper, "England and the Mediterranean, 1570–1670," in *Essays in the Economic and Social History of Tudor and Stuart England in Honour of R. H. Tawney*, ed. F. J. Fisher (Cambridge, UK: Cambridge University Press, 1961), 117–37.

40. Prynne includes photocopies of Ralph Davis's reply (dated May 19) as well as Prynne's subsequent reply to Davis (dated May 20). In the copy of Prynne's reply to Davis, Prynne adds a note to Olson at the bottom: "*This, Charles, is a DEVICE, to get him (I hope) to tell me about SHIPS rather than NAMES, and about their origins in the ship-yards rather than yet more registers of shipping and excise documents. We work for what we want."

Quickly, and I'm still taking in
the new matter of your last note,
about the book (The Book)

Love,
Jeremy

May 23, 1966

Prynne sent a photocopy of M. J. T. Lewis, Temples in Roman Britain *(Cambridge: Cambridge University Press, 1966), pp. 9–10, as well as the jacket of Karl W. Butzer,* Environment & Archaeology *(Chicago: Aldine, 1964).*

May 27, 1966

*Prynne sent a typescript of his poem "The Glacial Question, Unsolved" (*Poems, *65–67).*

May 28, 1966

Jeremy: agree entirely with you that date has now entered calendar for work by the person himself, there; here of course and will in fact accomplish that—+ advantage wld seem to be materials here plus that postage-stamp character of sd. scene as pasted directly on the eye can be, deo volente, brought shortly under control.

Simply also therefore to acknowledge help still [on matter in from you this past week of earlier question on sd Royal Merchant

Will I hope shortly therefore [though that it would be the summer may be too soon I of course mean only that I don't think that I can do it that rapidly—tho please don't give up holding open to me the pleasure—

Charles (Saturday night May 28th)

Gonville and Caius College
Cambridge
June 2, 1966

Dear Charles,

I was going to write a new piece on to the glaciation poem, which is the first touch of what I hope to bring much closer. One of the experts, a man called West, is right here in Cambridge, and I've written to him for several of his papers (hoping not to encounter that odd & "curious" glance).[41] But having come back from that trip to London with Ed & Helene (of which you by now have received our conjoint salute), and having found Bob Creeley so easily distracted by airy mention of "names," I sat up in Ed's kitchen after they had gone to bed, with that specific intention. But could not find the glaciation text, as Ed had secreted this in some pocket; and so I started into something else, this other thing.[42] Our setting is more and more dense, the lines of increasing intricacy, "to prevent the living from entering the infernal regions, and the dead from escaping from their confinement."[43] And when in the Chester Play of Christ's Descent into Hell the Kinge of blisse approaches Hell gates, the stage directions read: "Tunc veniet Ihesus et fiet Clamor vel sonitus materialis magnus, et dicate Ihesus: 'Attolite portas principes vestras et elevamini portae aeternales, et introibit Rex gloriae.'" And then Iesus says to Adam:

Peace to the *[sic]*, Adam, my Darlinge,
and eke to all thy ofspringe,
that righteous were in eirth lyvinge;
from me you shall not sever.[44]

Jeremy

---

28 Fort Square
Gloucester, MA
June 3, 1966 [postmarked]

Wow now that means they'll have to listen like Andrew says, for I am sure The Glacial Question, Un(answered! is what he means will haul Wivenhoe 2 more "ours," he says (meaning of course yours!

Wow, the syntax, and the line: like Baudelaire said is there [I have to go look, from my very first poem: Voila, a Tide in the affairs of man to discern!

And isn't it beautiful the question that Pleistocene isn't over? That the

41. Prynne wrote to the Cambridge botanist R. G. West for copies of his recent papers, including "The Glaciations and Interglacials of East Anglia," *Quarternaria* 2 (1955): 45–52; with J. J. Donner, "The Glaciations of East Anglia and the East Midlands: A Differentiation Based on Stone-Orientation Measurements of the Tills," *Quart. Journ. Geol. Soc.* 112 (1956): 69–91; "The Pleistocene Epoch in East Anglia," *Journ. Glac.* 3 (1958): 211–16; with R. P. Suggate and B. W. Sparks, "On the Extent of the Last Glaciation in Eastern England," *Proc. Roy. Soc.* B: 150 (1959): 263–83; and "Interglacial and Interstadial Vegetation in England," *Proc. Linn. Soc. London* 175 (1961): 81–90.

42. Prynne enclosed a typescript of his poem "Die a Millionaire (pronounced "diamonds in the air")," *Poems*, 13–16.

43. See John Lemprière, "Cerberus," *A Classical Dictionary* (London: Printed for T. Cadell and W. Davies, 1804).

44. See Dr. Matthews, ed. *Chester Plays, XVII: Christ's Descent into Hell*, 11. 189–92, 326.

intervallic is the short wonder of man—that poetry commands that he as a Winter's Business resemble his own movements, that he not continue to treat all he knows as high-fallutin? get his nose to what he does?

And Jeremy think of it: you have a bigger island than like mine! It is that romance, of the Atlantic—Norfolk, wow

It must be, that all the lights will go on. They do, + the noses: I am swept into the stream Fantastic. And like take it away!

Yrs,
An
Admirer

Gonville and Caius College
Cambridge
June 5, 1966

Prynne sent a copy of Morris Swadesh, "Linguistic Overview," in Prehistoric Man in the New World, *ed. J. D. Jennings & E. Norbeck (Chicago, 1964).*

Gonville and Caius College
Cambridge
June 7, 1966

Dear Charles,

Very excited—and pleased to overflowing—to have your letter: and as by now you will know the issue is one of continuance, or how to keep up with, rather than back, in the hoop of that question. And as for your question (properly also ours), here is another sketch of the rim.[45]

Ever,
Jeremy

---

45. Prynne enclosed a photocopy of Davis's reply (dated June 6), which was pessimistic about the prospect about tracing individual ships in the New England trade in the early seventeenth century. He also enclosed a copy of the first part of his assemblage, "A Pedantic Note, in Two Parts," later published in the *English Intelligencer*, series 2, 346–51; reprinted in Neil Pattison, Reitha Pattison, and Luke Roberts, eds., *Certain Prose of the "English Intelligencer"* (Cambridge, UK: Mountain Press, 2012): 124–29.

28 Fort Square
Gloucester, MA
June 7, 1966

Jeremy

Your mailing of Swadesh [June 5th] is most valuable [isn't it?]—I cldn't delay to thank you, the usefulness—again for me he is [I ran into him applying glottochronology in 1964, + thus identifying the Cherokee as Iroquois—+ the Iroquois as originally then the city of Montreal when Cartier—+ which, when Champlain etc—all not there. [This, by the way, is in Wm Fenton, ed. Symposium on Cherokee + Iroquois Culture, 1961, Bulletin 180 Bur. of Am. Ethnology, Smithsonian.]

I also rec'd your reader—Monday—your new poem, + note how my deceased wife's sister, Jean, came in just as I was sitting down to my mail—+ stayed unhappily late + I have been unable yet Today to get back. Will—+ love, + altogether thanks for further "awning" me.

Charles

PS: better than that—posted Cambridge—4 VI 66 [oh I see here VII yr note is 5 VI]

June 10, 1966

Dear J.P.

Davis's letter is of course it—and the pleasure when a man has made himself able to be that complete, and capable.

I have it, then, and I am obliged to you. If my ship—and my man—[he refused to take the oath when Charles 2 succeeded, saying etc.—and that God did not, require him to. The General Court of still the Massachusetts Bay Company, of course, treated him: as in fact each boy of warrior age here in the later "States" grown of that union and from the purchased abscinding of the requirement that the Governor and offices of that Company be "London"—became Boston, though this too was not then for some years [if ever??] actual [in Whitehead's immaculate measure
no actuality no
reason

—if I cannot find then register via subsidy of

Wm Ste[ph]/[v] ens Stepney in Middlesex, Ship's carpenter, succeeding in part played by John Hawkins in improving and revising design of England's vessels at Deptford yards was it just before sd Wm Stephens or Stevens was born [date of birth unknown, but recorded here as alive at some short time after Charles 2's—and the Stuart's restoration

and for a ship called The Royal Merchant both words ring as though Thomas Gresham were and had succeeded,

then this jetty I occupy directly overseeing the Beach that Stevens was granted as his for ship-construction 2 mo 42 does not also look out its
front-window to a
PAINTED TYPE-FACE white paint on brick I can't
duplicate for you but my mind is to sign this
[will will [[verb]]

Friday June 10th Charles

Gonville and Caius College
Cambridge
June 12, 1966

Ed tells me I can't have "brother" in the Diamonds poem (penultimate line), either by will, trust, or the current decadence of language.[46] I hate to believe him, and I almost don't: by what NAME is one to call those whom one loves before one knows? I thought of "friend," but there must be a question of birth. Is "brother" really too corrupt? I think I have to recognise that it is, but the taste is incredibly bitter in the mouth: the last portion of wish taken from me. Brother is like Choice, I thought it could be put up as a sail without being ripped to bits. But Eduard *[sic]* is right, though I feel much the poorer for it.

Jeremy

Gonville and Caius College
Cambridge
June 13, 1966

Throw the first copy of this poem away: it had a misprint in the penultimate line.[47]

With selected & hand-picked *compliments*

[the error was "fes" for "few"]

46. Prynne enclosed a revised page three of "Die a Millionaire" as well as his poem "Numbers in Time of Trouble." See *Poems*, 17–18.
47. Prynne refers to "fes" instead of "few" in the penultimate line of "Numbers in Time of Trouble."

Gonville and Caius College
Cambridge
June 24, 1966

Prynne sent a copy of W. F. Albright, The Amarna Letters from Palestine, Syria, The Philistines, and Phoenicia, *vol. II, ch. XX, (Cambridge, UK: Cambridge University Press, 1966).*

June 26, 1966

Jeremy: Failure to respond—or even get to have read your further poem solely rushing to amor at future—

Love, O

Also 4 day visit with + from my daughter now about to be—15! And whereby suddenly is a long-legged [+ her father's] + a face which cld at least launch a Wicking fleet: Scandinavian possibility, coming up!

Charles

A good nose, for example—from somewhere neither father nor northern

---

Gloucester, MA
July 4, 1966

Can't leave the 4th of July go without greeting you. Now that you have made England green again—

Love, O

Gonville and Caius College
Cambridge
July 6, 1966

Chiare, fresche e dolei acque
ove le belle membra
pose colei che sola a me per donna . . . (PETRARCA)

Dolce e chiara è la note e senza vento,
Equeta sovra i tetti e in mezzo agli orti
Posa la luna, e di lontan rivela
Serna ogni montagna . . . (LEOPARDI)

Leopardi had a querulous mind and the feelings of a shopkeeper's daughter, but he was tuned in exactly to the history of the race vested in the lyric language of Latinium: nobility is thus a practised art, as birth is one of the highest
With the English 'Apiru's *compliments*
forms of attainment ('Generosity' is being born into the gens, of high birth and the munificence is style, just as the lyric flower of this Italian speech is music as memory. Cf. Leopardi's Zibaldone, II, pp. 384–390.) Thus his speech is beautiful like Sir Arthur George and also a moving art like the great letters (Keats Sc). The nearest to that is John Wieners, specifically his reading at Berkeley, which is the most white and chastened nobility to come out of modern USA.

Not so?
Jeremy

[and more on the Týr thing][48]

Gonville and Caius College
Cambridge
July 7, 1966

What is the Outer Prêdmost?

JP

July 12, 1966

Do you have

Human Universe? [Auerhahn edition? pp 81–94 (specifically p. 81–82)

As of "argument" there [previously unpublished 50pp. ms. essay on Quantity in Verse, + the Late Plays of Shakespeare] noted this sequence just now, in a new hook on John So.:

> 1600, Eliz creates East India Co.
> 1606, Muscovy Co.—+ Hudson sails for them E, 1607
> Jan 1st 1607, Susan Constant + others sail, hung up 6 weeks Donus, arr. Chesapeake April 26th, establish JAMES' TOWN May 14th, 1607

48. Prynne includes two photocopied excerpts: "Tiw," in A. H. Smith, *English Place-Name Elements*, vol. II (Cambridge, UK: Cambridge University Press, 1956), 180; and Karl Schneider, *Die germanischen Runennamen: versuch einer Gesamtdeutung* (Meisenheim am Glan, 1956), 363–65. He also advises consulting R. V. W. Elliott, *Runes: An Introduction*, 2nd ed. (Manchester, UK: Manchester University Press, 1963), 55.

The Outer is as though it were an India State; Prêdmost was a Pleistocene site [Czechoslovakian? or Hungary??]

Gloucester, MA
July 14, 1966

Jeremy [as regards your DIE A MILLIONAIRE—+ please abide again—+ hopefully a last time—my scratched handwriting]

It is beautifully argued. And in fact exciting, to see you use all that new knowledge even to their words—McNamara's Band, + the Presidency. Especially—I had not learned that one, self-optimising, system—

Equally the beauty, of your own claim, and prayer—+ equally exciting, how you came from it, in the duplicity of the Irish monks 7th century, though (to the Know the [names—and further! know them.

The problem must be—and you'd know how much I have erred too, and care to [I mean care not to, but equally care to carry the, thing as though—like you do Northumberland, there

Picts [today's
card in for you [I've posted
already with photos
Ed sent me of
fr the Times I'd judge Stonehenge [and
Newsweek— Le-roy
Jones—and one also I fathered

by John Smelan's wife (fr. Wieners) taken Berkeley last summer of Creeley John Linsley + I in the very real beer joint there on the Avenue coming out from the University [Plus one color picture of a detail of Carpaccio's painting of the arrival of the German ambassadors, + one very fine sundry bell also hanging from a tack of one of the cards on the wall so the canvas clothing or seems to show Venice—how to keep it properly mixed. It will get harder [and harder (I imagine, having without any connection to coming home and reading

satisfactorily [for myself] your
poem here, now, tonight
it is, like, feeling can't

register itself as a subject except on some one or else—even your shoulders there is, even with that rank neck:

It is an essay. And not a poem (Isn't it? Any way not at all to abuse, or be the less grateful, myself! or [interfere with your own process or feeling, surely to acknowledge [what up to now I hadn't been able successfully to read—due to my own preoccupations, only, as I had so junkily the Pleistocene One] and to give you my own best sense [and of the nicest sense I can bring of what is all there—and isn't, not because etc but I dare say because there's like no getting around that one the Gods wld say—+ they are ours—Love, O [Thursday night July 14th—+ hope it hasn't gone cold on you or you've raced ahead + I'm wasting my breath [Any way, of course, it being one of—like you—like (us!)

Yrs [in this case it must be a month late! Inexcusable; but believe me I am just now bothered (unhappily—+ unnecessarily

Hope soon to be quite over
any—by the way [over)
the 'shit' in that poem
used—+ you'll know I
can speak—just about as

with the single exception of what we are talking about as fine as I have had reason or occasion to see it. And that's not, praise! Wow. I really treasure it. Very much takes me several hitches alm the daily fucking dawn bloody ugly + more difficult Present, I do de-klare! Creeley too in-cluded! or It is a stincer *[sic]* of a clinker of a Greek unheard of I swear time. Never before—+ one wld act so it is the last time—For sure!

Gonville and Caius College
Cambridge
July 16, 1966

Předmost: 'epipalaeolithic' site in Moravia—I had searched in the European gazetteer, but the actual place must have changed its name! Neither *[V. Gordon]* Childe (The Danube in Prehistory, Oxford 1929) nor *[Grahame]* Clark & *[Stuart]* Piggott (Prehistoric Societies, London, 1965) includes any map shewing the position of the site (the latter spells the name without the diacritical, but I am less inclined to trust these authors over such matters). Childe writes: "It is, indeed, clear that Předmost represents a peculiar culture that may be closer akin to the Solutrean than to the Aurignacian" (p. 13; and see ch. II, passim). Childe can't now be the most trustworthy, at this late date, but in case you don't have it I enclose his comparative chart from the Danube book; presumably Předmost precedes Danubian 1a.[49] Clark & Piggott call this site "Gravettian" and comment on the elaboration of its burial ceremonies (pp. 76ff.); they date it as "Advanced Palaeolithic."

JP

Gonville and Caius College
Cambridge
July 18, 1966

Dear Charles,

Briefly, a postscriptum to that chart of Childe's—it's fine the way he runs right down to the Scyths, but the earlier parts are the crucial thing, and his evidence was mostly all from artifacts rather than geochronology. And so here's another more recent chart with the C^{14} dates alongside and the glacial oscillations set in provisional order (he's juxtaposed, in vertical columns, several different solutions to the problem of sequence, as you can see). This is affixed to the main article, by Hugo Gross, "Der gegenwärtige Stand der Geochronologie des Spätpleistozäns in Mittel- und Westeuropa," Quartär, 14 (1962/63), 49–68.[50] The journal carries the sub-title: "Annals for the story of the Pleistocene and associated stone age cultures," and it's a curious pleasure to see the top line of the chart called simply "Nacheiszeit"! This other journal, Eiszeitalter und Gegenwärt, I have not seen yet.

Jeremy

---

28 Fort Square
Gloucester, MA
July 20, 1966

Dear Jeremy:

My source (as I should, perhaps, have told you) is Hawkes. You will see that he gives Předmost—in the neighborhood of Brüna, by the way—a lot more interest, at least, than your sources, apparently, for one thing using the narrow on Brüna-face skeletons there, and the shouldered point ("a blade with an offset

49. Prynne encloses a photocopy of the "Table Giving Correlations of the Several Cultures in Time and Space," in V. Gordon Childe, *The Danube in Prehistory* (Oxford, UK: Clarendon Press, 1929), facing p. 418.

50. Prynne encloses a photocopy of the chart in Gross' article (62–63).

tang for hafting"), to distinguish even an East-Gravettian from—or with a West, in such later Gravettian as at Fort Robert—and, in fact at the Pin Hole Cave in Creswell Crags, in Derbyshire.[51]

What seems to me attractive entirely—even about Outer—Palaeolithic, of this group (or jump!) of men, coming toward Mesolithic, even with my love for the more Sioux-like faces of Aurignacians of Crô-Magnon, is that these were of this shoulder-blade + narrower face—Hawkes ever dramatizes Gravettian anyway as the "first known blade-culture of the steppe—corridor out of Asia beyond" [the mountain gone confused on Asia Minor], "in the loess land sites of the South Russian plain" [again: "While the Aurignacian never ranges far from the Eurasiatic mountain spine, the Gravillian appears thus in the gateway from Asia across the frigid steppes, a hunting-culture with the mammoth and horse as its major quarry"—][52]—it is also an unguessed matter that the best likeness to the so-called Lyngby axe [as the oldest thing of its kind known in Europe, or the world] is, the great Danish predestinarian Sophus Müller thought, [was] the sharp antler clubs used by some North American Indians for finishing off captured game—somewhat like the halibut club, here!—[which I have used myself to conk swordfish]—and it is this club, as Hawkes is interesting enough to note, which, away the equipment of antler, ivory, and bone, appears much earlier than 'Lyngby,' at Předmost. "Předmost even yields bone hafts perforated apparently for an axe-like head, and a deer-antler socket or 'sleeve' for a similar tool-head has been geologically dated, along with a human skull-cap, to the Würm 2–Würm 3 inter-glacial at Hengelo in Holland"—in other words, that long before the time flint axe-head made possible the Mesolithi 'Forest Cultures' of Northern Europe—and of North America![53]

Ok? Isn't he a gem? And now will you tell me where I do (did I) use Outer-Předmost? (!!

Yours,
Thursday and with joy to hear from you,
again—July 20th LXVI [and still here—Charles

July 21, 1966

Jeremy [Friday

Nacheiszeit has, that advantage (that say Gothic has, a language more than German for as, simple that a law—

51. C. F. C. Hawkes, *The Prehistoric Foundations*, 30.
52. Hawkes, *Prehistoric Foundations*, 30.
53. Hawkes, *Prehistoric Foundations*, 54.

I had it as the
fine-pointed Fortification
inserted by Capt. John Smith, Jamestown

+ thereafter sd to have been used throughout the Colonies—in that case as of Indo-European language—mythology [material also applicable in chronology, that say German comes into our use already earlier than, by way of Anglo-Saxon [closer to Gothic?

And Ice [as you have yourself so successfully shown—exhibited] is history in the powerful sense of both

I, what you have shown, there, that that Island bounces—floats—up + down. And is ridged

+ II, what is conceivably the most compelling new condition, that a human Pleistocene wall (of people) has suddenly started pre-1650 AD—mounted in fear of us. Yrs, in exchange

C

Gonville and Caius College
Cambridge
July 26, 1966

Dear Charles,

Here is the Předmost text, from Trobar (1964); I assume it's a Maximus letter, though it's not in the copy I have of the next instalment.[54] Those heavy brow ridges are exciting, as any ridged bone is an extension of landscape and its necessities: change as deformation and the crustal folding. Such folding is a concentration, of course, and a real poignancy, which is why the Asian steppe-areas must still be ice-covered (ice being the primal level, holding the water to those few inches a season and scouring the ridge

which is rim, time-check, the break of day (ðœgrima in AS) as the sun rises over the back of "the foe of the gods, /The girdler of all the earth beneath" [Hymiskvitha][55]

"Til Þess aetla vitrir menn Þat haft, at Ísland se Týli kallat, at Þat er vída á landinu er sol skírm um naetr, Þa er dagr er sem lengstr, erm Þat er viða um daga er sól sér eigi, Þa er nótt er sem lengst" [For this reason wise men consider that it is Iceland which is called Thule, where throughout the land

54. See Olson, *Maximus* III, 381.
55. See Bellows, trans., *The Poetic Eddas: The Mythological Poems*, 145.

the sun shines during the night when the day is longest, yet when night is longest the sun keeps aloof even in the broadest part of the day]—LANDNÁMABÓK, Prologue added by Þórðarson[56]

[A reference to Bede followes, & Bede is known to have used the lost book Pythias. The Prologue is 13th cent.]

I don't know why this matter of ice has not been properly got to before, as the Gulf Stream offers that exilic or borrowed warmth which makes frost into the history of the English spirit (i.e., even desire for truth, what is our primal matter, in which we are so clumsy when just this borrowing or ridge on the isotherm chart could point us to where we are as the possible; ice is the totally serious condition, history of time:

Forþon wāt sē þe sceal   his winedryhtnes
lēofes lārchridum   longe forþolian,
ðonne sorg ond slǣp   somod aetgoedre
earmne ānhogan   oft gebindað,
þinceð him on mōde   þæt hē his mondryhten
clyppe ond cysse   ond on cnēo lecge
honda ond hēafod   swā hē hwilum ǣr
in geārdagum   giefstōlas brēac.
Ðonne onwæcneð eft   wineleas guma,
gesihð him beforan   fealwe wēgas,
baþian brimfuglas   brædan feþra,
hrēosan hrīm ond snāw   hagle gemenged.
Þonne bēoð þӯ hefigran   heortan benne,
sāre æfter swæsne.
(WANDERER, 11.37–50)

[For this he knows who must long forgo the counsel of his dear lord, when sorrow and sleep together lay hold on the wretched solitary man, that it seems in his mind that he is embracing and kissing his liege lord, and laying hands and head on his knee, as sometimes in former days he enjoyed the bounty from the throne. Then the friendless man awakens; he sees before him the dark waves, the seabirds dipping, and spreading their wings, frost and snow falling, mingled

56. The translation appears to be Prynne's own; however, see Ari the Learned, *The Book of the Settlement of Iceland*, trans. Rev. T. Ellwood (London: Kendal, 1898), 1.

with hail. Then the wounds of his heart are the heavier, in grief for his loved one.][57]

Hrīm connects directly with rim, in the first sense of crust (of a wound, which is again history as pain, the infliction of time)—which leads to AS hrūse, earth, ground, the crust on which we walk. The ridge here is welt, what we join to as we go in our shoes; Ralegh has the whole linkage very exactly:

"Thus home I draw, as deaths longe night drawes onn.
Yet every foot, olde thoughts turne back myne eyes.
Constraynt mee guides as old age drawes a storm
Agaynst the hill, which over wayghty lyes

For feebell armes, or wasted strenght to move.
My steapps are backwarde, gasinge on my loss,
My minds affection, and my sowles sole love,
Not mixte with fancies chafe, or fortunes dross."
(THE 11TH: AND LAST BOOKE OF THE OCEAN TO SCINTHIA)[58]

"My love is not of tyme" he says earlier, but the ridge of it is, and not for nothing is that pilgrim-image so much in his mind. Pokorny takes it all back to I. kreu-, kreud-: krū, thick, clotted blood, leading to kreus-, krus-, ice, crust (or scab), and in verbal forms, free (pp. 621–622). And to confirm Ralegh's knowledge, Tucker glosses L. solum as "the ground, floor; land, country; sole of shoe" (p. 226).

"The 19. of July we fell into a great whirling and brustling of a tyde, setting to the Northwards: and sayling about halfe a league wee came into a very calme Sea, which bent to the South southwest: Here we heard a mighty great roaring of the Sea as if it had bene the breach of some shoare, the ayre being so foggie and full of thicke mist, that we could not see the one ship from the other being a very small distance asunder: so the Captaine and the Master being in distrust howe the tyde might set them, caused the Mooneshine to hoyse out her boate and to sound, but they could not find ground in 300. fathoms and better. Then the Captaine, Master, and I went towards the breache, to see what it should be, giuing charge to our gunners that at every glasse they should shoote off a musket shot, to the intent that we might keepe our selves from loosing them: Then comming nere to the breach, we

57. The translation appears to be Prynne's own.
58. See Raleigh, *The Shepherd of the Ocean*, 40.

met many Islands of yce floting, which had quickly compassed us about: then we went upon some of them, and did perceiue that all the roaring which we heard, was caused onely by the rouling of this yce together."

(The first voyage of Master Iohn Davis, vndertaken in Iune 1585. for the Discouerie of the Northwest Passage, written by Iohn Ianes Marchant, Servant to the worshipfull M. William Sanderson, in Hakluyt, Principall Navigations [1589], p. 777)

27th July: This letter was going to progress to a different argument, but I've just finished the enclosed poem as part of it, and this will hold me off for a few more days.[59] I'll try to pick it up again soon, & meanwhile entrust this to the post.

| [that's the ice-rune in
every one of the runic alphabets] — As ever & before,
Jeremy

Gonville and Caius College
Cambridge
July 29, 1966

Prynne sent Frank Debenham, "The Ice Islands of the Arctic: A Hypothesis" The Geographical Review *44 no. 4 (1954), 495–507, and a photocopied excerpt from John de Plano Carpini,* The Voyage of Johannes de Plano Carpini vnto the Northeast Parts of the World, in the Yeere of our Lord, 1246, *trans. Richard Hakluyt [from the abridgement of Carpini's narrative by Vincent of Beauvais], in* The Texts and Versions of John de Plano Carpini and William de Rubruquis, *ed. C. R. Beazley (London, 1903), pp. 117–18.*

Stonehenge
August 2, 1966

"Suppose an initially correct configuration for M, N and S is known. The prescriptions enable us to predict ahead what the positions of M [the projection of the moon on to the ecliptic], N [the ascending node of the lunar orbit] and S [the position of the sun] are going to be, and thus to foresee

59. Prynne enclosed a typescript of his poem "Frost and Snow, Falling," whose title was likely inspired by his translation of *The Wanderer*: "the seabirds dipping, and spreading their wings, frost and snow falling, mingled with hail." See *Poems*, 70–71.

coming events—but only for a while, because inaccuracies in our prescriptions will cause the markers to differ more and more from the true positions of the real Moon, Sun, and ascending node. The lunar marker will be the first to deviate seriously—the prescription gives an orbital period of 28 days instead of 27.32 days. But we can make a correcting adjustment to the M marker twice every month, simply by aligning M opposite S at the time of full Moon, and by placing it coincident with S at new Moon. The prescription for S gives an orbital period of 364 days, which is near enough to the actual period because it is possible to correct the position of S four times every year, by suitable observations made with the midsummer, midwinter, and equinoctial sighting lines that are set up with such remarkable accuracy at Stonehenge."

Fred Hoyle, "Stonehenge—An Eclipse Predictor," Nature, 211 (July 30, 1966), p. 455.]

---

28 Fort Square
Gloucester, MA
August 8, 1966

Jeremy—Ed (Monday, August 8th: just to home-in on yr double experience!)

Very excited by your joint expedition (and evidenced to me by your paired cards) of those earliest (?) Indo-Europeans, to England—and that it was a sea transgression obviously making Frisia no longer tenable [suggesting, crazily, that "English" even then, like (!__ "Frisian" its notable distinct counterpart, language-morpho-wise] which both dates Beakers A's surely to the Essex coast and opens Bhutan as a land-route between what has since been classic North Atlantic Civilization + "Olde Europe"! [from 1900 or 1800BC to_____?]

Jeremy: been bad two weeks, + in the traffic [peoples, + my owne own selfe] two letters to you

(acknowledging delightful letter (with last poem) and Frank Debenham's Ice island piece

[had you followed ARLIS II, went from SW corner of Ellesmere in April 1959 passed across Lomonosov Ridge eastward + ended up meeting only in Denmark Strait + south of Reykjavik June 1965!?

Will be more on, I pray, from here
henceforth, Charles

Gonville and Caius College
Cambridge
August 9, 1966

On ridge, further to the last note:

This is a term in ancient use, referring to a raised strip of cultivated land and thus used in Anglo-Saxon (hrycg). Land can also be used in this local sense, as a measure delimiting the unit of rise & fall in arable terrain (see the additional entries under land in Toller's Supplement to Bosworth-Toller's Anglo-Saxon Dictionary). This ridging must depend on techniques of ploughing, but there is quite adequate evidence of ridge-and-furrow tillage pre-dating the Roman invasions. The best simple display of the language in view is by M. W. Beresford, "Maps and the Medieval Landscape," Antiquity, XXIV (1950), who advances an "equation" by means of which open-field maps may be reconstructed from currently existing landforms. "The controversial equation is the simple one that the single strip of the medieval fields is represented exactly by the ridge and furrow of the modern English landscape. From one green furrow, up and over the curved ridge, and down to the next furrow: this twenty-two feet or so is the selion, the land, the ridge of all open-field documents from the 12th century to the 19th. The length of the strip, very roughly approximating to the furrow-length (or furlong) of 220 yards is the length of the ridge-and-furrow" (p. 115).

This argument is effectively only a reduced survey of the same man's "Ridge and Furrow and the Open Fields," Economic History Review, N. S. I (1948–1949), where Beresford says: "The word commonly found in Midland land-terriers [written surveys in which the territory forming the Church lands were recorded and sent to the bishop] of the seventeenth and eighteenth centuries is 'land.' The medieval equivalent was 'terrae' for strips which Professor Stenton [Documents Illustrative . . . of the Danelaw] notes in the twelfth century, and it appears alongside 'seliones' as the word for strips in many medieval documents." Beresford's EHR argument was broken into by Eric Kerridge, "Ridge and Furrow and Agrarian History," Economic History Review, N. S. III (1950–1951), who took the linear gatherings of soil to be no more than the consequence of the most recent deep ploughing & not medieval or even necessarily pre-enclosure. The writing is finely technical, and it's possible not to be too involved with his intention to demolish Beresford's "equation," since the turning and returning curvature of tillage is part of the language, our metric of repetition, tribal response as an immediate response to landform: the condition of being. The great banks around the sanctuary at Avebury were set in horizontal shelves, just like those described by *[William]* Cobbett (Rural Rides) and quoted in Kerridge's piece (p. 23). Whether tilled or not, this would define a condition of being, just as those terraced vineyards in northern Italy perpetuate the intense localism in any theory of fertility. The ridge is the assertion and presence of style, land held like a tent or the ridge-pole of a shamanistic lodge. In the Buryat initiation there are erected, after the initial arrangements, "nine birches, grouped in threes, tied together by a rope of white horsehair and with ribbons of various colors fastened to them in a particular order—white, blue, red, yellow (the colors perhaps signify the various levels of the sky). . . . The chief birch—the one inside the yurt—is connected with all the other outside by two ribbons, one red, the other blue; these symbolize the 'rainbow,' the road by which the shaman will reach the realm of the spirits, the sky" (Mircea Eliade, Shamanism; Archaic Techniques of Ecstasy [English trans, London, 1964], p. 118).

All this idealised ridge-work is the touch of that sidereal presence, tracked in the heavens or some notion of level as where we are (standing forth, as a mode of ek-stasis). The myth and extent of this terrain is entirely literal; compare the clan river of the Evenk Shamans, described in the brilliant article by A. F. Anisimov, "The Shaman's Tent of the Evenks and the Origin of the Shamanistic Rite," trans. from the original Russian in H. N. Michael (ed.), Studies in Siberian Shamanism (Toronto, 1963): to prevent the displacement of the clan's dead souls from their proper zones, "the clan shaman barred all the approaches to the upper part of the clan river of life in a most careful way. At every tributary, ridge, and crevice, the shaman set up numerous gates of watchmen-spirits. In the air, at the head of the river, were the shaman's bird-spirits. At the mouths of tributaries and on the river itself stood the shaman's fish-spirits in the form of a weir. The passage from the lower world into the middle world the shaman barred with an impassable weir resembling a fishing seine, in the middle of which he placed an ingenious snare from which the pernicious spirit, he thought, could not escape once it had entered" (p. 113).[60] The point about ridge being not that it's some ego-term hoisted into the highest centre, but the lie of our world, how far we can raise the entire condition: tillage is the shamanic relation to land and the ridge is its metric achievement. The description of its modes can be an entirely ritual one: "Ridge and furrow ploughing can be in many forms, of which the most common are gathering-up from the flat, twice- and thrice-gathering, crown-and-furrow ploughing, coupling ridges, casting down ridges, slitting or cleaving down ridges and ploughing two-in-and-two-out. Ridges are composed of furrow slices laid beside and parallel to one another. The middle of the ridge receives the name of 'crown,' the two sides, 'the flanks,' the divisions between the ridges, the 'open

60. Prynne would refer to the Buryat shaman's spirit-theater in his poem vis-à-vis Anisimov's article in the poem "Aristeas, in Seven Years," *Poems*, 90–96.

furrows,' the edges of the furrow slices next the open furrows, 'the furrow brows,' and the last furrows ploughed in the open furrows are named the 'mould' or 'hint-end' furrows . . ." (Kerridge, p. 15). The consequences of this are laid out in a very exact & perceptive book, The Making of the English Landscape by W. G. Hoskins (London, 1955). Hoskins has a real sense of presence, and this stabilises all the varia of chronology and economic condition, &c, which so usually reduce any notion of being to an anxiousness about limits.

The land is king and the
ridge crowns it, in
this spiritual estate,
raised on the brow of middle earth

Jeremy

Gonville and Caius College
Cambridge
August 15, 1966

Prynne sent a copy of Stuart Piggott, "From Salisbury Plain to South Siberia," the Wiltshire Magazine *58 (1962): 93–97.*

Gonville and Caius College
Cambridge
August 16, 1966

Prynne sent a copy of J. Tuzo Wilson, "Did the Atlantic Close and then Re-Open?," Nature *211 (August 13, 1965): 676–81.*

Gonville and Caius College
Cambridge
August 19, 1966

Dear Charles,

This is just to send you another poem, going on with the recent sequence of notes, as I do want the whole thing unfrozen or something broken out of it at long last.[61] At the moment I sense this immense pressure, the Jurassic invasion leaving not enough time for the ice to form to proper place nor the time itself to become memorable. We are even setting (and breaking) our wage freeze. Engels wrote to

61. Prynne enclosed a typescript of his poem "In Cimmerian Darkness" (*Poems*, 74–75).

Henry Lloyd (in 1893) that "It is only in industrially young countries like America and Russia, that Capital gives full fling to the recklessness of its greed."[62] The older greed is more intricate, here they want all those minor feelings of trust and well-being sieved up in the National Plan. Maybe some release or outlet is what I need, but really at this moment there is no useful hope for us, we will never get across to the Secondary Neolithic or anything else, as there are no main locations yet in place. The small hopes are all running sores: festering expectancy. The radical turning-point just isn't there, and how long do we have to wait? Who they are, the sequence of tenses. The ice-floe is a model gerund but loose pack-ice is just mush, I can't even get the hours going back in the right order. It's not our time makes the weakness; perhaps that hopelessly premature pattern of rescue.

I don't know why I go on with this. How does anyone get on out or make the line, at least for himself? But the decay is multivalent, a complete system of values taking over the links of being and thus also the connections of language. To what does it connect? The condition is reticulate, there is almost nothing to strike. There must be, but there isn't. And no end in sight, though I don't know what it means to say this. Useless threat, perhaps. Anyway I just thought this evening that I'd say something very general about the condition here, without specific festivity; and there it is.

CHRISTOPHER SMART	'Good is his cause, and just is his pretence,' (Replies the god of theft and eloquence.)[63]
J.M.W. TURNER	Hope, Hope, fallacious Hope! Where is thy market now?[64]

Jeremy

London
August 23, 1966

London, 23rd August 1966; Charles: just been looking at the David Smith exhibition here at the Tate Gallery—about 40 pieces including several of the stainless steel cubi and the assemblages from Italy. There's something quite native about

62. Friedrich Engels to Henry Demarest Lloyd [May 27, 1893], in Karl Marx and Frederick Engels, *Collected Works* 50, 146.

63. Smart, from *The Hilliad*, 11.162–63.

64. These lines accompanied Turner's painting *Slave Ship (Slavers Throwing Overboard the Dead and Dying, Typhoon Coming On)* (1840). See A. J. Finberg, *The Life of J. M. W. Turner*, 2nd ed. (Oxford: Oxford University Press, 1961), 474.

this work, not to any location but as an inherent quality—he is strong by it but never does for me get quite clear into the air. The cubi seem the best, making that frontal fix (almost a stance, e.g. at the work-bench) into image; reminding me of Juan Gris (something dark in both their accuracy, like a fillet of laurels). But the scale isn't somehow it, not fully "just"; the menands (menaeds?) shown are too small. What I do admire is the work, and l'esprit; the quality of his mind must have been terrific. Zig III was not there but looks great from the photo; the 1961 Sentinel was magnificent except for a tiresome disc wilfully added to the base (maybe the native, again). But, a PROFESSION—what that would be worth, for keeping to it, as clearly he did; even Rilke envied that. Did you ever meet him, in the NY backwoods? Jeremy[65]

Gonville and Caius College
Cambridge
September 1, 1966

Ne willeþ ȝee nouȝth greuen þe erþe.
Ne þe Cee. Ne þe trees vntil þat we
merken þe tokne of þe lorde in þe
foreheuedes of his seruauntz.
[Rev. vii. 3][66]

Gonville and Caius College
Cambridge
September 3, 1966

Prynne sent a photocopied excerpt of Emile Benveniste, <<Hiver>> et <<neige>>en indo-européen," MNHMHE XAPIN I: Gedenkenschrift Paul Kretschmer *(Vienna, 1956), 31–39; W. F. Albright and T. O. Lambdin,* The Evidence of Language *vol. I, ch. IV [Cambridge Ancient History Fascicle 50] (Cambridge, UK: Cambridge University Press, 1966); and D. R. Hughes and D. R. Brothwell,* The Earliest Populations of Man in Europe, Western Asia and Northern Africa, *vol. I, ch. V [Cambridge Ancient History Fascicle 54] (Cambridge, UK: Cambridge University Press, 1966).*

65. The picture on this postcard from the Tate features the work not of Smith, but of Amédée Ozenfant, "Glass and Bottles" (1926). Prynne also enclosed a copy of Ronald J. Mason, "The Paleo-Indian Tradition in Eastern North America," *Current Anthropology* 3.3 (1962): 227–78.

66. The photograph on the front of the postcard shows the "Gate of Honour" at Gonville and Caius College. Prynne quotes from a fourteenth-century version of the Apocalypse of St. John (Revelation), a manuscript of which is held at Gonville and Caius. See also Elis Fridner, *An English Fourteenth Century Apocalypse Version with a Prose Commentary* (Lund: C. W. K. Gleerup, 1961).

Gonville and Caius College
Cambridge
September 7, 1966

Dear Charles,

Just to enclose a few more things and to hope you are O.K. 'West' is very elegant, and of course dealing with exactly the same question; it's good to have it there, like that.[67]

I hope you are O.K.
Jeremy

The enclosed report from The New Scientist is just a preliminary notice, in immediate reference to Hughes & Brothwell, The Earliest Populations, pp. 6–7.[68] From Flint's human/glacial chart also enclosed (Tab 26-G) you can get some idea of the extension hereby involved. It's not clear whether Homo sapiens palaeo-hungaricus does pre-date Heidelberg man, but it looks probable. The scalar force of this discovery, considered in relation to the time-line, carries the species back over two massive temperature ridges (see Flint's Fig 25-2, also enclosed). Flint says of the term interstadial (as used, for instance, in the New Scientist report) that it "is used not only as a time term but also in a time-stratigraphic sense" (Glacial and Pleistocene Geology, p. 386). Butzer is prudishly dismissive about time/temperature correlations prior to late Pleistocene (pre-Riss), and also sceptical about the stratigraphy of Mindel (Environment and Archeology, p. 284), 23 note). But now that it's (perhaps) also a human zone, that "scientific" disinterest can hardly stand.

Despite the climate, the human presence may thus (if it's true) have complicated itself right back into that overlapping series of obliquely intersecting scales and functions, outwards from which (coming up the other way) the first regimens were composed for a theory of "future." Which is of course the deepest enforcement to language still to be carried across the ice and into the public gaze.

J.P.

---

67. Prynne refers to Charles Olson, *'West'* (London: Goliard Press, 1966). See *Collected Poems*, 593–600.
68. Prynne enclosed a photocopy of "Quite the Oldest of Our Species" [Notes and Comments] *New Scientist* 31 (September 1, 1966), 463–64; and two photocopied charts from R. F. Flint, *Glacial and Pleistocene Geology* (New York: Wiley, 1957), 439 and 478.

28 Fort Square
Gloucester, MA
September 9, 1966

Jeremy

Whatever the future now holds (I mean, of results of the plain practice + advantage of pragmaticism) you must yourself be likewise convinced we do have now a picture both clear + useful. I am also lately dazzled that 1900 say—or 1950!—or let us act on the chronology + allow 1945! does [round off[69]

The Pond House
Hadstock
Cambridge
October 10, 1966

Dear Charles,

No news for over a month now, and although I try not to find this disturbing it in fact is so. Which is to say only, that I hope very much you are all right, and that you should know & remember how you have friends whose anxiousness is not self-importance but a much more old-fashioned form of brotherhood. For my own image the way is precarious but still fully live: the personal has invaded the public, private and all the rest, so that happily I am now married and living at the address above. A light back into the world of reflection, that is, some special question of source about which I had scarcely dreamed, but from which the flow is a cool and crystal stream. Ed is also well, and whatever theory there might have been in our hopes for you, our own matter therein is now shaped to a specific & directed shaft: that you should in fact be whole & beyond danger. And that the smallest sign would be a star quickened and restored to its course.

Jeremy

Gonville and Caius College
Cambridge
November 23, 1966

Dear Charles,

Here are passports to the two deepest dredges of matter which you now have easily within reach. I thought you might find them useful.[70] I hope we can meet

69. Olson enclosed an offprint of his poem "Across Space and Time," *Set* 1 (Winter 1961–1962). See *Collected Poems*, 508–9.

70. It appears that Prynne sent this letter to Olson in London, then staying at 90 Piccadilly. Prynne

again (& perhaps rather more completely) before you leave for Berlin; would you like to make an excursion to Cambridge?

Jeremy

=+G11 1.59 LONDON T S/W 46
MR JEREMY PRYNNE GONVILLE AND KAIUS *[sic]* COLLEGE CAMBRIDGE

IMPOSSIBLE PERIOD OF TIME AND I HAVE HAD TO CUT IT OFF TONIGHT I DO SEND YOU MY APOLOGIES AND HAVE ALSO SENT TO THE PERSE DINNER PERSON MY REGRETS LOVE AND WILL BE IN TOUCH SOON = CHARLES

+ PRYNNE GONVILLE AND KAIUS *[sic]* COLLEGE PERSE DINNER PERSON MY REGRETS LOVE AND ETC +[71]

Gonville and Caius College
Cambridge
December 12, 1966

Dear Charles,

Have a good trip, into the outer darkness of Europe; and if when you return you ever want to be at any time *rescued* from Mount Street, just let me know.

As ever,
Jeremy

Hotel Steinplatz
Berlin
December 24, 1966

Out of the light of Heaven the flower
grows down, the air
of Heaven

So: my dear Jeremie I have, here, stumbled on the 7th or 9th century rune-alphabet (RUNENREIHE)—Norman, + from St. Gallener Mss.

enclosed a recommendation to the British Museum that would give Olson access to the Reading Room, as well as another to the Public Record Office; both are dated November 22, 1966.

71. Prynne had invited Olson to dinner at Gonville and Caius College as part of a commemoration of Dr. Perse to be held on December 9, 1966.

Or two, actually: in the Footnotes to this book [Insel-Bucherei Nr. 432, Älteste deutsche Dichtungen, by Karl Wolfskehl + Friedrich von der Leyer. No date, but new, I believe], there is another version p. 128. Maybe this one is the 7th century.

In any case the importance (+ its use, especially in Sweden, for the messager on the sea-serpent of those Sigurd-memory stones especially the Remsun bergit[72] [?]—stone [SW of Stockholm], to my own taste) of the meaning of this alphabet again leads me to ask or hope actually that you still entertain—or have not given up [?] that wish I had that you in particular wld do such a little sharp clear clean swift utter book on this whole subject. The mystique of which I am sure is bull-shit. And the worth of which—as was the Chimiya it seems, strangely, to have lived beside [taking Geber as c. 800 (?), and both runes + alchemy lasting through 1700—or 1600 + or—: 1597 is my own arbitrary date for the writing of Wm Dorn![73]

In any case greetings from this enormously provincial city—Big Dumb Formal City where I am holed up—Hölle, for sure, in the Ende!

Love + feelings for the New year [If you wld write it's a fair chance I'll still be at this Hotel.

Yours,
Charles

St. Gallener 9 Jahrhundert

Feu forman ·
Ur after ·
Thuris thristen stabu ·
Os ist himo oboro ·
Rat ritan endost ·
Chaon thanne cliuot ·
Hagal habet Naut ·
Is · Ar endi Sol ·
Tiu · Brica endi Man midi ·
Lago the leohto ·
Yr al bihabet ·

[—7. Jahrhundert??]

Feu froma
Ur anmot

72. Olson refers to the Ramsundberget, or Ramsund carving, one of the Sigurd stones, found in Södermanland, Sweden.

73. On "Wm Dorn," see Olson's poem, "Color . . . ," in *Collected Poems*, 593.

Thuris thri staba
Os obana
Rat rismit
Can cliuvit
Hagel hardho
Naut nagal
Is ar
Sol skinnit
Tiu Birka birit
Lagn leohto
Manne middi (!)
Yr al[74]

Hotel Steinplatz
Berlin
December 30, 1966

Dearest Jeremy,

It is a kind of genetic capital for me, perhaps more in fact to my surprise than England. Or this maybe why England herself appropriates German royal houses since (the Georges, was it) to alleviate or distance the guilt of being—since when?—so English! In any case I only today rec'd your delicious 'ticket' of delivery—dated December 13th, + only forwarded by my Lady *[Panna]* Grady yesterday! So I of course wrote previously to you without benefit of such aid + abutment professed—and, if I hadn't my own resources, would have been of course the first to be taken!

I say only any of this to give you token that despite some useless continuing negligibleness I do find my 'position' here—isolated in a Proust-ish quiet hotel room in Berlin an advantageous one. I feel almost like Regelsburg, wld it be—or Regens this outer darkness, next to the East

In fact the air of Berlin is in fact good and in some sense like Kansas City (RR Station gives, that you are at the center of railpoints in as many directions as at present my spirit does have prompts me.

Anyway, to greet, to yourself + wife the
Great Year,
O

---

74. Olson transcribes two different versions of the *Abecedarium Nordmannicum*, a short poem using the runes of the Younger Futhark found in the ninth-century Codex Sangallensis 878.

Hotel Steinplatz
Berlin
December 31, 1966

Sat Dec 31st (last day of this year 1966

J: I did not, in that sense mean, to speak against England I solely do think that she has been 'up' since some time say surely since 1593, and as you'd well know—even talking to that boy Harwood, that if she [as you well laid it out for her in Draft about England etc. which I have with me, + I treasure—any thought you'd blast them, + publish?[75] e.g.—seems like Robt. Ingersoll practically (doing funeral oration Whitman's burial)—or of course as you so excellently place it, Ralegh. She goes downward on her own ground and in time or she'll continue to get slicker + slicker.

And I hope I'm not at all at least to you something like some fucking foreigner: I mean language of course + more + more am utterly devoted to the rule language is life that poets + princes—+ now poets alone are any of those stupid nation's instructors—+ leaders

OK. No push, solely further feeling. Very moved—+ may, thank God at last have, some entrance to the: Germanic. Which was what I was—+ by genetic of course meant not race but 'history' [exactly in Whitehead's careful alphabet, that anything has to be seen in the complementarity of the genetic and the morphological, anything anyone any time event including the Future + that be both the Universe + God etc.

Ok. Talking like a Norse or his grandmother,

Yr Edda Charles Olson

Keep me posted.

75. Perhaps referring to Lee Harwood (1939–2015), English poet and translator.

CHAPTER 7
1967–1970

Hotel Steinplatz
Berlin
January 2, 1967

(the New year,
the Year of Saturn, 1967

My dear Jeremy:

I wonder if I could trouble you to feed my engines by say opening an account for me at your favourite bookstore there, Cambridge: + letting me have post[1]

RWV Elliot's Runes [Manchester, in the '50's]

+ if it by chance wld be available—

H. M. Chadwick's The Origin of the English Nation [Cambridge, 1924]

Having a fine time—amorously, with the neue film people!: which is relieving! And looking forward to further work, improvement—+ travels! Love, O.

Ja—excuse me—also: if you are due + can afford the time—

S. B. F. Jameson's The Runes of Sweden [-?-, 1962]

plus, if available M. Olsen's Farms + Fanes of Ancient Norway [-?-trans. Th. Gleditsch, 1928]

Hotel Steinplatz
Berlin
c. January 1967 [undated]

J(e!

To make myself wholly impossible cld you also see if Foyles had J. K. Bostock, A Handbook on Old High German Literature?,—?, 1955—?

O(h!

1. Prynne wrote to Blackwell's on January 5 to request their most recent catalogues on "ENGLISH, GERMAN, LINGUISTICS & EUROPEAN PHILOLOGY, AND ICELANDIC" and also to request that they open an account for Prynne's "American friend, currently in Berlin."

Gonville and Caius College
Cambridge
January 4, 1967

Certain personal matters adjust to their wavelength and then may, quite suddenly, be thrust out of it, so that the whole amplitude is broken. One should be cautious about this perhaps, not letting a chance movement shatter the abstractions of space. And language is the rate of this ability, so little in this resort to do with vocalism, thus we keep with it and our hopes for the chief purity, the cleanest water. Not at all to be confused with staying, since neither support nor rest are how we keep so, thus, and which is then the better part, of that. Keep to the rate and hope that the rest be in continual danger.

I don't think I can use the Germanic affair at this moment, though I have at it enough, and am also I suppose inside it too. Those extensions of place and time twisted down out of history (that's our Black Death, circa now), are too loose in the matter of travel. They can at one level be openly moved, and I come less & less to like that: or cannot use it. I would prefer a theologic placing of quality

[Here I was interrupted by a
visitation of friends and must
stop there, for now
Jeremy

Gonville and Caius College
Cambridge
January 14, 1967

Prynne sent a photocopy of Heffer's Linguistics Catalogue 802, Blackwell's European Philology Catalogue, *and a handwritten copy of his poem "On the Matter of Thermal Packing"* (Poems, *84–86).*

Gonville and Caius College
Cambridge
January 16, 1967

For Charles, now
in the temperate
climate of this age & in wit-
ness to the language
of this one

fact[2]
Jeremy

---

17 Hanover Terrace
London
January 18, 1967

Dear Jeremy: I abhor *[Ernest]* de Selincourt of course (+ all the sticky feeling of + bet. DW [Dorothy Wordsworth] (shit) etc + STC [Samuel Taylor Coleridge] (germ)

Equally I assume you yourself see what ice especially doth do to morning waters—wow, isn't it unconscionable how self-fatheaded good seasons are to stiff-nesses

Your grateful + chummy Friend
Charles Olson

Gonville and Caius College
Cambridge
February 7, 1967

Prynne sent a photograph with a short note: "Birthplace of E. P. [Ezra Pound], *Hailey, Idaho, taken in August 1965."*

London
February 20, 1967

My dear Jeremy,

Just, really, to cover my shame, not to have been in touch with you as well as to thank you for several recent mailings.—Things actually nerving, + visit of Harvey and Polly Brown from the States—plus Londoners—plus of course my own natural habits—keep eating time—or its surplus I believe in so much—away.

Hope all is well with your own self, + yrs, + feel actually, even though this may seem slight as though I were in my own kitchen—a little!

Love, + best
thoughts + feelings
Charles

---

2. Prynne enclosed Wordsworth, *The Prelude*, ed. E. de Sélincourt, 2nd rev. ed. (Oxford, 1959), iii (title), 633–42; and *The Early Letters of William and Dorothy Wordsworth*, ed. E. de Selincourt (Oxford: Oxford University Press, 1935), 203–11 (all of letter 89).

Gonville and Caius College
Cambridge
February 28, 1967

Dear Charles,

Here is your letter of 24th December as you ask, and also a listing of the books you asked me about, at that same time (which in fact I sent off to my bookseller & which produced the information I have already sent on to you).[3] Don't go too far away, we are as it is already too much out of touch—we should not so easily be offset by small difference, I feel that strongly, as of just this moment, having myself recently been preoccupied with older things (Buriat ceremonial *[sic]*, as some kind of cut back to the nomadic, or semi-that condition: which the sillier reform schools would call totemism). Ha.

Write when you can
Jeremy

March 3, 1967

My dear Jeremy

I believe the letter I was referring to is another either a following one—yes—or why I feel then [Berlin] in the "East"—+ that advantage [the letter opening in fact on some 'change' of such?

Cld you also add that to what you have already sent? And I do thank you.—I also know how we are differently travelling at the moment. I shld imagine that is more than anything else—at least I am so bugged by too many purposes + also visitors. I love my compendium! Love O

Gonville and Caius College
March 14, 1967

Dear Charles,

Sorry to be so long, I've been occupied with trying to make something of

3. I have not found any record of a previous letter indicating Olson's wish for a copy of his letter of December 24, 1966. It may be lost or the request may have been communicated via some other medium. Prynne inquired about the following books from Heffer's bookshop in Cambridge on January 12, 1967:

J. K. Bostock, *A Handbook on Old High German Literature* (Oxford: Clarendon Press, 1955).
H. M. Chadwick, *The Origin of the English Nation* (Cambridge, UK: Cambridge University Press, 1907).
R. W. V. Elliott, *Runes: An Introduction* (Manchester: Manchester University Press, 1959; revised ed., 1963).
S. B. F. Jansson, *The Runes of Sweden*, trans. P. G. Foote (Stockholm: Norstedt & Förlag, 1962).
Magnus Olsen, *Farms and Fanes of Ancient Norway: The Place Names of a Country Discussed in Their Bearings on Social and Religious History* (Oslo: H. Aschehoug, 1928).

it, as we now are (and as I suppose you do already know). So that here's the whole sequence from Berlin (i.e. that strip of muscle which pulled on English bones).[4]

Write soon,
Jeremy

Gonville and Caius College
March 17, 1967

Dear Charles,

Hope you got the last packet OK. I've just finished this longer piece, & thought you might like to see it.[5]

Yours again,
Jeremy

Lamb House
Rye, Sussex
July 27, 1967

If you live & write in a walled garden (the sea present but not seen) then maybe the enclosed order of feeling is 'natural' to that, each element of the possible a bracket around some notional essence of 'the real thing.' Thereby always to reserve the detriment!

Jeremy

Gonville and Caius College
Cambridge
July 31, 1967

Dear Charles,

I thought you might like to look at this.[6] It's only two fragments, or pointers to a whole extent of neglected intensity, but whereas I think I've already sent you the first part, the 2nd stage (P.S.) is probably new. I wish there was some real working interest in these parts of the whole, some city we could share with

4. Prynne enclosed photocopies of all of Olson's letters written from Berlin.
5. Prynne enclosed a typescript of "Aristeas, in Seven Years" (without the list of "References"). See *Poems*, 90–96.
6. Prynne enclosed a photocopy of his assemblage "A Pedantic Note in Two Parts," *The English Intelligencer* series 2, 346–51 (completed June 3, 1967). See Pattison, Pattison, and Roberts, 124–35.

all this, but mostly it's lip-service & those who remember how they used to be interested, once.

I hope it's good to be back

Love
Jeremy

---

28 Fort Square
Gloucester, MA
August 4, 1967

Dear Jeremy,

It is like opening a package to sit here writing to you . . . 28 Fort Square August 4th—having lost last night, before the City Council, my deepest wish to have that land "over the Car" like they say—and open up your letter, just gathered from the P.O., on + as of those R-U-N-E-S

I am so obliged to have your work land on my diving board the very moment I catch breath for the 1st time in—obviously—about a year.

This is only quickly—+ with thanks as well for Blake's remarkable "last words—to ask you also, if Ed + Helene have not yet gone to Ibiza to tell them I am writing to them there.

Collected love,
O

The Pond House (with the red door)[7]
Hadstock,
Cambridge
September 24, 1967

Dear Charles, thinking of you here tonight & in fact momentarily quite overcome with memory of Massachusetts and all the places we are—that day of change to cold in the air & the touch thereby of distance: the loyalty we cannot want to afford. How are you? I hope OK and would be warmer here for a word of what you're doing or thinking, so near to us across the ocean & still in the same house.

Jeremy

---

7. Prynne colored in the front door of the Pond House with red ink on the front photograph of this postcard.

28 Fort Square
Gloucester, MA
October 9, 1967

My dear Jeremy—Many beautiful thanks for your picture (again, now colored) of your house [like so much else I didn't do, in England. What a year! Or more I am the utterest stick in his own house.]—Been back here actually only two weeks, and only in the last two days—or once more for a day, felt that hold + pull from below, without which I am so susceptible + a waster it's as though I did not know that I was alive. Ridiculous hyper over responsiveness. Which only here in this one stupid tenement you have regard for ya say I gather sometimes some self help.

Very exciting actually when it comes to taboo or totem + the perils of the soul. I at least hope or was recently seeking to say in what way a man might at this stage have something so picayune, with the shore these few feet down the alley + unto the street the extent practically of what has argued of ataxia: last night I was again overwhelmed at the thought that shore is 'racing' NNW at 1 1/2′ a century!

Or only Lake Van measure contents me still?[8] (I am back chasing the out lines of this Neri, Gloucester—which happily, despite my total defeat on that house by the City Council, + most personal of all the wharfers + neighbors: I fled in fact in houses that I had that once laid myself open—The lovely thing is + it may be of course only October, which is good enough for me, that returning I had no sense of the bakery food spoiled, and eat again of my own pie.

I regret so much so much time + chance was spent in the past year—or that in any case I am buried in this single posture like Leonidas' stick which holds the Vine [both ways, now!] But tant pis it's once again off + on + I am at least with it! My daughter, who is now—will be 16 next weekend—visits me from school near Boston and that too seems mine. Love, + as often as you can do please let me hear from you.

Charles

Gonville and Caius College
Cambridge
October 15, 1967

Dear Charles,

I was pleased to have your letter though I am somewhat wary of that single-wavelength feeling—how it works through this precise component of dispersion, even polarity. I want in fact to cut away this strange 3000-mile domesticity

8. On "Lake Van measure," see Olson, "The Vinland Map Review," in *Collected Prose*, 330, as well as *Maximus* III, 551, and Butterick, *Guide*, 687–88.

which will not really support even the glimmer of a real feat at close quarters. We do of course both realise that we were held off, here, and you most poignantly from as you say even the normal purchase of gravity, from what should have been the closing or reach over of a fantastic accident: the mid-atlantic cordilleras could have been ours, we could have stood there without drowning or defeat (or any of that female Hapsburg nonsense) and even Europa herself could have settled into something called the re-emergence of land.

Instead there's a slice of meat, severed and bleeding at both shores, and we talk of home. A week ago it was clear and frosty for the first time, the earth beginning solid and giving that free movement through the air, not invited with old summer persistence: chaste weather, indeed. I mean, I thought about children of certain particular ages & tempers, and I was also homesick for the United States of America. Of course in part and biographically, but actually (like they say) for all of it. Some unexpected release from approximation must have triggered it, the iron under foot (though I was in a car at the time and driving down a road to London that I know well). Even the rise & fall of the land surface was an alien image, home deferred, I was lifted by some barometric flip into a notion of what, by now, we uniquely should already have had.

And seen right there, for us. Andrew Crozier is held off from just that by warmth of feeling he can only contain by technical antagonism, in that middle earth of ours he would flower like the green bay tree. John Temple might even save his own life (to name only two you've met). At such a pace Robert Creeley might be rejoined to his language (he says he likes London but when here the stereotypes of nervous inanity drop from his mouth like pearls into pigswill) and Ed Dorn's elegant drift, already commencing on the too elegant, could be kept from blowing itself inside out. That's the land I mean & which we should have, if we have to build an ark to find it. I know where I am and where I think you say you are, but where are we in that other and more fearful sense? Not in our houses, god I so hope, not in our houses.[9]

Jeremy

---

28 Fort Square
Gloucester, MA
October 18, 1967

Dear Jeremy,

Talk abt house I shld say: just put phone down—to Sears!—having got myself

9. Prynne enclosed a copy of *The English Intelligencer*, 482–504.

for 425 bucks into hell itself earwise buying yesterday a FROSTLESS ETC + + + [the other having broken down during the night before while I was out

So this is in the midst of every kind of impossible etc immediately to respond to yrs of the 16th in [today Wednesday the 18th—[+ etc. leaving in 48 hrs to speak etc on etc POETRY 500 miles away—[10]

I need therefore (1) to excuse myself for both, obviously, my previous letter as well as + (2) to respond only in these terms which, as in fact you remind me, are those which I do obviously still think are those particulars. I can't in fact see image or Man in that hopeful sense, of more than they are etc, any more than either (1) I find them or (2) I am able to.

So I must in fact, I guess, disappoint you—at least I am not at all embarrassed that I did, still, write you from my home (address.

That other 'we' still as you'd well know I think it is still too grand for the likes of myself, yours in haste + full of pain and distress that I can offer you nothing more than this in this moment,

Charles

November 7, 1967
(Election Day,
Cities Thought
The Nation)

My dear + loved Jeremy—

You aren't going to leave it just like that, are you?

You ought (oughtn't you?) to respect my deep Catholic World sense more than that, no?

Anyway love O

Gonville and Caius College
Cambridge
February 26, 1968

Prynne sent R. A. Crossland, Immigrants from the North *[Fascicle 60], in* Cambridge Ancient History (Cambridge, UK: Cambridge University Press, 1967).

---

10. Olson gave a talk and reading at the State College of New York at Cortland on October 20. See *Muthologos*, 229–335.

28 Fort Square
Gloucester, MA
March 6, 1968

My dear Jeremy,

Thank you, though Crossman *[sic]* again, as in that earlier one you sent me in Past and Present, seems always to dim the subject curiously simply by leaving or not actually apprehending the peaks or levels within the incredibly huge landscape Indo-European is. . . . . as though the earth wasn't also a part of the top it does eventually throw up: it wld be like digging a tell ignoring that the evidence of it wasn't the fact that it shows.

In any case it is very helpful to be put on to what he does have there that is now—and his decisiveness at least to say how he best takes the argument at any given point in fact. (It is always only that I remain convinced that this particular broad subject, as you'd well know I do, is the dust & business best made known today to give the present a past which for sure is more than its own knowledge or ability to get up on its own lame & miseryish values. . . . .

or there cld be socialism (Crossman of course makes me feel as though I am reading his father is it??????

In any case blessings, and greetings, and hopefulness beyond belief that all is well with you, and your own,

Charles

PS: I guess it's <u>Crossland</u> I'm making the confusion with, huh?

January 3, 1969

For Charles, warmly saluted
as the time sweetens & we
recall so well, we are no other
& cannot ever be less so:

3rd Jan. 69 Jeremy[11]

mid sereingum Ic wæs & mid seringum[12]

---

11. This was inscribed on the frontispiece to Prynne's *Aristeas* (London: Ferry Press, 1968), a copy of which Prynne sent to Olson.
12. Line 76 from the Anglo-Saxon poem "Widsith."

1969 APR 18 04:26
CAMBRIDGE 53275
SYA702 BU499
B LLE273 DG INTL TDB GLOUCESTER MASS 37 17
LT J H PRYNNE, GONVILLE CAIUS COLLEGE
CAMBRIDGE (ENGLAND)

NO CAPITAL F FOREIGN POLICY ALL CAPITAL H HOME CAPITAL D DEPARTMENT CAPITAL K KINGDOM OF CAPITAL H HEAVENLY CAPITAL E EMPEROR THE HABITUDES THE HABITATIONAL JEREMY LOVE CHARLES

Gonville and Caius College
Cambridge
December 29, 1969

Dear Charles,

I write this quickly, to get it off before we are launched into the new decade—new only by that pallid reckoning which nowadays passes as <u>time</u>, but still enough for the more popular festivals. They tell me that things are uncertain with you at this moment, and so rather than anything so coy & forced as hopefulness this is just another presence from over the ocean, keeping the gain switched full on, knowing you'll know how to read exactly what this will not say. Take it at all the right speed, & remember maybe that <u>season</u> is one of the talismans to guide us out of <u>time</u>: as Whitman wrote of the seashore, "that suggesting, dividing line, contact, junction, the solid marrying the liquid—that curious, lurking something (as doubtless every objective form finally becomes to the subjective spirit) which means for more than its mere first sight, grand as that is—blending the real and ideal, and each made portion of the other."[13]

So anyway the real & ideal come to you with this note as cheerful influence, figures for the patch of ceiling above your head. "Humana uero natura est illa, que est supra omnia Dei opera eleuata, & paulominus Angelis minorata, intellectualem & sensibilem naturam complicãs, ac universa intrà se cõstringens."[14] The <u>shoreline</u>.

Keep close to where you belong:
Jeremy

---

13. Whitman, "Sea-Shore Fancies" in *Specimen Days*, 95.

14. Nicholas de Cusa, *De docta ignorantia*, book III, ed. Raymond Klibansky (Hamburg: Felix Meiner, 1977), 198. "Now, human nature is that [nature] which, though created a little lower than the angels, is elevated above all the [other] works of God; it enfolds intellectual and sensible nature and encloses all things within itself . . ." See *On Learned Ignorance*, 119.

Gonville and Caius College
Cambridge
January 1, 1970

Scribed on the first day of the new decade I send this by faithful messenger who now from me salutes you—hey, and some of those little red guide-books as well, to keep your eyes popping.[15] Wherever you are I hope you're right up in front with it: I mean, from this you really ought to feel loaned a really haughty stare for anything around you that's boring or obnoxious; because the force of my demand that you be free of such is inalienably magical.

LOVE
Jeremy[16]

15. Prynne includes a copy of his poem sequence *Fire Lizard*, which was written on New Year's Day 1970 and inscribed "For Charles, across the / water, with love, New Year's / Day." Prynne also included a bundle of fascicles: G. L. Huxley, *Achaeans and Hittites* (Belfast: Queen's University, 1968); M. E. L. Mallowan, *The Early Dynastic Period in Mesopotamia*, vol. 1, ch. 16 (London: Cambridge University Press, 1968); Margaret S. Drower, *Ugarit*, vol. 2, ch. 21 (b) §§ 4 and 5 (Cambridge, UK: Cambridge University Press, 1968); Robert H. Dyson Jr., *The Archaeological Evidence of the Second Millenium B.C. on the Persian Plateau*, vol. 2, ch. 16 (Cambridge, UK: Cambridge University Press, 1968); H. J. Franken, *Palestine in the Time of the Nineteenth Dynasty* (*b*) Archaeological Evidence, vol. 2, ch. 26 (b) (Cambridge, UK: Cambridge University Press, 1968); R. D. Barnett, *The Sea Peoples*, vol. 2, ch. 28 (Cambridge, UK: Cambridge University Press, 1969).

16. Olson passed away on January 10, 1970 just days after this letter was posted to him at the Cornell Medical Center.

Bibliography

Anisimov, A. F. "The Shaman's Tent of the Evenks and the Origin of the Shamanistic Rite." In *Studies in Siberian Shamanism*, edited by H. N. Michael, 84–123. Toronto: University of Toronto Press, 1963.

Ari the Learned. *The Book of the Settlement of Iceland*. Translated by T. Ellwood. London: Kendal, 1898.

Bailyn, Bernard. *The New England Merchants of the Seventeenth Century*. Cambridge, MA: Harvard University Press, 1955.

Bailyn, Bernard, and Lotte Bailyn. *Massachusetts Shipping, 1697–1714: A Statistical Study*. Cambridge, MA: Harvard University Press, 1959.

Barnes, William. *An Outline of English Speech-Craft*. London: Kegan Paul, 1878.

Beresford, M. W. "Maps and the Medieval Landscape." *Antiquity* 24, no. 95 (1950): 114–18.

———. "Revisions in Economic History: XI. Ridge and Furrow and the Open Fields." *Economic History Review* n.s. 1, no. 1 (1948): 34–45.

Bloomfield, M. W., and L. Newmark. *A Linguistic Introduction to the History of English*. New York: Alfred A. Knopf, 1964.

Boisacq, Émile. *Dictionnaire étymologique de la langue Grecque*. Paris: Klincksieck, 1938.

Bosworth, Joseph. *An Anglo-Saxon Dictionary*. Oxford: Clarendon Press, 1898.

Brinton, Ian. "'His brilliant luminous shade.'" In *A Manner of Utterance: The Poetry of J. H. Prynne*, edited by Ian Brinton, 11–22. Exeter: Shearsman Books, 2009.

Butterick, George F. *A Guide to the Maximus Poems of Charles Olson*. Berkeley: University of California Press, 1978.

Chang, Tung-Sun. "A Chinese Philosopher's Theory of Knowledge." *ETC: A Review of General Semantics* 9 (1952): 203–26.

Chomsky, Noam. *Current Issues in Linguistic Theory*. The Hague: Mouton, 1964.

Clark, G. N. *Guide to English Commercial Statistics, 1696–1782*. London: Royal Historical Society, 1938.

Clark, Tom. *Charles Olson: The Allegory of a Poet's Life*, 2nd ed. Berkeley: North Atlantic Books, 2000.

Comenius, J. A. *Naturall Philosophie Reformed by Divine Light: or, A Synopsis of Physicks. . . . Being a View of the World in Generall, and of the Particular Creatures therein Conteined; Grounded upon Scripture Principles*. London: Printed by Robert and William Leybourn for Thomas Pierrepont, 1651.

Creeley, Robert. *Collected Essays*. Berkeley: University of California Press, 1989.

Cusa, Nicholas de. *De docta ignorantia. Die belehrte Unwissenheit*, Book III. Edited by Raymond Klibansky. Hamburg: Felix Meiner, 1977.

———. *On Learned Ignorance*. Translated by Jasper Hopkins. Minneapolis: Arthur J. Banning Press, 1981.

Davidson, H. R. Ellis. "Weland the Smith." *Folklore* 69, no. 3 (1958): 145–59.

de Bruyne, Edgar. *Etudes d'esthétiques* médiévales. 3 vols. Bruges: De Tempel, 1946.

Defoe, Daniel. *The Works of Daniel Defoe, with a Memoir of His Life and Writings*. 2 vols. Edited by William Hazlitt. London: John Clements, 1841.

de Vries, Jan. *Altnordisches etymologisches Wörterbuch*. Leiden: Brill, 1961.

———. "Germanic and Celtic Heroic Traditions." *Saga-Book* 16 (1962): 22–40.

———. *Heroic Song and Heroic Legend*. Translated by B. J. Timmer. London: Oxford University Press, 1963.

Doblhofer, Ernst. *Zeichen und Wunder: Die Entzifferung verschollener Schriften und Sprachen*. Berlin: Paul Neff, 1957.

Dorn, Edward. *Collected Poems*. Edited by Jennifer Dunbar Dorn with Justin Katko, Reitha Pattison, and Kyle Waugh. London: Carcanet, 2012.

———. Papers. Thomas J. Dodd Research Center, University of Connecticut.

———. *What I See in the Maximus Poems*. Ventura, CA: Migrant Press, 1960.

Dryden, John. *Virgil's Husbandry, or an Essay on the Georgics: Being the First Book. Translated into English Verse*. London: Sold by William and John Innys . . . and John Pemberton, 1725.

Duncan, Robert. *A Selected Prose*. Edited by Robert J. Bertholf. New York: New Directions, 1995.

Eliade, Mircea. *Myths, Dreams and Mysteries: The Encounter between Contemporary Faiths and Archaic Realities*. Translated by P. Mairet. London: Harvill Press, 1960.

———. *Shamanism; Archaic Techniques of Ecstasy*. Translated by Willard R. Trask. London: Routledge and Kegan Paul, 1964.

Engels, Friedrich. Letter to Henry Demarest Lloyd [May 27, 1893]. In Karl Marx and Frederick Engels, *Collected Works*. Vol. 50, *Letters 1892–1895*, 146. London: Lawrence & Wishart, 2004.

Fenollosa, Ernest, and Ezra Pound. "The Chinese Written Character as a Medium for Poetry." In *Ezra Pound's Poetry and Prose: Contributions to Periodicals*. Vol. 3. Edited by Lea Baechler, A. Walton Litz, and James Longenbach. New York: Garland, 1991.

Finberg, A. J. *The Life of J. M. W. Turner, R.A*, 2nd ed. Oxford: Oxford University Press, 1961.

Fisher, F. J. "London's Export Trade in the Early Seventeenth Century." *Economic History Review*, 2nd ser., 3 (1950): 151–61.

Flint, R. F. *Glacial and Pleistocene Geology*. New York: John Wiley and Sons, 1957.

Fridner, Elis. *An English Fourteenth Century Apocalypse Version with a Prose Commentary*. Lund: C. W. K. Gleerup, 1961.

Fung, Yu-Lan. *A History of Chinese Philosophy*. Vol. 1. Translated by Derk Bodde. Princeton, NJ: Princeton University Press, 1937–1953.

Gilbert, G. K. "Contributions to the History of Lake Bonneville." In *Second Annual Report of the United States Geological Survey, 1880–1881*, edited by J. W. Powell, 167–200. Washington, DC: US Government Printing Office, 1882.

Giuseppi, M. S. *A Guide to the Manuscripts Preserved in the Public Records Office*. 2 vols. London: HMSO, 1923–24.

Goetze, Albrecht. "Warfare in Asia Minor." *Iraq* 25 (1963): 124–30.

Golding, Arthur, trans. *The excellent and pleasant worke, Collectanea rerum memorabilium of Caius Julius Solinus* [1587]. Gainesville, FL: Scholars' Facsimiles & Reprints, 1955.

Gordon, I. L., ed. *The Seafarer*. London: Methuen, 1960.

Grosseteste, Robert. *Exameron secundum Lincolniensis*. British Museum Royal MS. 6 E.V.

Hakluyt, Richard. *The Principal Navigations, Voiages, Traffiques and Discoveries of the English Nation*, 3 vols. London: George Bishop, Ralph Newberie, and Robert Barker, 1598/99–1600.

The Hávámal, with Selections from Other Poems of the Edda, edited by D. E. Martin Clarke. Cambridge, UK: Cambridge University Press, 1923.

Hawkes, C. F. C. *The Prehistoric Foundations of Europe to the Mycenean Age*. New York: Routledge, 1940.

Heidegger, Martin. *Elucidations of Hölderlin's Poetry*. Translated by Keith Hoeller. Amherst, NY: Humanity Books, 2000.

———. *Erläuterungen zu Hölderlins Dichtung*. 2nd ed. Frankfurt: Klostermann, 1951.

———. *Holzwege*. Frankfurt: Klostermann, 1950.

———. *Off the Beaten Track*. Edited by Julian Young and Kenneth Haynes. Cambridge, UK: Cambridge University Press, 2002.

Herrick, Robert. *Hesperides; or Works Both Human & Divine*. 1648. London: George Newnes, 1905.

Hickman, Ben. "'A Big Kiss for Mother England': *The New American Poetry* in Britain." In *The New American Poetry: Fifty Years Later*, edited by John R. Woznicki, 81–107. Bethlehem, PA: Lehigh University Press, 2014.

Ho, Ping-Yü, and Joseph Needham. "Theories of Categories in Early Medieval Chinese Alchemy." *Journal of the Warburg and Courtauld Institutes* 22 (1959): 173–210.

Hofmann, J. B. *Etymologisches Wörterbuch des Griesischen*. Munich: R. Oldenbourg, 1949.

Hopkins, Gerard Manley. *Poems of Gerard Manley Hopkins*. Edited by Robert Bridges. London: Humphrey Milford, 1918.

Horneck, Anthony. *Delight and Judgment: or, a Prospect of the Great Day of Judgment, and Its Power to Damp, and Imbitter Sensual Delights, Sports, and Recreations*. London: Printed by H. Hills, 1683.

Hoyle, Fred. "Stonehenge—An Eclipse Predictor." *Nature* 211 (1966): 454–56.

Humboldt, Alexander von. *Cosmos: A Sketch of a Physical Description of the Universe*. Translated by E. C. Otté. 5 vols. London: Henry G. Bohn, 1848–1858.

Hutton, James. "The Theory of Rain." *Transactions of the Royal Society of Edinburgh* 1 (1788): 42–86.

———. "Theory of the Earth; or an Investigation of the Laws Observable in the Composition, Dissolution, and Restoration of Land upon the Globe." *Transactions of the Royal Society of Edinburgh* 1, no. 2 (1788): 209–304.

Jonson, Ben. *The English Grammar*. c. 1619. London: N.p., 1640.

Judah, C. B. *The North American Fisheries and British Policy to 1713*. Urbana, IL: University of Illinois Bulletin, 1933.

Keats, John. *Letters*. 4th ed. Edited by M. B. Forman. Oxford: Oxford University Press, 1952.

Kenny, Herbert. "Charles Olson: A Memoir." *New Boston Review* (Summer 1976). Reprinted in *Minutes of the Charles Olson Society* 58 (May 2006). http://charlesolson.org/Files/Kenny.htm.

Kerridge, Eric. "Ridge and Furrow and Agrarian History." *Economic History Review* 4, no. 1 (1951): 14–36.

King, C. A. M. *Beaches and Coasts*. London: Edward Arnold, 1959.

Klaeber, Friedrich, ed. *Beowulf and the Fight at Finnsburg*. Boston: D. C. Heath & Co., 1922.

Latter, Alex. *Late Modernism and "The English Intelligencer": On the Poetics of Community*. London: Bloomsbury, 2015.

Lehnert, Martin. *Poetry and Prose of the Anglo-Saxons*. Halle: M. Niemeyer, 1956.

Lempriere, John. *A Classical Dictionary*, 7th ed. 1788. London: T. Cadell and W. Davies, 1809.

Lewis, Wyndham. *Time and Western Man*. Boston: Beacon Press, 1957.

Lipscomb, George. *The History and Antiquities of the County of Buckingham*. 4 vols. London: J & W Robins, 1847.

Matthews, Dr. [J.], ed. *Chester Plays*. London: Kegan Paul, Trench & Co., 1916.

Maud, Ralph. *Charles Olson at the Harbor*. Vancouver, BC: Talonbooks, 2008.

———. *Charles Olson's Reading: A Biography*. Carbondale: Southern Illinois University Press, 1996.

McClure, Michael. "Phi Upsilon Kappa." *Kulchur* 8 (Winter 1962): 65–74. In *Meat Science: Essays*. 2nd ed. San Francisco: City Lights, 1963.

McGrath, Patrick. *Merchants and Merchandise in Seventeenth-Century Bristol*. Bristol: Bristol Record Society, 1955.

———. "Merchant Shipping in the Seventeenth Century: The Evidence of the Bristol Deposition Books, Part I." *Mariner's Mirror* 41, no. 1 (1954): 23–37.

———. *Records Relating to the Society of Merchant Venturers of the City of Bristol in the Seventeenth Century*. Bristol: Bristol Record Society, 1952.

Mellors, Anthony. *Late Modernist Poetics: From Pound to Prynne*. Manchester: Manchester University Press, 2005.

———. "Literal Myth in Prynne and Olson." *Fragmente* 4 (Autumn/Winter 1991): 36–47.

Mill, John Stuart. *A System of Logic, Ratiocinative and Inductive, Being a Connected View of the Principles of Evidence, and the Methods of Scientific Investigation*. 3rd revised ed. 2 vols. 1843. Reprint, London: John W. Parker, 1851.

Milne, E. A. *Vectorial Mechanics*. London: Methuen, 1948.

"Names and Things." *Spectator* July 28, 1961.

Needham, Joseph. *Science and Civilisation in China*. Vol. 2, *History of Scientific Thought*. Cambridge, UK: Cambridge University Press, 1956.

Olson, Charles. *A Bibliography on America for Edward Dorn*. San Francisco: Four Seasons, 1964.

———. *Collected Prose*. Edited by Donald Allen and Benjamin Friedlander. Berkeley: University of California Press, 1997.

———. *The Maximus Poems*. Edited by George F. Butterick. Berkeley: University of California Press, 1983.

———. *The Mayan Letters*. Palma de Mallorca: Divers Press, 1953.

———. *Muthologos: Lectures and Interviews*. Revised 2nd ed. Edited by Ralph Maud. Vancouver, BC: Talonbooks, 2010.

———. *Selected Letters*. Edited by Ralph Maud. Berkeley: University of California Press, 2000.

Oppen, George. "Three Poets." *Poetry* 100 (August 1962): 329–33.

Owens, Richard. "'The Practical Limits of Daylight': Charles Olson and J. H. Prynne." *Worcester Review* 31 (2010): 135–48.

Parkinson, John. *Paradisi in Sole Paradisus Terrestris. Or, a garden of all sorts of pleasant flowers which our English ayre will permit to be noursed vp*. London: Printed by Humfrey Lownes and Robert Young, 1629.

Partridge, Eric. *Origins*. London: Routledge Kegan and Paul, 1958.

Pattison, Neil, Reitha Pattison, and Luke Roberts, eds. *Certain Prose of the "English Intelligencer."* Cambridge, UK: Mountain Books, 2012.

The Poetic Eddas: The Mythological Poems. Translated by Henry Adams Bellows. 1923. New York: Dover, 2004.

Pokorny, Julius. *Indogermanisches etymologisches Wörterbuch*. Bern: Franke Verlag, 1947–1959.

Pound, Ezra. *Confucius: The Great Digest, the Unwobbling Pivot, the Analects*. New York: New Directions, 1951.

———. *Literary Essays of Ezra Pound*. Edited by T. S. Eliot. London: Faber & Faber, 1954.

Prynne, J. H. *Force of Circumstance and Other Poems*. London: Routledge and Kegan Paul, 1962.

———. "Its Own Intrinsic Form." Review of Robert Creeley's *For Love: Poems 1950–1960* (New York: Scribner's, 1962). In Dorn, Papers, I. A. Box 19, Folder 328.

———. "Lie of the Other Land." *Prospect* 6 (Spring 1964): 36–37.

———. *Poems*. Northumberland: Bloodaxe Books, 2015.

———. "Resistance and Difficulty." *Prospect* 5 (Winter 1961): 26–30.

———. Review of *Maximus IV, V, VI*. *The Park* 4/5 (1969): 64–66.

———. "Salt Water, Fresh Water." *Prospect* 6 (Spring 1964): 34.

Raleigh, Sir Walter. *The Shepherd of the Ocean*. Edited by Frank Hersey. New York: Macmillan, 1916.

Rodríguez, Andrés. "Enlarging History: The Poetry of J. H. Prynne." *Sagetrieb* 10 (1991): 83–107.

Ruskin, John. *Works*. Vol. 3. Edited by E. T. Cook and A. Wedderburn. London: George Allen, 1903.

Sainsbury, W. N., ed. *Calendar of State Papers, Colonial Series, 1574–1660, Preserved in the State Paper Department of Her Majesty's Public Record Office*. London: H.M.S.O., 1860.

Sapir, Edward. *Language: An Introduction to the Study of Speech*. New York: Harcourt, Brace, 1949.

Selerie, Gavin. "From Weymouth Back: Olson's British Contacts, Travels and Legacy." In *Contemporary Olson*, edited by David Herd. Manchester: Manchester University Press, 2015, 113–26.

Sheppard, Robert. *The Poetry of Saying: British Poetry and Its Discontents, 1950–2000*. Liverpool: Liverpool University Press, 2005.

Simpson, J. "Mímir: Two Myths or One?" *Saga-Book* 16 (1962): 41–53.

Skeat, W. W. *An Etymological Dictionary of the English Language*. Oxford: Clarendon Press, 1882.

Smart, Christopher. *The Hilliad*. London: D. Job, 1753.

South, Robert. *A Sermon Preached at the Cathedral Church of St. Paul, Novemb. 9. 1662*. London: Printed by J.G. for Tho. Robinson, 1663.

———. *Sermons Preached upon Several Occasions*. London: Lintot, 1744.

Sturluson, Snorri. *The Prose Edda: Tales from Norse Mythology*. Translated by Jean I. Young. Berkeley: University of California Press, 1954.

Sutherland, Keston. "XL Prynne." In *Complicities: British Poetry 1945–2007*, edited by Robin Purves and Sam Ladkin, 43–73. Prague: Litteraria Pragensia, 2007.

Tatarkiewicz, Wladyslaw. *History of Aesthetics*. 2 vols. London: Continuum, 2005.

Tencer, Michael. The Bibliography of J. H. Prynne. http://prynnebibliography.org.

Timoshenko, S., and D. H. Young. *Engineering Mechanics*. 4th ed. New York: McGraw-Hill, 1956.

Tolstoy, Leo. *Anna Karenin*. Translated by Rosemary Edmonds. London: Penguin, 1954.

Tomlinson, Charles. "From Both Sides of the Atlantic." *New Statesman* 61 (March 3, 1961): 352.

Traherne, Thomas. *Traherne's Poems of Felicity*. Edited by H. I. Bell. Oxford: Clarendon Press, 1910.

Turville-Petre, E. O. G. *Myth and Religion of the North: The Religion of Ancient Scandinavia*. London: Weidenfeld and Nicolson, 1964.

von Hallberg, Robert. *Charles Olson: The Scholar's Art*. Cambridge, MA: Harvard University Press, 1978.

Walcot, P. Review of Jacqueline Duchemin, *La Houlette et la Lyre*. *Journal of Hellenic Studies* 82 (1962): 154–55.

Whitehead, Alfred North. *Process and Reality*. Edited by David Ray Griffin and Donald W. Sherburne. New York: Free Press, 1978.

Whitelock, Dorothy, David C. Douglas, and Susie I. Tucker. *The Anglo-Saxon Chronicle*. London: Eyre and Spottiswoode, 1961.

Whitman, Walt. *Leaves of Grass*. Philadelphia: David McKay, 1900.

———. *Specimen Days & Collect*. Philadelphia: Rees Welsh, 1883.

Wilkins, John. *An Essay Towards a Real Character, and a Philosophical Language*. London: Sa. Gellibrand, 1668.

Williams, N. J., ed. *Descriptive List of Exchequer, Queen's Remembrancer, Port Books: Part I, 1565 to 1700*. London: Public Record Office, 1960.

———. "The London Port Books," *Transactions of the London & Middlesex Archaeological Society* 18 (1956): 13–26.

Woodward, John. *An Essay toward a Natural History of the Earth: and Terrestrial Bodies, Especially Minerals: As also of the Sea, Rivers, and Springs. With an Account of the Universal Deluge: And of the Effects That it Had upon the Earth*. London: Printed for Ric. Wilkin, 1695.

Index

www.ingramcontent.com/pod-product-compliance
Lightning Source LLC
Chambersburg PA
CBHW060820310726
48980CB00002B/355
* 9 7 8 0 8 2 6 3 5 8 3 2 5 *